# Praise for *The Web Game Developer's Cookbook*

"*The Web Game Developer's Cookbook* is a fun hands-on introduction both to building games and to web technologies. Learning through making is an empowering, exciting first step."

**—Jonathan Beilin**
DIY.org

"It is not only a book about libraries: it teaches how web pages work, how games work, and how to put everything together. Study one, learn three: best deal ever."

**—Francesco "KesieV" Cottone**
Web Alchemist, and Technical Advisor at Vidiemme Consulting

"A wonderful overview of the HTML5 Game Development landscape, covering a wide range of tools and 10 different game genres."

**—Pascal Rettig**
Author of *Professional Mobile HTML5 Game Development*

"With a friendly and reassuring tone, Burchard breaks down some of the most well-known gaming genres into their basic ingredients. *The Web Game Developer's Cookbook* transforms a seemingly daunting task into an approachable crash course even for those who've never written a line of code before."

**—Jason Tocci, Ph.D.**
Writer, Designer, and Researcher

# The Web Game
# Developer's Cookbook

# The Web Game Developer's Cookbook

## Using JavaScript and HTML5 to Develop Games

Evan Burchard

✦✦ Addison-Wesley

Upper Saddle River, NJ · Boston · Indianapolis · San Francisco
New York · Toronto · Montreal · London · Munich · Paris · Madrid
Capetown · Sydney · Tokyo · Singapore · Mexico City

The publisher offers excellent discounts on this book when ordered in quantity for bulk purchases or special sales, which may include electronic versions and/or custom covers and content particular to your business, training goals, marketing focus, and branding interests. For more information, please contact:

U.S. Corporate and Government Sales
(800) 382-3419
corpsales@pearsontechgroup.com

For sales outside the United States, please contact:

International Sales
international@pearsoned.com

Visit us on the Web: informit.com/aw

*Library of Congress Cataloging-in-Publication Data is on file.*

Copyright © 2013 Pearson Education, Inc.

ISBN-13: 9780321898388
ISBN-10: 0321898389

Text printed in the United States on recycled paper at RR Donnelley, Crawfordsville, IN.
First printing: March 2013

**Editor-in-Chief**
Mark Taub

**Acquisitions Editor**
Laura Lewin

**Development Editor**
Songlin Qiu

**Managing Editor**
Kristy Hart

**Project Editor**
Andy Beaster

**Copy Editor**
Apostrophe Editing Services

**Indexer**
Cheryl Lenser

**Proofreader**
Sarah Kearns

**Technical Reviewers**
Jonathan Beilin
Rich Jones
Jason Tocci

**Editorial Assistant**
Olivia Basegio

**Interior Designer**
Kim Scott

**Cover Designer**
Chuti Prasertsith

**Compositor**
Nonie Ratcliff

*For Jade*

# Contents

# PREFACE

When I was little, I learned that fun comes in plastic cartridges from Japan, stamped with the "Official Nintendo Seal of Quality," and smelling of Styrofoam. Challenge, discovery, and companionship were all bundled together in a magical box that output entertainment when you put these littler boxes in it and pressed "POWER." Later, I uncovered something shocking: These games (and games like them) could be made by mortal humans, sometimes only one or a few of them, but the team sizes were growing. As I was watching, what had started with small teams of hackers was becoming the 50-billion-dollar video game industry we know today.

But now, even as large studios dominate the market, a renaissance is brewing of small, independent teams working on games. Distribution platforms supporting these efforts have sprung up by the dozens, but nowhere is this revolution more pronounced than in the humble-and-often-overlooked web browser arena. Backed by advancements in browser technology, hundreds of free game engines are available that enable even a solo game designer to create games that are memorable, personal, fun, and potentially lucrative. All you need is a browser, a text editor, and the kind of information in this book. It's a few more button presses than turning on a console, but it has never been easier to make this kind of fun for yourself and others.

"POWER"

# ACKNOWLEDGMENTS

First of all, you. Seriously. You are reading a book that I wrote. That blows my mind. Thank you so much.

I want to thank the team at Pearson, and especially Laura, Olivia, and Songlin for giving me the chance and the guidance I needed to be able to write this book.

Thanks to my friends and reviewers, Jon, Rich, Jason, Greg, BBsan, Pascal, Tim, and Tony.

To my mom, for her wisdom of people. To my dad, for his appreciation of nuance. To Amy, for her patience and perspective. To Gretchen and Max, my first play testers and the most candid, hilarious people I know.

To everyone who made the games that I loved growing up. And to everyone in the ROM hacking community of the '90s who first showed me how to break those games into pieces.

To open source contributors. I wouldn't be able to have fun or work in nearly the same way if there weren't people so committed to making the world awesome. Thanks especially to the people who built the tools that I use in this book (see Appendix C, "Resources"). This book absolutely couldn't exist without their efforts. And a special thanks to Kesiev for his early work in synthesizing and presenting the promise of HTML5 gaming.

I want to thank Mr. Morris for simultaneously justifying rebellion and paying attention; Dr. Jamison for teaching me to value breadth and depth of understanding; and Dr. Hatasa for giving me a chance to see the world from a completely new perspective.

Thanks to all the choir and theater kids, punks, weirdos, nerds, hackers, engineers, entrepreneurs, researchers, designers, dreamers, and polyglots who have kept me sane, entertained, and in just the right amount of trouble over the years. And a special thanks to the one theater kid who has put up with me for so long.

Finally, thanks to everyone who believed in me and told me why, and to everyone who didn't and told me why.

# ABOUT THE AUTHOR

**Evan Burchard** recognizes that he is not the first or last person driven to learn programming by an interest in creating games, and seeks to empower others to take full advantage of the modern, free, and game-friendly web. In addition to designing games with electricity, ice, fire, and the latest browser technologies, he enjoys extremely long walks (his current record is Massachusetts to Iowa).

# INTRODUCTION

Games used to require specialized tools to produce. Now all you need is a browser and a text editor. Even outside of HTML5 games, the time and cost to make a game has dropped so dramatically that people can now build games in hours or days. The indie game developer scene is growing, as are game jams, the online and in-person get-togethers for rapid game making.

The typical time frame for a game jam is 48 hours, as codified by larger distributed events such as Global Game Jam and Ludum Dare. But game designers (by definition) like to invent their own rules, so some jams can be as short as 1 hour long. Besides the social and collaborative benefits, game creators forcing themselves to create a game quickly can make them faster the next time around, which are great skills for long-term or short-term projects.

"Building things quickly" isn't just for those indie developer punks. In the corporate world, it's called productivity. Finding and learning to use good tools is a much easier path to productivity than the ill-defined goal of "getting smarter." And it passes quite convincingly as intelligence, especially if your definition of "tool" encompasses things such as mathematics.

This book tracks down some of the best HTML5 game engines available, whittled down from an initial list of more than 100. These, and the other tools in this book, enable you to create games quickly in the browser. All of them are accessible in that nothing is required beyond loading their JavaScript into an HTML file and occasionally adding a few lines of code. Overall, the chosen few have great documentation and a thriving community around them. Some of the engines are bigger than others. They all expose a unique set of functionality for game making, and through learning to use a few, you can start to see what is common among them as well as what is different.

Each engine is paired with a complementary game genre in each chapter. The complexity of the genre informs the requirements for increasingly feature-rich engines as you progress through the book. By the end, you should feel comfortable learning a new game engine or even hacking together your own.

Each game can be created in a few hours. Will these be your favorite games of the given genre? It's highly unlikely. This book demonstrates how to break down genres of games into their basic elements. This lays the foundation, puts up the frame, and installs the drywall. In some cases, the author has decorated sparsely. There might be a big hole in the roof and the author's favorite pictures are hanging on the wall. Don't hesitate to build a courtyard, install shag carpeting, or plant some ginkgo trees if you want. Take down my pictures. You'll see where to get all of the materials you need, but it's your house. Do whatever you want with it. These are your games as soon as you load them up.

When you finish this book, you should be able to easily think of a scene from your favorite game, break it into a list of features, and know how you would create a similar experience by using the toolset you use throughout this book. You might even have a sense of how difficult it is or how long it would take. If you are productive with these tools, and you have a good story to tell, you should be able to create something that someone loves in no time.

## Audience for This Book

There are many paths that may have brought you here. If you have an interest in games, and are just learning to code, this book is for you. If you are a web developer or designer who is looking for exposure to tools, techniques, or templates for making games, or you want to go from beginner to intermediate level JavaScript coding, this book is for you. If you are a game designer or developer for flash, native mobile/desktop applications, or some other platform, investigating how to build things in an HTML5/JavaScript context, this book is for you also. If you have a tattoo of the HTML5 shield, regularly present about your open source contributions to game engines, and can jam out an HTML5 Mario 64 clone with a native iPhone port in a weekend, this book might not be what you're looking for.

## Coding Style Conventions Used In This Book

To indicate that a line is new or has changes, bold text is used. When code is omitted from a listing, an ellipsis (...) is used in place of 1 or more lines of code. To explicitly call out removed or changed lines of code, a commented (begins with //), bolded line of code is used in its place. If an entire listing shows new code, the text will not be bold.

The continuation character (➡) indicates that code is continued from the previous line.

When code appears inside of the text, `it will look like this`.

> ### note
> When there is something that requires a bit more explanation, it is called out in a "note" that looks like this.

> ## tip
> When there is something that doesn't quite fit in the text, but is helpful to know, it appears as a "tip" that looks like this.

> ## warning
> **WARNINGS LOOK LIKE THIS**  A "warning" is used when there is something that may not be obvious and could cause problems if you did not know about it.

# How This Book Is Organized

This book is broken up into 11 chapters, with one game per each in Chapters 1 through 10, along with three appendixes (A, "JavaScript Basics," B, "Quality Control," and C, "Resources"). Chapter 1, "Quiz," assumes no knowledge of HTML, CSS, JavaScript, or a functional toolset. The rest of the chapters assume that Appendix A and Chapter 1 are well understood by you. From a code standpoint, none of the chapters rely on tools built in previous chapters. That said, the genres are ordered roughly by their complexity, so gaining experience in the simpler genres may be of benefit in creating the games in the later chapters. Chapter 11, "Leveling Up," serves as a guide to what you might want to do after completing this book. It is complemented by the list of resources in Appendix C, which also supports Chapters 1 through 10 by highlighting what tools are needed to create the games in this book.

Each game is broken up into "recipes," which, in addition to breaking up games into understandable chunks of code and text, are reflected in the source files provided at jsarcade.com. What this means is that every recipe contains a complementary folder within the code that can be downloaded on the companion site. If you get lost or want to warp ahead, you can start fresh with the code in a later recipe. Also, if you want to preview what the game will be like when you finish a chapter, you can warp straight to the "final" directory for the given game/ chapter and see what it is you are making.

If you find yourself getting lost a lot, and you have a good understanding of the material in Chapter 1 and Appendix A, Appendix B is there to provide more context around how to prevent getting stuck, and what to do about it when you are.

# How To Use This Book

To make full use of the text, you need to download the source code files for each chapter. This includes JavaScript, HTML, CSS, images, and any additional files needed for each recipe. They are linked to at jsarcade.com. Code is organized first by chapter title. Inside of each chapter's directory is a full copy of the code you need to make the game run, with three different types of directories. "initial/" marks the minimum amount of code you need to have a game running. "after_recipe<x>/" directories specify "checkpoints" after each recipe (most headings in each chapter) so that in case you get lost along the way somehow, you can be confused for only a page or two. The "final/" directory specifies the finished game after you complete a chapter. While inside any of the chapters' recipe directories, you can see an index.html file. If you double-click it or otherwise open it in a browser by some other means, you can see the game as it exists after following the recipe that is indicated by the directory name. Demos of all the final versions of each game are available at jsarcade.com, so you can preview a game and choose which one you want to implement next.

> ## note
>
> The source files for all the games, game engines, and other required software are available to download at jsarcade.com and the Publisher's website at informit.com/title/9780321898388

You can skip around, but keep in mind that the games get more complex as the book progresses. If you have trouble understanding anything, make use of the checkpoint (after_recipe<x>) code, and pay special attention to Chapter 1 and Appendix A. If you have trouble understanding why something is going wrong, read through Appendix B.

You may notice that after finishing a chapter, you still feel like the game is missing something. It could be an explosion, a great storyline, or a boss battle. You can find suggestions at the end of each chapter of things that you could add to them—whether you have different ideas or like the suggestions provided, go for it. These become your games as soon as you get the code running on your computer. They are templates, and meant to be hacked, extended, and personalized. I will applaud and definitely not sue you for beating me at my own game making.

# CHAPTER 1

# QUIZ

This type of game has simple rules. There is a right answer. You either know or you guess. From trivia nights at restaurants to the SAT, it would be an understatement to call this genre of game "pervasive" in today's world. TV game shows often find their way into an interactive format. Even when there are more elements to a game than simple questions and answers, every piece of software operates on some kind of underlying logic. When the king asks if you want to fight the dragon, and you have to say "yes," that's a fairly small, easy quiz. It would be a stretch to say that falling in a hole in a platformer, or losing all of your hit points in an RPG, is the same experience as missing a question on a quiz, but programming the rules and consequences of each is similar in all game genres.

# Recipe: Making the Questions

To accommodate various levels of web development experience among readers, this chapter is intended to be as clear as possible for people just starting out. The following chapters become more complex, but this chapter's material is meant to ensure an appropriate level of understanding early. We all started somewhere, and for some it might be here. If the information presented in this chapter seems extremely simple to you, you can skim it or skip it entirely. Things will become more complicated and difficult later.

There are three primary goals in developing this chapter's game. First, we want to establish a baseline understanding of HTML, CSS, and JavaScript. The knowledge of JavaScript required for this book is the deepest of the three. If you're unsure about JavaScript basics along the way, check out Appendix A, "JavaScript Basics," for a reference. Second, we use a lot of external libraries throughout the book, so we want to ensure at this point that you have no trouble bringing them in. Third, we want to establish a comfortable, repeatable pattern for creating, editing, saving, and opening files that are fundamental to using this book.

If you don't have a text editor, you will need one now. You can use any number of tools to create and edit the JavaScript, HTML, and CSS files in this book. If you don't know what text editor is right for you, see Appendix C, "Resources," to get an idea of your options.

To start, open your text editor, and add the code in Listing 1.1 to the quiz/initial/index.html file. If you haven't downloaded the files for this book yet, see the Introduction for details on getting the code.

**Listing 1.1**   index.html Showing the html Structure

```
<!DOCTYPE html>
<html>
  <head>
    <meta charset="utf-8">
    <title>Quiz</title>
    <link rel="stylesheet" type="text/css" href="main.css">
  </head>
  <body>
    <h1>Quiz</h1>
    <div id="quiz">
    </div>
  </body>
</html>
```

> **note**
>
> HTML stands for HyperText Markup Language. Way back when, *links* were also called *hyperlinks*, and there were a few other *hyper*-related things that amounted to being able to jump from document to document. HyperText is kind of like normal text with these hyperlinks in it. Markup is auxiliary text around the HyperText to give a bit more context. So HTML is a collection of syntax guidelines for combining different types of text to produce linkable pages that end up having an .html extension.
>
> An HTML tag is text that appears in <angle brackets like these>, and an HTML *element* is anything that appears between a <beginning tag> and a </closing tag>, including the beginning and closing tags. Notice the "/" used in the closing tag.

You start by declaring the DOCTYPE. This lets the browser know that the document it is parsing and presenting is HTML. There are other file formats that browsers can open, from XML documents to audio files and images, so this makes it clear that you want this file processed as a normal web page. You might be wondering about the consequences of not doing this. The truth is that it depends on what browser you are using, and the effects can be anywhere from subtle to terrible. Effectively, they are unknown, which is a good enough reason not to forget this preamble in your document.

Next, you have an <html> tag. This wraps the document with a global container, and its typical contents are one <head> tag and one <body> tag, just as you have here. You might notice that all three of these tags having ending tags with a slash (for example, </body>). This is how you specify what inner elements the element is wrapping.

What goes inside of the <head> tag is, generally speaking, information that is important for the browser to know about, but not directly related to what the user sees within the main part of the browser window. The <meta> tag serves many purposes. Here it is describing what the text encoding should be for the document. If you don't have this, characters that are outside of a fairly limited (although common) set will be treated in unpredictable ways. Most day-to-day characters for English speakers will render correctly, but if you work with international characters, you could have a problem. Additionally, you see a warning in the JavaScript console (Firebug or Chrome developer tools) saying that you should have this. That said, this tag has been omitted in many cases throughout this book so that you can focus on what is original in each chapter.

The <title> tag describes what text displays in the uppermost part of the browser (depending on the browser, this could be the header bar, the tab, or both) and is also often used by applications providing shortcuts and bookmarks to give an "at a glance" idea of the page.

Next is a `<link>` tag that specifies its `rel` attribute as a `stylesheet`, the `type` attribute as a css file, and the `href` to describe the path of where the file is stored on your computer. This path (just the filename) indicates that it is sitting next to index.html in the same directory. You see this tag frequently to link an external style sheet (CSS file), and except for the path, it will stay the same most of the time. One additional thing to note about the `<link>` tag is that it, like the `<meta>` tag, does not have a closing tag (like `</link>`). For tags that are not acting as containers, these are not always necessary.

In the `<body>` tag, you have two nested elements. The first is a header (`<h1>`) tag that has default styling to make the text inside appear larger. The `<div>` tag is a major organizational element for containing chunks of marked-up information. In this case, it has an attribute, `id`, which, along with the tag name and the attribute `class`, forms the three most common ways to specify styles with CSS (for example, new colors and text sizes) and behavior with JavaScript (for example, when this is clicked, turn the page upside-down).

You don't yet have anything in your `<div>` element, but before you start adding anything new, check to see that you're on track. Save your file as index.html, and open a browser. Then, either type the file path for the file into the URL bar, drag it from the desktop into the URL bar, or double-click it.

After you get the file to open in a browser, you should see something like Figure 1.1. Notice that "Quiz" appears as the name of the tab because of the `<title>` tag you specified earlier.

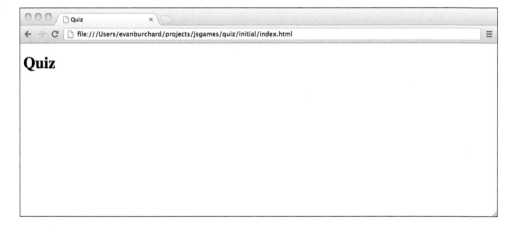

**Figure 1.1**  Opening the html file in Chrome

If you don't have Chrome or Firefox, you should download both now. They highlight different issues that arise when developing HTML5 games, and you will use both. They are not treated as completely interchangeable throughout this book.

Now head into your `<div>` tag, and add some questions to your index.html file with the bold code in Listing 1.2. This sample is rather long but regular. If you want to save yourself some typing, this file can be copied from quiz/after_recipe1/index.html.

**Listing 1.2**   The Questions of the Quiz

```
...
<div id="quiz">
  <div id="question1">
    <div class="question">Which is not a main file type that we
➥use to make websites?</div>
    <input type="radio" name="question1" value="a"/>
    <label>.html</label>
    <input type="radio" name="question1" value="b"/>
    <label>.exe</label>
    <input type="radio" name="question1" value="c"/>
    <label>.js</label>
    <input type="radio" name="question1" value="d"/>
    <label>.css</label>
  </div>
  <br />
  <div id="question2">
    <div class="question">A JavaScript object is wrapped by what
➥characters?</div>
    <input type="radio" name="question2" value="a"/>
    <label>[]</label>
    <input type="radio" name="question2" value="b"/>
    <label>;;</label>
    <input type="radio" name="question2" value="c"/>
    <label>{}</label>
    <input type="radio" name="question2" value="d"/>
    <label>()</label>
  </div>
  <br />
  <div id="question3">
    <div class="question">Moles are which of the following?</div>
    <input type="radio" name="question3" value="a"/>
    <label>Omniverous</label>
    <input type="radio" name="question3" value="b"/>
    <label>Adorable</label>
    <input type="radio" name="question3" value="c"/>
    <label>Whackable</label>
    <input type="radio" name="question3" value="d"/>
    <label>All of the above</label>
  </div>
  <br />
  <div id="question4">
```

```html
    <div class="question">In Japanese "か" is prounounced...</div>
    <input type="radio" name="question4" value="a"/>
    <label>ka</label>
    <input type="radio" name="question4" value="b"/>
    <label>ko</label>
    <input type="radio" name="question4" value="c"/>
    <label>ke</label>
    <input type="radio" name="question4" value="d"/>
    <label>ki</label>
  </div>
  <br />
  <div id="question5">
    <div class="question">The gravitational constant on earth is
➡approximately...</div>
    <input type="radio" name="question5" value="a"/>
    <label>10m/s^2</label>
    <input type="radio" name="question5" value="b"/>
    <label>.809m/s^2</label>
    <input type="radio" name="question5" value="c"/>
    <label>9.81m/s^2</label>
    <input type="radio" name="question5" value="d"/>
    <label>84.4m/s^2</label>
  </div>
  <br />
  <div id="question6">
    <div class="question">45 (in base 10) is what in binary
➡(base 2)?</div>
    <input type="radio" name="question6" value="a"/>
    <label>101101</label>
    <input type="radio" name="question6" value="b"/>
    <label>110011</label>
    <input type="radio" name="question6" value="c"/>
    <label>011101</label>
    <input type="radio" name="question6" value="d"/>
    <label>101011</label>
  </div>
  <br />
  <div id="question7">
    <div class="question">4 << 2 = ...</div>
    <input type="radio" name="question7" value="a"/>
    <label>16</label>
    <input type="radio" name="question7" value="b"/>
    <label>4</label>
    <input type="radio" name="question7" value="c"/>
    <label>2</label>
    <input type="radio" name="question7" value="d"/>
    <label>8</label>
```

```
    </div>
    <br />
    <div id="question8">
       <div class="question">Given the lengths of two sides of a
➥right triangle (one with a 90 degree angle), how would you find
➥the hypotenuse?</div>
       <input type="radio" name="question8" value="a"/>
       <label>Pi*Radius^2</label>
       <input type="radio" name="question8" value="b"/>
       <label>Pythagorean Theorem</label>
       <input type="radio" name="question8" value="c"/>
       <label>Calculator?</label>
       <input type="radio" name="question8" value="d"/>
       <label>Sin(side1 + side2)</label>
    </div>
    <br />
    <div id="question9">
       <div class="question">True or False: All games must run at at
➥least 60 frames per second to be any good.</div>
       <input type="radio" name="question9" value="a"/>
       <label>True</label>
       <input type="radio" name="question9" value="b"/>
       <label>False</label>
    </div>
    <br />
    <div id="question10">
       <div class="question">Using a server can help you to...</div>
       <input type="radio" name="question10" value="a"/>
       <label>hide your code.</label>
       <input type="radio" name="question10" value="b"/>
       <label>have a performant game.</label>
       <input type="radio" name="question10" value="c"/>
       <label>create shared experiences for players.</label>
       <input type="radio" name="question10" value="d"/>
       <label>all of the above.</label>
    </div>
 </div>
 ...
```

Each question in this quiz has the same structure but with different indicators of the question number and different question and choice text. Now pretend that you are concerned only with the first question. In this case, you start with a `<div>` tag with the `id` of `question1`. This is a unique identifier that you can use later. This `<div>` tag wraps the entire question and answer block. Next, another `<div>` tag contains the text of the question. This has a `class` of `question`. Recall that `class`, like tag name (for example, `<div>`) or `id`, is a way to reference this element later. The major difference between `class` and `id` is that an `id` is unique but classes can be shared.

Next, you have an `<input>` tag with three attributes. The `type="radio"` means that it is a radio button. If you don't know what that looks like, see Figure 1.2. The second attribute, `name`, must be unique among all the choices that ask the same question. The `value` stores what is typically passed during html form submissions in a similar way that text entered into a text field gets passed along. You won't be submitting any forms, but you will be using JavaScript later to check the answers on this page via these values. So far, you have seen tags that don't require an ending tag and ones that do. This input tag is a third type that ends with a `/>`, indicating that it is acting as its own closing tag.

The `<label>` tags are used for text that sits outside of an input element. Their main function is to give focus to their complementary input when clicked. You don't implement that here, but if you want that functionality, add a unique `id` to each answer, such as `id="question-10-"answer-b"` and give the corresponding label a `for` attribute like `<label for="question-10-answer-b">`.

Between each question is a break tag (`<br />`) that ends with a slash and acts as its own ending tag. The break tag puts vertical space between things. How much space is not consistent from browser to browser, so in cases in which the layout matters (most but not here), this space should be added with CSS styling instead.

If all went according to plan, if you save and open this file in your browser, you should now see something like Figure 1.2.

## Recipe: Hiding and Showing Your Quiz

Games frequently have a notion of unlockables. Some examples are unlockable characters, unlockable side quests, and unlockable levels. Here, you have unlockable questions. It may seem like you're headed backward, but it is only because your content is so simple and perceivable. You would not expect to play every level of a Mario game at once, right? If your quiz were 100 questions instead of 10, you might feel the same way about showing all the questions at once.

So how should you lock down your content? You have many options, including putting questions on separate pages, but for the sake of starting out simple, just add a CSS file that can prevent the content from showing. Next, you need a new file called main.css with the code in Listing 1.3 to sit in the same directory as index.html.

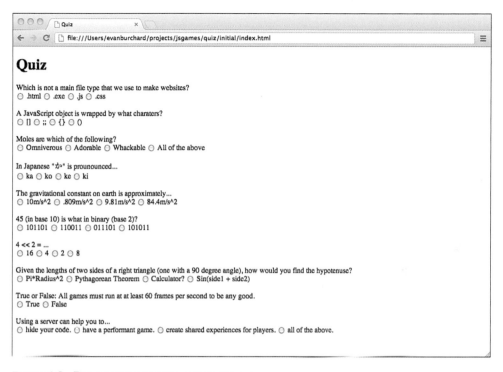

**Figure 1.2**  The questions and answers for the quiz

**Listing 1.3**  main.css to Hide the Content

```
#quiz{
   display:none;
}
body{
   margin-left:50px;
}
```

`#quiz` refers to everything inside a container element such as a `div` with the `id` of `quiz`. The `display:none` here is what hides everything inside of the `div` with the `id` of `quiz`. If you were selecting an element with the `id` of `another-quiz`, your style selector would be `#another-quiz`. If you were selecting the elements with a `class` of quiz, you would use a dot instead of a # symbol for your selector, so it would be `.quiz`.

Tag-based selectors have nothing in front of their names, so to select the `body` tag, you don't need a dot or a # symbol. Adding `margin-left:50px;` here bumps the page to the right a little bit. Notice the format of both of these styling blocks. You have a selector, an open brace, styling information, and then a closing brace. In the styling format, you have the label for the css attribute name on the left, followed by a colon, followed by the value of the css attribute you want to affect, and followed by a semicolon to terminate the line.

If you're just starting out with web development, this syntax can be tricky, especially when paired with html tags, along with their ids, classes, and other attributes being introduced simultaneously. The good news is that you have just covered basics of CSS and HTML. You will be exposed to new attributes and selectors, but the fundamentals are right here. In the short term, if you make a mistake, it's probably something simple like swapping a dot for a # symbol, not terminating with a semicolon or curly brace, or some other form of typo. Truthfully, those are the most common mistakes that professionals make, too. If something isn't working, slow down and carefully read what you have written.

At this point, if you save the files and open index.html in a browser, it will look like you are back at Figure 1.1, but with the indenting from the styling you added to `body`.

# Recipe: Getting Your Questions Back

With all your questions gone, you need a way to get them back. You can do this in a roundabout way by adding packages used in each of the later chapters. For each package you add, you'll add a question back in.

Before you ensure that packages can be loaded, first you need to make sure that you can load any JavaScript whatsoever. At almost the bottom of your index.html file, add the bold line in Listing 1.4.

**Listing 1.4**  Loading Your First External JavaScript File

```
...
    <script src="game.js"></script>
  </body>
</html>
```

This loads the game.js JavaScript file. Next, you need to create that file. Create a file called game.js in the same directory as main.css and index.html and add the code in Listing 1.5.

**Listing 1.5**  The game.js File

```
alert('Hello world');
console.log('Hello world');
```

This code prints information to two places. If you open the index.html file in your browser, the first place, the alert box, is obvious. The second line with `console.log` prints to the JavaScript console, an indispensable tool for development. If you need more information about getting a JavaScript console up and running, see Appendix B, "Quality Control."

With that out of the way, next let's take on jQuery. To get this, going to jquery.com is probably the fastest route. How you get it from its website into your file system is up to you. The author simply hit the biggest, shiniest button, which led to a page that showed only the text of the code. He then copied and pasted that into a new file that he created and called jquery.js. Then he saved that file.

There are buttons on the site that just give you a file to download in a more traditional way as well. How you do it is up to you, but make sure that you get it into the right directory on your file system (the same one where index.html, main.css, and game.js are located).

After you have the file in the proper directory, add the bolded line in Listing 1.6 to the bottom of the index.html file. Make sure that your filename matches what is listed in this file.

**Listing 1.6**   Adding jQuery to the index.html File

```
. . .
    <script src="jquery.js"></script>
    <script src="game.js"></script>
  </body>
</html>
```

If your file is called something other than `jquery.js`, you must change this to load the file properly.

Before we go any further, we need to adjust our CSS file a bit. We were too aggressive before. Instead of hiding the entire quiz, let's be more specific and hide every question individually with the code in Listing 1.7.

**Listing 1.7**   Hiding the Questions, Not the Quiz

```
body{
  margin-left:50px;
}
#question1, #question2, #question3, #question4, #question5,
#question6, #question7, #question8, #question9, #question10{
  display:none;
}
```

You deleted the #quiz id selector from before and replaced it with a comma-separated list of id selectors to affect. Instead of doing it this way, you could have declared a common class for all these elements and used a dot selector. However, using a list of selectors in this way is good to be aware of.

Now that you changed how your hiding works with the CSS acting as the bad guy, use jQuery as the good guy to help you unlock a question. To do this, change your game.js code to that which is found in Listing 1.8. This should replace the code previously written in this file.

**Listing 1.8**   Showing Your First Question if jQuery Is Loaded

```
if(jQuery){
  $("#question1").show();
};
```

In the first line, you check to see if jQuery is loaded. If it is, you execute the second line. On the second line, you use jQuery's $ function, passing in the CSS selector #question1, surrounded by quotes and parentheses. Then, you execute jQuery's show function to change display:none to display:block for the first question.

If you save the files and load index.html in your browser, you see that your first question is back in action.

# Recipe: The Shopping List

In this recipe, you have nine more files that you need to import. You might be wondering why you would hide questions only to show them again if you are able to load a file. Downloading files and including them in other files might seem like a repetitive or unnecessary exercise to many of you, but understanding how to access and leverage other peoples' code is crucial. Few projects are built from scratch, and learning how to build games by "standing on the shoulders of giants" is well worth your time if you don't have this skill yet. In addition, this section gives a preview of what kinds of files you will use in later chapters.

That said, if you are comfortable with integrating JavaScript libraries into a system and have a good understanding of version control, much of what follows will be a review. Feel free to skim or skip this recipe.

Here are the files that you need, and what they are used for in the book:

1. **jquery.js:** You already have this one. It's used by a few different chapters to easily select and manipulate page elements.

2. **impress.js:** In Chapter 3, "Party," you use this presentation tool (like PowerPoint, but in JavaScript) as a game engine for managing the "pages" of your interactive fiction game.

3. **atom.js:** Weighing in at an uncompressed 203 lines of coffeescript, this is certainly one of the smallest game engines there is. You use this to build the party game.

4. **easel.js:** This provides a nicer interface to the canvas API that we use when exploring how to draw elements for the puzzle game.

5. **melon.js:** This is the engine that you use for Chapter 5, "Platformer."

6. **yabble.js:** When you build the fighting game, this is the library that you use to load the "game.js" game engine (not to be confused with your game.js file in this chapter and others).

7. **jquery.gamequery.js:** This is a jQuery plug-in that is also a game engine. You use it to make the side-scrolling shooter.

8. **jaws.js:** This is an all-around solid game engine that you use (with old-fashioned trigonometry) to build the first person shooter.

9. **enchant.js:** Hailing from Japan, this game engine has a ton of features and great support for mobile. You use this for the RPG in Chapter 9, "RPG."

10. **crafty.js:** This is a fully featured extremely well-supported game engine that you use to build the RTS. (If the author had to pick just one game engine to take to a deserted island, it might be this one.)

So, now that you have the main library that you use in this chapter, jQuery, taken care of, let's go shopping for the rest. If you were feeling particularly adventurous, you could try grabbing them all from their project pages listed in Appendix C, "Resources." Alternatively, they are available in the after_recipe4 section of this chapter's files. Just make sure to put the files in the same directory as your index.html file.

If you took a look at Appendix C, you may have noticed that these files are also hosted on github. For getting files from github, you have three options. The first is that you can download the entire project as a zip file, unzip it, and then use the files you need.

The second is that you make your way through the project, click the relevant file, create a new empty file on your computer, and copy and paste the code as it appears on github into your local file. This might seem convoluted, but it can be a fast process.

The third option is a little more complicated but could provide you with a better process while you work, now and in the future. The third option is to install git, use it to download (clone) the project, and head to the chapter's directory to get the files for this chapter. You can work out of this directory or just copy the files you need from it.

git is a "version control system" that enables you to keep track of the changes you make to your files. github is a website where people (many programmers working with many languages) who use this tool can find other projects and manage their own. It is free to use with public projects. The author highly recommends taking this path. The best instructions for installing git are at help.github.com/articles/set-up-git.

After getting all the required files, one way or another, you should end up with a file system containing files so that it looks like Figure 1.3.

With that in place, you can start requiring these JavaScript files by adding the bolded lines in Listing 1.9 to the bottom of index.html.

**Listing 1.9**  Requiring Your JavaScript Files in index.html

```
<script src="jquery.js"></script>
<script src="impress.js"></script>
<!-- atom needs this to run -->
<canvas></canvas>
<script src="atom.js"></script>
<script src="easel.js"></script>
<script src="melon.js"></script>
<script src="yabble.js"></script>
<script src="jquery.gamequery.js"></script>
<script src="jaws.js"></script>
<script src="enchant.js"></script>
```

```
<script src="crafty.js"></script>
  <script src="game.js"></script>
</body>
</html>
```

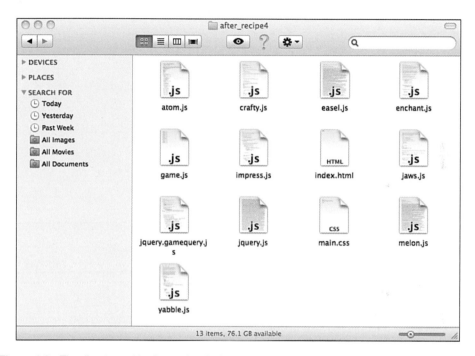

**Figure 1.3** The directory with all your JavaScript files in it

Make sure that the names of the files that you are including match the names of your files as referenced in index.html. The process of requiring JavaScript files from html usually follows this simple pattern of using `<script>` tags. One oddity within this section is the `<canvas>` element that you added above atom.js, along with the `<!-- -->` line above that. You add this `<canvas>` element because without it, atom.js cannot work. In most game engines, you must indicate that you want to start the engine by calling an initializing function or referencing a particular `<canvas>` element to work with. atom.js starts hunting for a canvas tag as soon as you require it. Rather than fight it (edit atom.js), just give it what it wants. The `<!-- -->` line is an HTML comment. The idea here is that you can make a note to yourself or others, but the comments are ignored by the browser. Keep in mind that these are still potentially user-facing, and anyone who "views the source" of the HTML page can see them. If you don't know what that means, see Appendix B.

Next, in the game.js file, get the rest of your questions back. You can accomplish this by adding the bold lines in Listing 1.10 to game.js.

**Listing 1.10**   Getting the Rest of the Questions Back

```
if(jQuery){
    $("#question1").show();
};
if(impress){
    $("#question2").show();
};
if(atom){
    $("#question3").show();
};
if(createjs){
    $("#question4").show();
};
if(me){
    $("#question5").show();
};
if(require){
    $("#question6").show();
};
if($().playground){
    $("#question7").show();
};
if(jaws){
    $("#question8").show();
};
if(enchant){
    $("#question9").show();
};
if(Crafty){
    $("#question10").show();
};
```

Here you can see that, like jQuery, the most common, immediately perceivable effect when importing a JavaScript file is that some object becomes available. One notable exception is the check for `playground` to show question number 7. gameQuery is a jQuery extension, and as such, it provides utilities on top of jQuery. For this reason, it does not come with a core object of its very own, so it looks for the `playground` function to be defined on the jQuery's `$()` instead.

**Listing 1.11**   Some CSS to Hide the Canvas in main.css

```
body{
  margin-left:50px;
}
#question1, #question2, #question3, #question4, #question5,
#question6, #question7, #question8, #question9, #question10{
  display:none;
}
canvas{
  display:none;
}
```

# Recipe: Which Answers Are Correct?

To figure out which answers are correct, you could simply add a "correct" class to each answer that is correct, but that seems a little too easy, both in terms of implementation and for a player's ability to figure it out. Everything that you have in these files, even a comment, is visible to the user, so if they didn't know the right answer, they could just view the source to find out what is right. To make this slightly more difficult for people with knowledge of programming, and impossible for those without it, you can implement a weak hashing function to check for correct answers.

A *hashing function* is something that takes one value and makes another value out of it. The strength of a hashing function is related to how easy it is to determine what the first value is just by having the second "hashed" value.

Before getting to that, let's create a style that makes it clear that something has happened when you get all the questions right. You can do this by adding the bolded lines in Listing 1.12 added to the end of main.css.

**Listing 1.12** A Winning Style in main.css

```
body{
  margin-left:50px;
}
#question1, #question2, #question3, #question4, #question5,
#question6, #question7, #question8, #question9, #question10{
  display:none;
}
canvas{
  display:none;
}
.correct{
  background-color:#24399f;
  color:white;
}
```

This style indicates a blue background and white text are added for elements with a `class` of `correct`. You can add this class when the player wins. In kindergarten or before, you probably heard once or twice about the color white, but the color #24399f rarely comes up in conversation, even in most graduate programs. This is a Red Green Blue (RGB) color. The first two numbers determine the red value, the middle two numbers determine the green value, and the last two determine the blue value.

But hang on a second. That last number looks like an "f." That's not a number. If you were using base 10 (the decimal system), that would be correct. And if you were using the decimal system, you would also be limited to 100 (0-9, 0-9 or 10 x 10) values for each color type. Someone decided that wasn't enough colors for the web, so you use base 16 here (hexadecimal), which gives you 256 (16 x 16) shades of each RGB value. There are a limited number of color names as well, but you can also call white `#ffffff` and black `#00000` instead. By the way, someone else at some point decided this might be too many colors, so you can also just use 3 hex values (one for each value of red, green or blue), making black #000 and white #fff.

With the CSS changes out of the way, you now have one small addition to your index.html file. You must replace the opening body tag with the bold line of code in Listing 1.13.

**Listing 1.13**   Adding an onclick Handler to Body in index.html

```
<!DOCTYPE html>
<html>
  <head>
    <meta charset="utf-8">
    <title>Quiz</title>
    <link rel="stylesheet" type="text/css" href="main.css">
  </head>
<body onclick="checkAnswers();">
```

Instead of a plain `<body>` tag, you now have one with an `onclick` attribute that contains a string of JavaScript in quotes. If the word "string" was confusing, read through Appendix A and come back. This string in an `onclick` handler says to run the `checkAnswers` function any time any element inside of the page is clicked. Note that when calling a function, you use the parentheses. If they are omitted, you simply refer to but do not call the function.

Now for your last code sample of the chapter, Listing 1.14, see what happens when the function is called. This bolded code can go at the top of the game.js file, in between the jQuery check and showing question 1.

**Listing 1.14**   Checking for Right Answers

```
if(jQuery){
  var checkAnswers = function(){
    var answerString = "";
    var answers = $(":checked");
    answers.each(function(i) {
      answerString = answerString + answers[i].value;
    });
    $(":checked").each(function(i) {
      var answerString = answerString + answers[i].value;
    });
    checkIfCorrect(answerString);
  };

  var checkIfCorrect = function(theString){
    if(parseInt(theString, 16) === 811124566973){
```

```
        $("body").addClass("correct");
        $("h1").text("You Win!");
        $("canvas").show();
      }
    };

    $("#question1").show();
  }
  . . .
```

Here, you define two functions in bold. The first, `checkAnswers`, sets an empty string that you will be adding to. Next, the value of each one of the radio buttons that has been clicked is added to the answer string (in order). After that loop is executed, the second function, `checkIfCorrect`, is called to verify the string is equal to a long number. Why do you use this number?

Recall when talking about CSS colors that hexadecimal values can range from 0–f. That means that a–d, which is what your answers are, are all valid hexadecimal numbers. (You can think of them as 10-13.) So you just string them together, and the long number is just the decimal form of your hexadecimal string.

If it matches, you add the class of "correct" to the body element, which triggers the background and text color change. Next the text at your h1 tag, "Quiz," is replaced with the words "You Win!" Finally, you use that canvas element that you hid before to lock mouse input on the screen. Rather than this, a more typical approach would be to disable the inputs with jQuery's `disable` function, but this is kind of an interesting hack to get some value out of that canvas tag you weren't using for anything. This canvas element could end up being a game, built with atom.js where the quiz simply serves as a barrier to playing.

When all is said and done, if you save the files and load index.html into a browser, you should end up with something like Figure 1.4.

## Summary

In this chapter, we created a simple quiz game with questions pertinent to each chapter in the book. You set up an extra challenge for yourself by making the questions unlockable by adding JavaScript libraries used throughout the book. To check the answers, you implemented a weak hashing function to convert the hexadecimal values in the quiz values into a long decimal value.

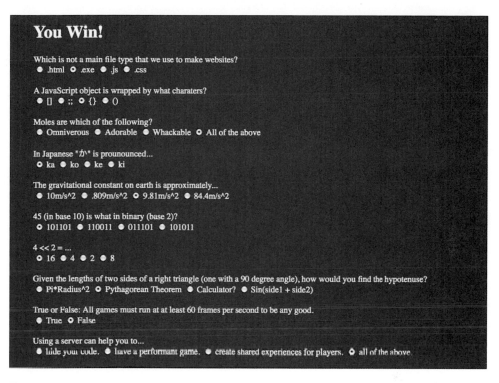

**Figure 1.4** All the right answers with a winning state

On our way to completing this game, we covered basic HTML/CSS/jQuery, git, and software licensing. This chapter also highlighted some game engines and other libraries that you will use throughout the rest of this book.

If you want to take the quiz game further, you could see if you could make a second page of questions that are only available if you get the first ones correct. Chapter 2 covers one possibility for displaying more dynamic information, so that may serve as inspiration. Alternatively, you ended this game by covering everything with a canvas. You could put another game on there. After all, atom.js is watching that canvas, waiting for you to come back after you read about it in Chapter 3, "Party."

If this chapter was difficult, take some more time with it and Appendix A. If this chapter was a breeze, don't worry. The gloves come off in Chapter 2. And by Chapter 6, "Fighting," we put on the brass knuckles.

# INTERACTIVE FICTION

For readers who grew up in the age of modern games, MMORPGs, real-time first person shooters, and sports games that have actually informed how play happens on a real-life football field, it may be easy to dismiss very early games created without the benefit of sophisticated hardware and software. The genres of interactive fiction, *gamebooks* such as the Choose Your Own Adventure series, and point and-click adventures had to rely on different elements to engage their players. For some games such as *Zork*, it was the novelty of presenting an expansive world with a rich set of interaction verbs from a command line, paired with a large amount of objects to pick up, inspect, eat, and go along in your quest.

With point-and-click adventures on the NES such as *Shadowgate* and *Maniac Mansion*, this feeling of an immersive, interactive world is preserved, and horror and comedy are presented richly, especially given the limitations of technology at the time. Incidentally, if you are a fan of *Maniac Mansion*, JavaScript, games in general, or this genre, read Douglas Crockford's post-mortem about his work on the NES version of that game (http://www.crockford.com/wrrrld/maniac.html). If you don't know who he is, he wrote *JavaScript: The Good Parts*, *JSLint*, and is an all-around hero in the JavaScript community.

This type of game might seem a bit old-school, but there are a few contexts where it is valuable. *Double Fine Adventure*, the latest from the people who created *Monkey Island* and yes, *Maniac Mansion*, raised nearly 3.5 million dollars in 2012. Japanese dating sims have been extremely popular for a while, and even spill into other genres like the initially original RPG *Harvest Moon* for SNES with its quest of courtship running alongside the main goal of building a farm. A word of warning here: Themes such as "getting the girl" or "rescuing the girl" are considered by many to be trite and offensive. Check in with other peoples' perspectives in general, but especially when you make a game for them because it is possible to make a game *against* them if you don't make an effort in this way. More options are available technically and culturally than ever before, and it is a waste not to explore and understand all your options. Within this genre, you have a great deal of potential to explore input that is free form, or restricted, and set a mood that can be extremely dark, whimsical, or anything in between.

For the game in this chapter, we'll be using impress.js, which typically serves as a library for creating slideshow demonstrations. It creates an interface similar to a book, with a simple linear traversal, but standard web page navigation means that you can implement the "go to page 45" style functionality of a game book quite easily. You also get access to some CSS3 features such as transitions, scaling, and rotation effects without having to implement them by hand. We'll get a bit closer to a *Maniac Mansion*-style game by creating items that can be collected in an inventory and applied later using a native HTML5 drag-and-drop style interface. A truly expressive engine that understands an arbitrary verb matched with one or two arbitrary nouns is surprisingly complex to build. Even a script for that type of engine can be difficult. We will take a shortcut and just bind certain objects together so that there is only one result from their interaction. That feature will make aspects of the game play a little like *Minecraft*, but in story-board form.

# Recipe: Styled Pages

If you open up the initial/index.html page from the interactive_fiction folder, there is not much going on. You're loading the impress library, but you're not yet creating the divs that serve as pages (referred to throughout this chapter as *slides* as well) in your story. Now add some of these as shown by the bold lines in Listing 2.1.

**Listing 2.1** Adding Pages to Your Story in index.html

```
<!doctype html>
<html lang="en">
<head>
    <meta charset="utf-8" />
    <title>Interactive Fiction</title>
     <link href="main.css" rel="stylesheet" />
</head>
<body>
<div id="impress">
    <div id="1" class="step slide">
        <q>You're on the first slide (page).  The down and right arrow
➥keys will take you to the next page. The left and up arrow keys will
➥take you back. </q>
    </div>
    <div id="2" class="step slide">
        <q>You can also use the spacebar instead of the right or down
➥key to go to the next page.</q>
    </div>
    <div id="3" class="step slide">
        <q>Now you're on the last page.  Right will take you back to
➥the beginning.</q>
    </div>
</div>
<script src="impress.js"></script>
<script>impress().init();</script>
</body>
</html>
```

First, consider the nonbolded boilerplate code first. You can get away without the `charset="utf-8"` line, but having it there will stop you from getting the errors you see in the console even when you display simple English. It has not been included in many of the code samples in this book, so if you are annoyed by the errors, add this line. In addition, this attribute aids accessibility with screen readers (so that they can pronounce words correctly) and enables browsers to do things such as ask if the user would like the page to be translated. Also notice that you are loading the JavaScript at the bottom of the `body` tag instead of in the head. This is good practice because it gives the content a chance to load before loading the more time-intensive JavaScript and prevents blocking the initial page rendering. One other thing to notice here is that there is no `canvas` element, and there will not be one loaded by impress.js. You create this game using JavaScript, CSS3, and aspects of HTML5 that don't rely on `canvas`.

Next look at the code to create the pages. They are simple. You add an outer `div` with the `id` of `impress` and create inner divs with the classes `step` and `slide`. Right now, the slides describe how to navigate, but without some proper CSS in place, it will not be possible to go from slide to slide. You are loading a main.css file that currently doesn't exist. Now add that with the code in Listing 2.2.

**Listing 2.2**   Adding main.css for Navigation and Styling

```
html, body, div, span, applet, object, iframe,
h1, h2, h3, h4, h5, h6, p, blockquote, pre,
a, abbr, acronym, address, big, cite, code,
del, dfn, em, img, ins, kbd, q, s, samp,
small, strike, strong, sub, sup, tt, var,
b, u, i, center,
dl, dt, dd, ol, ul, li,
fieldset, form, label, legend,
table, caption, tbody, tfoot, thead, tr, th, td,
article, aside, canvas, details, embed,
figure, figcaption, footer, header, hgroup,
menu, nav, output, ruby, section, summary,
time, mark, audio, video {
    margin: 0;
    padding: 0;
    border: 0;
    font-size: 100%;
    font: inherit;
    vertical-align: baseline;
}

article, aside, details, figcaption, figure,
footer, header, hgroup, menu, nav, section {
    display: block;
}
ol, ul {
    list-style: none;
}
table {
    border-collapse: collapse;
    border-spacing: 0;
}
b, strong { font-weight: bold }
i, em { font-style: italic }
/* Reset ends here */
body {
    background: -webkit-gradient(radial, 50% 50%, 0, 50% 50%, 500,
➥from(rgb(0, 40, 200)), to(rgb(10, 10, 0)));
    background:    -webkit-radial-gradient(rgb(0, 40, 200), rgb(10,
➥10, 0));
    background:    -moz-radial-gradient(rgb(0, 40, 200), rgb(10,
➥10, 0));
```

```css
    background:      -ms-radial-gradient(rgb(0, 40, 200), rgb(10,
➡10, 0));
    background:      -o-radial-gradient(rgb(0, 40, 200), rgb(10,
➡10, 0));
    background:      radial-gradient(rgb(0, 40, 200), rgb(10, 10,
➡0));
}
.impress-enabled .step {
    margin: 0;
    opacity: 0.0;
    -webkit-transition: opacity 1s;
    -moz-transition:    opacity 1s;
    -ms-transition:     opacity 1s;
    -o-transition:      opacity 1s;
    transition:         opacity 1s;
}
.impress-enabled .step.active { opacity: 1 }
.slide {
    display: block;
    width: 700px;
    height: 600px;
    padding: 40px 60px;
    background-color: white;
    border: 1px solid rgba(0, 0, 0, .3);
    color: rgb(52, 52, 52);
    text-shadow: 0 2px 2px rgba(0, 0, 0, .1);
    border-radius: 5px;
    font-family: 'Open Sans', Arial, sans-serif;
    font-size: 30px;
}
```

There are two main things going on here. The first is that you are applying a "css reset" to the styling. You can find many examples of these online, some spanning hundreds of lines. The purpose of these is that browsers tend to have different defaults for how elements should be styled. This declares reasonable styling baseline behavior so that browsers can be trusted to work more similarly than they would otherwise.

From the line starting with body, you are actually styling your elements. The body tag is styled using a radial gradient, blue in the center and smoothly fading to a dark gray on the edges. There is a lot of overhead here because browsers have not agreed to a single implementation of some of the newer CSS elements. You can see this again in the next two sets of styles using the opacity feature. Here you set the active page to be visible, and the other pages to be invisible, with a 1-second transition to change them. For the slide element, you do some standard styling to make the pages show up against the black and blue background.

If everything went according to plan, you should open index.html in a browser and see something like Figure 2.1.

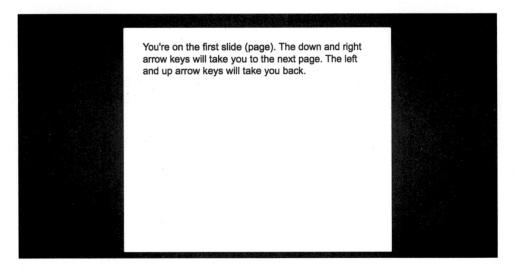

**Figure 2.1**  Slide styling in place

Next, add a basic story and some go-to-page functionality for the book to make it more like the form you want to achieve.

# Recipe: Goto Page

The ideal that you're going for is that on some pages you will have decisions to make, and on others you will have a game over, which could be good or bad. Let's deal with the decision page first by replacing the `<p>` tag in `div 1` with the bolded code in Listing 2.3 to index.html.

**Listing 2.3**  Decision Page

```
<div id="1" class="step slide">
  <div class="slide-text">
    <p>There's a time machine over there.  Flip the switch?</p>
```

```
    <p><a href="#2">FLIP</a> it.</p>
    <p><a href="#3">WAIT</a> for your dad, who is a scientist, to come
➡home</p>
  </div>
</div>
```

Here you introduce some links to other pages and wrap the p tags in a new `div` element with a class of `slide-text`. You will style those elements in just a minute. First, let's see where those links lead to by replacing the divs with ids 2 and 3 with the code in Listing 2.4.

### Listing 2.4  GameOver Pages

```
<div id="2" class="step slide" data-x="1500">
  <div class="slide-text">
    <p>You went back in time. It was fun.</p>
  </div>
  <div class="menu"><a href="#1">START OVER</a></div>
</div>
<div id="3" class="step slide" data-x="-1500">
  <div class="slide-text">
    <p>You hung around for a while, and then your dad came home.</p>
    <p>Then he helped you with your homework.</p>
    <p>It was kind of fun, but not that much fun.</p>
  </div>
  <div class="menu"><a href="#1">START OVER</a></div>
</div>
```

Here, you make a few adjustments to the second and third pages. We add the `data-x` attribute for reasons specific to impress.js. Without it, all the slides are essentially stacked on top of one another, and when you click, they all receive the priority of navigation. The clicks take the player to the last page. If you turn the `opacity` up on the `.impress-enabled .step`, you see this effect in action by clicking inactive pages and being taken to them. By setting the `data-x` attribute, you put the second and third pages in positions to the right and left of the first page.

Like in the first page, wrap the main text in a `div` with a `slide-text` class. Also add a `div` underneath the game over pages with the class `menu` that has a link headed back to the first page to play again.

These endings are not dramatic. You can explore more exciting endings, but part of what makes this style awesome is how cheaply you can create a new ending. Just add a slide with some text that says what happened. You don't need to create an all-new cut scene with music and animations for every ending. When a game such as the SNES RPG *Chrono Trigger* has multiple endings (and a NewGame+ option), it is respectable not only because it is thematically woven so elegantly, but also because between new writing, animations, and sound, it is a significant effort that gives diehard fans new possibilities to explore.

Because endings are so cheap to make in the mode you are working within, blasé endings can be explored alongside multiple good and bad endings. We'll be addressing these possibilities in a while, but for now, let's get back to styling the new elements that you added by adding the code in Listing 2.5 to the bottom of main.css.

**Listing 2.5**   Styling the Inside of Slides

```css
.slide p{
  margin-top:15px;
  margin-bottom:30px;
  line-height:45px;
}
.slide a, .slide a:visited {
  color: #071549;
  text-decoration:none;
  background-color: #abc;
  padding:5px;
  border-radius: 5px;
  border:1px solid #cde;
}
.slide a:hover, .slide a:active{
  background-color: #cde;
}
.slide .slide-text{
  height: 450px;
}
div.menu{
  border-top:2px solid black;
  padding-top:25px;
  text-align: center;
}
```

Most of this is standard CSS. If you're not sure what something is doing, try removing it or changing the values to see what happens. If you want to see these changes happen more quickly, editing the values through Firefox's firebug or the Chrome developer tools is a good option. Other than basic visual tweaks, the main thing that these styles accomplish is splitting the menu apart from the story portion of the page. For right now, just have a start over button there for game-ending slides, but you can use it for other things, too.

# Recipe: Adding an Inventory with Drag and Drop

You can travel from page to page now and create a choose your own adventure style experience. However, you can add images and an inventory to accomplish a style closer to click adventures like *Maniac Mansion*, with features that are a subset of the larger genre of interactive fiction.

For this recipe, you need to add three more files: bat.png, game.js, and dragDrop.js. You also need to make some changes to the index.html and main.css files. Start with the bold lines added to index.html in Listing 2.6.

**Listing 2.6** Adding the Item Containers to index.html

```
<body>
<div id="player_inventory" class="itemable">
  <span class="item-container"><h3>Inventory:</h3>
    <div class="inventory-box empty"></div>
    <div class="inventory-box empty"></div>
    <div class="inventory-box empty"></div>
  </span>
</div>
<div id="impress">
    <div id="1" class="step slide itemable">
      <div class="slide-text">
        <p>There's a time machine over there.  Flip the switch?</p>
        <p><a href="#2">FLIP</a> it.</p>
        <p><a href="#3">WAIT</a> for your dad, who is a scientist, to
➥come home</p>
      </div>
      <div class="menu item-container">
        <div class="inventory-box">
          <img src="bat.png" alt="bat" class="item" id="bat">
        </div>
      </div>
    </div>
    <div id="2" class="step slide itemable" data-x="1500">
      <div class="slide-text">
        <p>You went back in time. It was fun.</p>
      </div>
      <div class="menu"><a href="#1">START OVER</a></div>
    </div>
    <div id="3" class="step slide itemable" data-x="-1500">
      <div class="slide-text">
```

```
          <p>You hung around for a while, and then your dad came
➥home.</p>
          <p>Then he helped you with your homework.</p>
          <p>It was kind of fun, but not that much fun.</p>
        </div>
        <div class="menu"><a href="#1">START OVER</a></div>
      </div>
  </div>
</div>
<script src="impress.js"></script>
<script>impress().init();</script>

<script src="game.js"></script>
<script src="dragDrop.js"></script>

</body>
</html>
```

There are four major changes here. The first is that you now have a `div` with an `id` of `player_inventory`, with some elements nested beneath it. You style this in Listing 2.7. For now, think of it as a persistently on-screen list of items, and we'll get to the details of how to add and remove objects later in this recipe. The second change is that you have added an `itemable` class to your slide elements. This will be used for css styling and JavaScript hooks later. The third change is adding an `item-container` to your first slide with the bat inside, which contains the bat image that you added for this recipe. The last change is that you have two new files (game.js and dragDrop.js) to load before your closing body tag.

Now let's take a look at the new styling in Listing 2.7 that you can add to the bottom of main.css.

**Listing 2.7** CSS for Inventory and Drag/Drop

```css
img.item{
  width:100%;
  height:100%;
  cursor: move;
  padding:0px;
}
#player_inventory{
  position: fixed;
  text-align: center;
  width:180px;
  padding:15px;
  border-radius: 5px;
  top: 75px;
  left: 25px;
```

```
    background-color: white;
}
.menu .inventory-box{
    margin-right:20px;
}
.inventory-box{
    position: static;
    display: inline-block;
    height:130px;
    width:130px;
    border-radius: 5px;
    text-align:center;
}
.inventory-box.empty{
    border: 2px dashed #000;
}
h3{
    font-weight:bold;
    font-size:30px;
    margin-bottom:15px;
}
```

Here, you define styles for your inventory boxes, the containing elements, and the menu buttons at the bottom of each slide. You give a border to the empty class for when your inventory elements do not contain an image. Your reset function wiped out the default styling for the h3 heading tag, so you can add some styles for that as well.

Now, you need to create a dragDrop.js file to handle your interactions. This is a bit complicated, so we'll take it piece by piece. First, use the code in Listing 2.8 to start a new file called dragDrop.js.

**Listing 2.8** Adding Handlers to Inventory Boxes

```
var itemBoxes = document.querySelectorAll('.inventory-box');
[].forEach.call(itemBoxes, function(itemBox) {
    itemBox.addEventListener('dragstart', handleDragStart);
    itemBox.addEventListener('dragover', handleDragOver);
    itemBox.addEventListener('drop', handleDrop);
});
```

Taken line by line, we start by pulling all the elements with the class of inventory-box into a variable called itemBoxes. Next, we use a forEach loop to add drag handlers to each inventory-box. The addEventListener method is what we will be using to bind each individual event handler. Be aware when using this method that for older versions of Internet Explorer, you need to use the `attachEvent` method instead. In this `addEventListener` function, the first argument passed is the drag event. There are other event handlers such as `'click'` that you can bind to this element. The second argument is the name of the function that is bound to the element and executed when the event is triggered.

In the second line, you may be curious about the odd looping syntax. Using a more typical syntax, you could instead do something as shown in Listing 2.9. Note that this code does not belong to any file, it is simply here to contrast your functional style loop using `forEach`.

**Listing 2.9**  More Typical Way of Looping, Procedural Rather Than Functional

```
for (var i=0; i < itemBoxes.length; i++){
  itemBoxes[i].addEventListener('dragstart', handleDragStart);
  ...
}
```

Whereas Listing 2.9 is in a "procedural" style, Listing 2.8 is in a more "functional" style. The distinction may seem subtle, but the consequences, especially for large, complex programs, heavily favor the functional approach. This is because, generally speaking, using a functional style creates fewer variables and when necessary creates a new set of data rather than altering an existing one. In short, the system is simpler because you can more easily rely on the consistency of the values of variables and the behavior of functions throughout program execution.

## note

This book does not strictly adhere to a functional style but understanding its benefits is important as you master programming in JavaScript. There are efforts underway to encourage this approach in ECMAScript5 (the JavaScript specification) for modern browsers, with libraries such as `underscore.js` filling in the gaps for older browsers.

How the second line in Listing 2.8 actually works is a bit complicated. First, you apply the function `forEach` to an array literal, `[]`, which does not contain any elements. You do this because, although an array has a `forEach` function, `querySeletorAll` returns a `NodeList`, which does not have that function. Using the `call` function, you can pretend that it does. The first parameter in `call` is what the value of `this` will be during the execution of whatever function preceded `call`, in this case `forEach`. This will be `item_boxes` rather than `[]`. Subsequent parameters refer to parameters that are supplied to the `forEach` function. Because the first parameter of a `forEach` function is the function to be executed, the second parameter of call (everything from the `function` keyword to the closing `}`) serves as the function to be applied in each item (`item_box`) of `item_boxes`. `forEach` also allows us to bind the label `item_box` to a formal parameter that we use later. The reason that we are able to do this is because although a `NodeList` does not implement a `forEach` function, it does provide an `item` method that is what `forEach` relies on to set this formal parameter.

That is about the most complicated thing that appears in this book (at least until Chapter 8). If you understood it on the first pass, that is incredible. If not, don't worry. There are a lot of things to learn with JavaScript, and there is nothing wrong with writing `for` loops in most cases. For a given JavaScript implementation, which varies in the case of different browsers, `for` loops are even faster at times. And remember, even the most talented developer had to start somewhere, and no one who is civil will judge you too harshly while you're still learning. That said, this concept is a good thing to keep in mind when you're looking at other people's code or want to explore new and better ways of programming.

With that out of the way, let's get back to making games. To do that, you need to define those functions that you bound to the item boxes. Still in dragDrop.js, start at the top of the file, and define them one by one. First up is the `handleDragStart` function found in Listing 2.10.

**Listing 2.10**   Creating the handleDragStart Function

```
var draggingObject;
function handleDragStart(e) {
  draggingObject = this;
  e.dataTransfer.setData('text/html', this.innerHTML);
  var dragIcon = document.createElement('img');
  var imageName = this.firstChild.id;
  dragIcon.src = imageName + '.png';
  e.dataTransfer.setDragImage(dragIcon, -10, 10);
}
```

Here, you start by defining a variable called `draggingObject` in the global scope because you need it to be shared among various functions. For now, don't worry about the global scoping because you'll clean up that detail in a later recipe. You assign this variable to the inventory-box element that you are dragging from. Next, set the information to be transferred to be the html inside of the box. The last four lines create a tiny duplicate of the image that you are dragging to appear under the cursor. Without these lines, the drag still works, but how the image appears under the cursor will vary from browser to browser.

Next, in Listing 2.11, add the `handleDragOver` function to dragDrop.js.

**Listing 2.11    Creating the handleDragOver Function**

```
function handleDragOver(e) {
  e.preventDefault();
}
```

In the `handleDragOver` function, you're not doing much. Actually, all you're doing is stopping the default function from occurring.

In Listing 2.12, define the `handleDrop` function that does a lot more.

**Listing 2.12    Creating the handleDrop Function**

```
function handleDrop(e) {
  e.preventDefault();
  if (draggingObject != this) {
    var draggingGrandpa = draggingObject.parentElement.parentElement;
    var draggedToGrandpa = this.parentElement.parentElement;
    var draggingObjectId = draggingObject.firstChild.id;
    inventoryObject.add(draggedToGrandpa.id, draggingObjectId);
    inventoryObject.remove(draggingGrandpa.id, draggingObjectId);
    draggingObject.innerHTML = this.innerHTML;
    this.innerHTML = e.dataTransfer.getData('text/html');
    this.classList.remove('empty');
    draggingObject.classList.add('empty');
  }
}
```

Again, you need to call `e.preventDefault()` for this handler to execute properly. Set most of the code inside of a conditional that runs only if the object origin, `draggingObject`, is different from the drop target, `this`. In the next four lines, assign variables for the containing objects (the grandpas) and the ids of these elements. With the next two lines, move the object from the original `inventoryObject` to the inventory it is dragged to. You will see soon what this `inventoryObject` is, but first finish this function. In the next two lines, swap the `innerHTML` of the origin and target. The last two lines simply toggle the `empty` class.

You also have the ability to add handlers for `dragenter` and `dragleave`, but you do not need them for this recipe.

In Listing 2.13, address the `inventoryObject`. Add this code to a new file called game.js.

**Listing 2.13**  Creating an inventoryObject to Store and Retrieve Items

```
var inventoryObject = (function(){
  var inventory = {};
  var itemables = document.getElementsByClassName("itemable");
  [].forEach.call(itemables, function(itemable) {
    inventory[itemable.id] = [];
  });
  var items = document.getElementsByClassName("item");
  [].forEach.call(items, function(item) {
    var greatGrandpa = item.parentElement.parentElement.parentElement;
    inventory[greatGrandpa.id].push(item.id);
  });
  var add = function(inventorySection, newItem){
    inventory[inventorySection].push(newItem);
    return inventory;
  }
  var remove = function(inventorySection, itemToDelete){
    for (var i = 0; i < inventory[inventorySection].length; i++){
      if (inventory[inventorySection][i] == itemToDelete){
        inventory[inventorySection].splice(i, 1);
      }
    }
    return inventory;
  }
  return {
    get : function(){
          return inventory;
        },
    add : add,
    remove : remove
  }
})();
```

In the first line, we declare an inventory variable, and set it equal to the result of a function. You can tell that it is the result of a function because it ends with a parenthesis. As a consequence of the way JavaScript is parsed, the closing parenthesis on the last line requires you to have parentheses around the function like this: `(function(){...})`. Otherwise, you would have a syntax error.

Next, we initialize the `inventory` object with the empty object literal `{}`. Then, we use the functional pattern described earlier to initialize the inventory object with empty arrays at each index, where the slide id or `player_inventory` serves as the key name. In the next instance of the functional pattern, we populate the inventory with the objects that exist based on what is found in the html file.

We follow that with declaring two new functions: `add` and `remove`. They are more or less self-explanatory, but you should pay attention to the `push` and `splice` methods. They are among the most common in the JavaScript array API. One other thing to note about this function is the return values. In JavaScript, if you do not declare a specific return value, you will by default return `undefined`. There are times when you may want any number of different return values for various reasons, but in the case of manipulating objects in this way, it is reasonable to return the object being acted on (in this case `inventoryObject`). In addition to being a sensible choice overall, this allows you to chain calls such as the following: `inventoryObject.remove(…).add(…)`.

Some of the implications of what you need as a result of setting inventory equal to an imme-diately executing function are glossed over. Indeed, you ran the setup code, but you also have functions `add` and `remove` that will not be available outside of the context of the outer func-tion. What can you do in this situation? Well, the best option in this case is actually to make the outer function return an object, which you declare in the last few lines. This object consists of three methods: `get`, `add`, and `remove`. For `add` and `remove`, this has nothing to do with the implementation. Everything works the same, except these methods are now public, exposed outside of the context of the function through `inventoryObject.add()` and `inventoryObject.remove()`. What's great is that even though they may have public scope, they still have access to the private object `inventory` that is populated earlier in the function. This is known as *closure* and is an important concept for scoping information appropriately.

For the `get` function, rather than mapping to a private implementation outside of the `return` block, you inline your implementation, which simply returns the value of the private variable `inventory`.

The pattern demonstrated by this concept of private and public methods is known as the *module pattern*. It is one of the most fundamental patterns, and you will likely encounter it frequently in other people's code. If you are interested in methods of JavaScript code reuse and organization, there are a lot of exciting things going on in that area. Between MVC frameworks such as backbone, AMD/common.js for requiring extensions, increased usage of the pub subpattern, and applying the classical *Gang of Four* patterns to JavaScript, this is a great area to look into if you want to deepen your knowledge.

But this book is not about making games, not patterns. This has been a particularly difficult recipe, with lots of exposure to more esoteric knowledge than you'll be handling in general throughout the book. As proof that your hard work has paid off, you should see something similar to Figure 2.2 if you open index.html in your browser. And you can drag and drop the bat to and from the inventory.

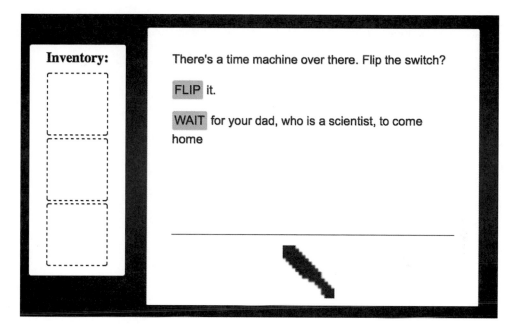

**Figure 2.2** First game slide after adding an inventory

# Recipe: Adding Complex Interactions

In this recipe, you create more complex interactions for your objects. Nothing will be as conceptually difficult as what you covered in the last recipe, but the code must be significantly changed to accommodate these new interactions. First, the bold lines indicate how your index.html file should change (see Listing 2.14).

**Listing 2.14** Updating the index.html File

```
...
<div id="player_inventory">
  <span class="item-container"><h3>Inventory:</h3>
    <div class="inventory-box empty"></div>
    <div class="inventory-box empty"></div>
    <div class="inventory-box empty"></div>
  </span>
</div>
<div id="impress">
  <div id="slide1" class="step slide">
    <div class="slide-text">
      <p>There's a time machine over there.  Flip the switch?</p>
```

```
      <p><a href='#slide2'>FLIP</a> it.</p>
      <p><a href='#slide3'>WAIT</a> for your dad, who is a scientist,
➥to come home</p>
        <div class="event-text"></div>
      </div>
      <div class="menu item-container"><div class="inventory-box">
➥<img src="bat.png" alt="bat" class="item" id="bat"></div></div>
    </div>
    <div id="slide2" class="step slide" data-x="1500">
      <div class="slide-text">
        <p>Woah.  A dinosaur.  I wonder if you can hit it with
➥something...</p>
        <div class="event-text"></div>
      </div>
      <div class="menu"><div class="inventory-box"><img src="dino.png"
➥alt="dino" class="item" id="dino"></div></div>
    </div>
    <div id="slide3" class="step slide" data-x="-1500">
      <div class="slide-text">
        <p>You hung around for a while, and then your dad came home.</p>
        <p>Then he helped you with your homework.</p>
        <p>It was kind of fun, but not that much fun.</p>
        <div class="event-text"></div>
      </div>
      <div class="menu"><a href="#slide1">START OVER</a></div>
    </div>
  </div>
  <script src="impress.js"></script>
  <script>impress().init();</script>
  ...
```

The ways of referencing elements have changed with this recipe. You no longer use the `itemable` class for your slides or the player inventory. It is difficult to reference and keep track of elements with numerical ids, so you also have prefixed the numbers with the word `slide`. As a consequence of this, your links to those slides have to change as well. You also add a `div` with an `event-text` class to every slide. Slide 2 gets a new object, a dino, placed inside of it, and it receives some new text about the presence of the dinosaur.

Although you are still loading impress.js in the same way, it requires a bit of customization for what you want. Let's address those changes in Listing 2.15.

**Listing 2.15**   Changes to impress.js

```
var game = {
  stepsTaken: [],
```

```
    updateAfterStep: function(stepId){
      this.stepsTaken.push(stepId);
    }
};
...
var getStep = function ( step ) {
  if (typeof step === "number") {
    step = step < 0 ? steps[ steps.length + step] : steps[ step];
  } else if (typeof step === "string") {
    step = byId(step);
  }
  if (!!step.id === true){
    game.updateAfterStep(step.id);
  };
  return (step && step.id && stepsData["impress-" + step.id]) ? step :
➥null;
};
...
```

There are two changes to note here. The first is that you are creating a game object that will be the only object of ours in the global scope until the end of the chapter. In this object, you have two attributes: an array that stores the slides that are visited and a function that adds a slide to that array. This code can go at the top of the file. The second change that you make is to invoke that function within impress.js every time a new slide is viewed by adding the bolded code where it is indicated in Listing 2.15. It will be near line 421 where it is added.

Next, revisit your dragDrop.js file in Listing 2.16.

### Listing 2.16  dragDrop Revisited

```
(function(){
...
  function handleDrop(e) {
    var dragAppliedTo = this;
    game.things.dropItemInto(draggingObject,
➥dragAppliedTo.parentElement.parentElement.id);
    e.preventDefault();
  }
...
})();
```

In this file, you have two main changes. First, you now wrap the entire code in a self-executing function. If you want this code to execute more than once (say if you need to rebind the event listeners), you could set this function to be an attribute on your global game object by changing the first line to `game.dragdrop = (function)(){`, but for this recipe, executing the code once is sufficient. The second change is that your `handleDrop` function has been simplified significantly. Now, you are simply passing the object being dragged and the `id` of the container where it is being dragged to into a `dropItemInto` function, which is a method defined on the `things` property of your global `game` object.

The changes required for game.js by Listing 2.17 are extensive, so start from scratch and take them piece by piece. This code should replace everything currently in game.js.

**Listing 2.17** Creating game.things

```
game.things = (function(){
  var items = {
    bat: {
      name: 'bat',
      effects: {
        'player_inventory': { message: "<p>You picked up the bat!</p>",
                              object: "addItem",
                              subject: "deleteItem"
        },
        'dino': { message: "<p>You hit the dino with the bat</p><p>Now
➥he's angry.</p>",
                  subject: 'deleteItem'
        },
        'empty': {
                  message: "<p>You set the bat down over there.</p>",
                  object: "addItem",
                  subject: "deleteItem"
        }
      }
    },
    dino: {
      name: 'dino',
      effects: {
        'player_inventory': { message: "<p>You can't move the
➥dino...</p>" }
      }
    }
  };

  var get = function(name){
    return this.items[name];
  };
  var dropItemInto = function(itemNode, target){
    var sourceContext = itemNode.parentElement.parentElement.id;
    if(sourceContext !== target){
```

```
        var item = itemNode.firstChild.id;
        var itemObject = this.get(item);

        if (target === 'player_inventory'){
          var effects = itemObject.effects[target];
        }else if(game.slide.getInventory(target)){
          var effects = itemObject.effects[game.slide.
➥getInventory(target)];
        }else{
          var effects = itemObject.effects['empty'];
        };

        var targetObject;
        if (!!effects.object === true){
          if(target==="player_inventory"){
            targetObject = game.playerInventory;
          }else{
            targetObject = game.slide;
          };
          targetObject[effects.object](itemObject);
        };
        if (!!effects.subject === true){
          if(sourceContext === "player_inventory"){
            var sourceObject = game.playerInventory;
          }else{
            var sourceObject = game.slide;
          };
          sourceObject[effects.subject](itemObject);
        };
        if (!!effects.message === true){
          game.slide.setText(effects.message);
        };
        game.screen.draw();
      };
    };

  return{
    items: items,
    get: get,
    dropItemInto: dropItemInto
  }
})();
```

There is quite a bit going on here. Structurally speaking, this entire object is wrapped up as a self-executing function and assigned as the `things` property of `game`. If you look at what the function returns (at the bottom), you can notice something that may look familiar. You return an object that maps public methods onto private methods, making them available at `game.things.items` for instance. The public interface of `game.things` now includes an `items` method that returns the `items` object, a `get` method that returns a specific item, and a `dropItemInto` method called from dragDrop.js and does most of the heavy lifting.

Going back to the top of the function, you can structure your item objects as data, including the methods to run when specific things happen. As for how this data is structured, your `bat` object has a `name` property of `bat`. The `effects` property of `bat` contains some additional JSON to dictate the effects of what happens when it is dragged onto various other object types and placements in the special case of `player_inventory`. The `dino` item has a smaller mapping because it will be dragged only into the player inventory. In all cases, you have three potential effects: `subject` indicates what function will be run on the object that you are dragging with respect to the place you are dragging it from; `object` indicates what function will be run on the object you are dragging with respect to the place you are dragging it to; and `message` describes the message that will be added to the slide as a result of the interaction.

Continuing down the file, the `get` method returns the item with the name given by the `name` parameter provided in the function call.

The final function, `dropItemInto`, is fairly complicated. It takes two parameters: the `itemNode` and the `target`. `sourceContext` is compared with `target`. If they are the same (the place dragged to is the same as the place dragged from), the function will not run any more code. Skipping to the `if`, `else if`, `else` branch, here you determine which effects of the given item that you want to execute. The next branch of `if` statements evaluates when there is an `object` property defined for the `effects`, determines the `targetObject` to execute the effect for, and executes the effect. The block beginning with `if (!!effects.subject === true) {` behaves in a similar way, executing for the `subject` rather than the `object`. The last `if` block at this level makes a call to `game.slide.setText`, which sets the `event-text` of the current slide to what is contained in the `message` property of `effects`. The last full line in `dropItemInto` calls `game.screen.draw` to update the screen after the inventories have been updated.

Now that you have seen the `dropItemInto` function, which drives most of the action, let's take a closer look at objects that it relies on to get work done. Listing 2.18 covers the `game.slide` object in game.js. This can immediately follow the code from Listing 2.17.

**Listing 2.18**   Creating the game.slide Function in game.js

```
game.slide = (function(){
  var inventory = {
    slide1: 'bat',
```

```
    slide2: 'dino',
    slide3: null
  };
  var addItem = function(item){
    inventory[game.slide.currentSlide()] = item.name;
  };
  var deleteItem = function(item){
    inventory[game.slide.currentSlide()] = null;
  };
  var findTextNode = function(slideId){
    return document.querySelector("#" + slideId + " .slide-text
➡.event-text");
  };
  var getInventory = function(slideId){
    return inventory[slideId];
  };
  var setText = function(message, slideId){
    if (!!slideId === false){
      slideId = currentSlide();
    }
    return findTextNode(slideId).innerHTML = message;
  };
  var currentSlide = function(){
    return game.stepsTaken[game.stepsTaken.length - 1];
  };
  var draw = function(slideId){
    if(!slideId === true){
      slideId = this.currentSlide();
    };
    var item = inventory[slideId];
    var inventoryBox = document.querySelector ('#'+slideId+'
➡.inventory-box');
    if (item === null){
      inventoryBox.innerHTML = "";
      inventoryBox.classList.add("empty");
    }
    else{
      inventoryBox.innerHTML = "<img src='"+item+".png' alt='"+item+"'
➡class='item' id='"+item+"'>";
      inventoryBox.classList.remove("empty");
    }
  };

  return {
    addItem: addItem,
    deleteItem: deleteItem,
```

```
    setText: setText,
    getInventory: getInventory,
    draw: draw,
    currentSlide: currentSlide
  };
})();
```

The pattern for how this property of game is defined and executed should begin to look familiar at this point. As before, you can get a good feel for this object by seeing what is made available in the public interface methods provided by the return block. Going to the top, you can see the inventory object contains your slides with the value of each being the name of the item they contain or null. Next, your addItem and deleteItem functions manage the inventory by adding the name of the item to a slide or setting it to null.

Next, you have a findTextNode method that finds the event-text div for a given slide. Because it is not mapped to an attribute inside of the return block, this is a private method, used only internally in the game.slide object. It is called by only one function, setText.

getInventory returns the item contained in a given slide based on the inventory object.

setText sets the message of a given slide based on the message and slideId that are passed in. If there is no slideId provided, it defaults to the currentSlide. If you're coming from a language with default parameters, you might expect something like the following to work when a slideId is not provided by the function call: function(message, slideId=currentSlide()). It doesn't. If you actually need default parameters, you need to pass in an object and handle it explicitly; otherwise, doing a null check works fine.

Next is the currentSlide method that you've heard so much about. This is the entire reason why you hacked into the impress.js library earlier. This function grabs the last element in the stepsTaken array that you append to every time you visit a new slide.

The last method in slide is the draw function. Again this starts with your hack for a default parameter that sets the slideId to currentSlide. It finds the inventory-box for the slide in question and sets it to contain what is described in the inventory object, be it null or a particular item. It also adds or removes the empty class depending on whether it contains an image.

You have one last large object to get through for this recipe, game.js's playerInventory, which you can find in Listing 2.19.

**Listing 2.19** Creating the playerInventory

```
game.playerInventory = (function(){
  var items = {
    bat: false
  };
  var clearInventory = function(){
    playerInventoryBoxes = document.querySelectorAll('#player_inventory
➥.inventory-box');
    [].forEach.call(playerInventoryBoxes, function(inventoryBox) {
      inventoryBox.classList.add("empty");
      inventoryBox.innerHTML = "";
    });
  };
  var addItem = function(item){
    if (this.items[item.name] === false){
      this.items[item.name] = true;
    };
    return this.items;
  };
  var deleteItem = function(item){
    if (this.items[item.name] === true){
      this.items[item.name] = false;
    };
    return this.items;
  };
  var draw = function(){
    clearInventory();
    var counter = 0;
    var inventoryBoxes = document.querySelectorAll('#player_inventory
➥.inventory-box');
    for(var item in this.items){
      if(this.items[item] === true){
        inventoryBoxes[counter].classList.remove("empty");
        inventoryBoxes[counter].innerHTML = "<img src='"+item+".png'
➥alt='"+item+"' class='item' id='"+item+"'>";
      }
      counter = counter + 1;
    };
  };
  return {
    items: items,
    addItem: addItem,
    deleteItem: deleteItem,
    draw: draw
  };
})();
```

Again, you use the same pattern for setting the object as an attribute and an immediately executing function as you've been doing all along in this file. No surprises there. Also as before, the `return` block illustrates the public availability of certain methods. Let's go to the top and get a better idea of what this object does.

`items` stores items in an object. You could make an argument that an array would be more appropriate than a standard object, but given a large array, it could be computationally expensive to check for the presence of an element by looking through the entire array rather than by finding the element by the index and determining presence based on a value of `true` or `false`. As a consequence of this, any item that can possibly appear in the player's inventory throughout the game should appear here with a value of `false`.

Next, the private function `clearInventory` takes all the images out of the `divs` of the player's inventory boxes. It is called before the `draw` method to start with a clean slate. This includes adding an `empty` class to each `inventoryBox`.

`addItem` and `deleteItem` are unremarkable. They simply toggle the `true/false` value of an item and return `this`.

The `draw` function kicks off by clearing the inventory. You set an explicit `counter` variable for your `for` loop, which has a syntax that you haven't covered in this chapter yet. When you have an object, not an array, it is preferable to use the `for...in` style loop syntax to gain access to individual items. You need the counter variable to reference specific html elements, both to add the html and to set remove the `empty` class.

As promised, you are out of large objects and just have one small one left. The `screen` property of game in Listing 2.20 must also be added to game.js.

**Listing 2.20**   Adding the screen Property to the Game

```
game.screen = (function(){
  var draw = function(){
    game.playerInventory.draw();
    game.slide.draw(game.slide.currentSlide());
  };
  return {
    draw: draw
  }
})();
```

`screen` is simply a wrapper object for the `draw` functions found in `playerInventory` and `slide`.

And that's it for this recipe. Figure 2.3 shows what happens when you hit the dino with the bat after opening index.html in your browser.

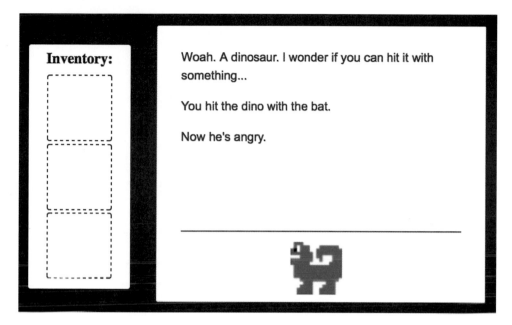

Inventory:

Woah. A dinosaur. I wonder if you can hit it with something...

You hit the dino with the bat.

Now he's angry.

**Figure 2.3** Hitting the dino

# Recipe: Breadcrumb Trail

The game seems to be shaping up quite nicely, but as of now, your navigation is limited by what you explicitly put into slides. The concept of a breadcrumb trail to keep a record of where you've been could be useful for flipping back to previous pages. For this, you need to make another adjustment to the impress.js library file and add a bit more html/css. Compared to the last two recipes, this is a breeze.

First, alter the impress.js code a bit. It will look almost exactly like the last version, but with the `updateAfterStep` method expanded somewhat. Add the bolded lines in Listing 2.21 to the impress.js file.

**Listing 2.21** Updating impress.js for Breadcrumb

```
var game = {
  stepsTaken: [],
  updateAfterStep: function(stepId){
```

```
        if (this.stepsTaken.length < 1 || stepId !== this.stepsTaken
➥[this.stepsTaken.length-1]){
        this.stepsTaken.push(stepId);
        var numberOfSteps = this.stepsTaken.length;
        var stepsElement = document.getElementById("steps");
        var newStep = document.createElement("li");
        newStep.innerHTML = "" + numberOfSteps +":
➥<a href=#"+stepId+">"+stepId+"</a>";
        var mostRecentStep = stepsElement.firstChild;
        stepsElement.insertBefore(newStep, mostRecentStep);
      };
    }
  };
```

Instead of simply pushing the step onto the array, now the method creates a new `li` element with a link to the slide last visited and adds it to the top of a list.

In the index.html file, you need to make two simple changes. Add the `stepsTaken` list. Also change your link to actually refresh the page. Now that you're dealing with items and inventories, this is a much easier option to manage them than cleaning everything up in the UI and background objects. Listing 2.22 should make this clear with the bolded sections indicating additions.

**Listing 2.22**   index.html Changes for Breadcrumb

```html
<div id="player_inventory"><span
class="item-container"><h3>Inventory:</h3>
  <div class="inventory-box empty"></div>
  <div class="inventory-box empty"></div>
  <div class="inventory-box empty"></div>
  </span>
</div>
<div id="steps-taken">
  <h3>Steps Taken:</h3>
  <ul id='steps'>
  </ul>
</div>
...
<div id="slide3" class="step slide" data-x="-1500">
  <div class="slide-text">
    <p>You hung around for a while, and then your dad came home.</p>
    <p>Then he helped you with your homework.</p>
    <p>It was kind of fun, but not that much fun.</p>
    <div class="event-text"></div>
  </div>
</div>
```

```
<div class="menu"><a href="#" onclick='location =
➥ window.location.pathname; return false;'>START OVER</a></div>
...
```

The last change for this recipe is simply to add the CSS in Listing 2.23 to main.css.

**Listing 2.23** Breadcrumb css

```
#steps-taken{
  position: fixed;
  text-align: center;
  width:180px;
  padding:15px;
  border-radius: 5px;
  top: 75px;
  right: 25px;
  background-color: white;
}
```

With all that in place, you should see something like Figure 2.4 after opening up index.html and visiting a few pages.

**Figure 2.4** Breadcrumbs in action

# Recipe: A Dramatic Ending

So far, there are two possibilities in the game: You either have not much fun or anger a dinosaur. Well, what if the dinosaur was so angry that he actually attacked you? You can make it happen with the wonderful and weird raptorize jQuery plug-in from http://www.zurb.com/playground/jquery-raptorize.

Put the sound files raptor-sound.mp3 and raptor-sound.ogg into the same folder as index.html. (You need both because different browsers support different audio codecs.) Also add the jQuery and jquery.raptorize files, along with the raptor.png image.

Now, in your index.html file, load the scripts, as shown in Listing 2.24.

**Listing 2.24** Raptorized index.html

```
<script src="impress.js"></script>
<script>impress().init();</script>
<script src="http://ajax.googleapis.com/ajax/libs/jquery/1.4.2/
➡ jquery.min.js"></script>
<script>!window.jQuery && document.write('<script
➡ src="jquery-1.4.1.min.js"><\/script>')</script>
<script src="jquery.raptorize.1.0.js"></script>
<script src="game.js"></script>
<script src="dragDrop.js"></script>
...
```

There are three new `script` tags. The first attempts to load jQuery from Google's content delivery network (CDN), which has some performance advantages for production apps. The second `script` tag loads the local jQuery library if Google's is unavailable. (This will most likely mean your Internet connection is bad because Google's CDN is reliable.) The third `script` tag loads raptorize.js.

Listing 2.25 shows some simple changes that you need to make to game.js.

**Listing 2.25** Raptorize Game

```
game.things = (function(){
  var items = {
    bat: {
      name: 'bat',
      effects: {
        'player_inventory': { message: "<p>You picked up the bat!</p>",
                              object: "addItem",
                              subject: "deleteItem"
        },
```

```
              'dino': { message: "<p>You hit the dino with the bat.
➥</p><p>Now he's angry.</p>",
                        subject: 'deleteItem',
                        object: 'deleteItem',
                        callback: function(){game.screen.callDino()}
...
var dropItemInto = function(itemNode, target){
...
if (!!effects.message === true){
  game.slide.setText(effects.message);
};
if(!!effects.callback  === true){
  effects.callback();
};
game.screen.draw();


...
game.screen = (function(){
  var draw = function(){
    game.playerInventory.draw();
    game.slide.draw(game.slide.currentSlide());
  };
  var callDino = function(){
    $('body').raptorise({ 'enterOn' : 'timer', 'delayTime' : 2000 });
  };
  return {
    callDino: callDino,
    draw: draw
  }
})();
...
```

First, in the `things` object, adjust the `bat`'s `effects` on the `dino`. Then make both the `dino` and the `bat` disappear, and add a `callback` function that calls the `dino`. Next, in the `drop-ItemInto` function, add a check to see if there is a `callback`, and then code to execute it if there is one. Lastly, add your `callDino` function to the `screen` object, and put a reference inside the `return` block to make it publicly available.

If all goes well, when the player hits the `dino` with the `bat` now, it gets REALLY angry and screeches across the screen, as shown in Figure 2.5.

**Figure 2.5** Dramatic ending

# Summary

So that's it for your foray into interactive fiction using the accidental game engine impress.js to explore the space. You covered a lot of material here, everything from JavaScript to patterns to functional programming to raptors.

If you found this chapter difficult, that is because it was. It is likely the hardest chapter in the whole book. JavaScript can be fairly opaque at times, which is part of the reason that libraries like jQuery are so popular, as well as why the chapters in this book that focus on using a game engine are simpler. In a given library, consistency and canonical documentation are more tractable, whereas in JavaScript, it's easy to get lost in the details of various specifications, implementations, and desecrations (the bad parts of JavaScript that Douglas Crockford warns against) of the language.

So where can you go from here? On the JavaScript side, learning all the patterns and functional programming capabilities, along with all the libraries associated with these techniques, is months of work. On the visual side, learning more about HTML5 and CSS3 is another reasonably sized bucket of educational possibility.

As for your game? Maybe you don't like dinosaurs. Maybe you want something more true to life, or something long with many branches. Perhaps you want a textual interface or North/West/South/East style navigation so that you can provide a different sense of exploration. Maybe you want to use this to make online greeting cards. More items. More consequences. More endings. Scarier, funnier, more meaningful. Go for it. After this chapter, you have a template game to adapt to tell a story in a way you might not have been able to before.

# CHAPTER 3

# PARTY

Games such as *Dance Dance Revolution*, *Mario Party*, and *Rock Band* make use of simplicity to create experiences that are accessible to new players, and well suited to playing in a casual group setting. This press a button fast/press the button at the right time/press the right button genre has attracted more interest lately as developers and publishers increasingly recognizing the appeal of these casual games to demographics that had not previously been emphasized.

In this chapter, we will be using the atom.js game engine to provide a thin game wrapper for game logic and exploring the native canvas interface for drawing graphics.

# Recipe: Creating a Sample Game in atom.js

This chapter uses the library atom.js as a minimal, lightweight engine to abstract some common gaming necessities. It does four main things: normalizes the concept of `requestAnimationFrame` across all browsers; provides an abstraction for key presses and mouse events; provides a handler to adjust the screen size when the window is changed; and most important, it defines a base object called `Game` with a few game loop-related methods that you will rely on in this game.

Looking in the party/initial/ folder, you notice two files: `atom.js` and `atom.coffee`, which have similar variables and structure but with completely different syntax. Assuming that you're unfamiliar with this approach to JavaScript, here's the purpose of the second file: It is written in a language called CoffeeScript. Some people find CoffeeScript (including, it would seem, the author of atom.js) easier to program in than JavaScript. There is some merit to this opinion. CoffeeScript provides a simpler syntax for parts of JavaScript and is more human-readable. For the atom.js library, there is an additional benefit of requiring 30 less lines of code in the CoffeeScript version.

So what's the downside to using CoffeeScript? Browsers cannot interpret CoffeeScript, only JavaScript. This means that every file written in CoffeeScript must be converted or "compiled" into the browser-readable JavaScript. You could do this with a program on your computer, but if you're just starting with CoffeeScript and don't want all that extra complexity, a site such as js2coffee.org/ can serve your conversion needs. Another downside is that debugging is potentially more difficult because a browser where the code runs will report errors in the JavaScript version, which is not the language that you write the code in originally. There are tools coming in from all directions to address this problem (source-mappers and in-browser CoffeeScript interpreters), but as of this writing, none have been accepted as a standard solution.

CoffeeScript files aren't included beyond this chapter, but because it has seen adoption in certain web development circles such as backbone.js and Ruby on Rails, it is worth understanding to some degree. It may be a fad or it may be here to stay, but at the end of the day, CoffeeScript is just an abstraction of JavaScript. That means that if your skills are solid on core JavaScript, you won't have much to worry about. That said, it's fun to learn new things. http://coffeescript.org is a great place to learn more if you are interested.

Okay, with that background on atom.js out of the way, start your index.html file with the code in Listing 3.1.

**Listing 3.1**   A Basic HTML File for atom.js

```
<!DOCTYPE html>
<html>
```

```
<head>
  <title>whackamole</title>
</head>
<canvas></canvas>
<script type="text/javascript" src="atom.js"></script>
<script type="text/javascript" src="game.js"></script>
</html>
```

In the first line, set the `doctype` with the html5-friendly doctype simply called `html`. Then, declare the title inside of the `head` tag. (This appears in the browser header and tab name.) Next, create an empty `canvas` tag and load the atom.js file along with your game.js file.

> **note**
>
> Depending on the game engine, `canvas` elements are used in various ways. Sometimes they are not written into the html directly because they are created by the engine, and sometimes the engine simply relies on the id of the `canvas` tag or the `canvas` tag. For atom, it needs a `canvas` tag to be there, and it grabs the first one it finds when it loads.

Clearly, your next step is to add a game.js file. With all game engines you encounter, it's incredibly useful to look for two things: example code and documentation. atom.js is somewhat Spartan on both, but you should make use of what is available. Listing 3.2 shows the example code included in the README.md file of atom.js.

**Listing 3.2** Example CoffeeScript Code from README

```
class Game extends atom.Game
  constructor: ->
    super
    atom.input.bind atom.key.LEFT_ARROW, 'left'
  update: (dt) ->
    if atom.input.pressed 'left'
      console.log "player started moving left"
    else if atom.input.down 'left'
      console.log "player still moving left"
  draw: ->
    atom.context.fillStyle = 'black'
    atom.context.fillRect 0, 0, atom.width, atom.height
game = new Game
window.onblur = -> game.stop()
window.onfocus = -> game.run()
game.run() }
```

It is CoffeeScript, so you need to convert it before it is useful, but first look at what want to accomplish in this code. You establish a `Game` variable that extends the `Game` property defined on `atom` in the atom.js code. With `super`, you say that when a method cannot be found on `Game`, it should refer to its parent object's implementation. Any keys that require binding (in this case, the left arrow) are also set in the constructor.

The update and draw methods run in a loop; the former waits for left-arrow key presses with the latter drawing a black background the size of the canvas (which fills the entire window). Then, a new `game` object is instantiated that inherits from `Game` (which extends `atom.Game`). Functions are bound to stop and start the game depending on whether the window is in focus. Lastly, the game is kicked off by executing the `run` function.

Listing 3.3 shows this game file converted to pure JavaScript after running it through a converter. Don't worry about saving this file; you change it in Listing 3.4.

**Listing 3.3**   Example Game in Pure JavaScript

```javascript
var Game;
var game;
var __hasProp = {}.hasOwnProperty;
var __extends = function(child, parent) {
  for (var key in parent) {
    if (__hasProp.call(parent, key)) child[key] = parent[key];
  }
  function ctor() {
    this.constructor = child;
  }
  ctor.prototype = parent.prototype;
  child.prototype = new ctor();
  child.__super__ = parent.prototype;
  return child;
};
Game = (function(_super) {
  __extends(Game, _super);
  function Game() {
    Game.__super__.constructor.apply(this, arguments);
    atom.input.bind(atom.key.LEFT_ARROW, 'left');
  }
  Game.prototype.update = function(dt) {
    if (atom.input.pressed('left')) {
      return console.log("player started moving left");
    } else if (atom.input.down('left')) {
      return console.log("player still moving left");
    }
  };
  Game.prototype.draw = function() {
```

```
      atom.context.fillStyle = 'black';
      return atom.context.fillRect(0, 0, atom.width, atom.height);
    };
    return Game;
  })(atom.Game);
  game = new Game;
  window.onblur = function() {
    return game.stop();
  };
  window.onfocus = function() {
    return game.run();
  };
  game.run();
```

You add a large amount of bulk through this conversion to JavaScript via some tool such as js2coffee.com. There are syntactic differences throughout, but most of the big scary new code happens above the `update` function. The way that classes and extensions are implemented in CoffeeScript appears to be complex when viewed in regular JavaScript.

First, `game` and `Game` are now defined at the top of the scope that they were defined in by the CoffeeScript file. Because there is no scoping function here, this means they are created in the global scope. This may seem like an odd choice, the thought being that variables might as well be defined at the same time they are set or immediately before. The reason for this convention of setting variables is simply because the alternative can be confusing if programmers expect a more traditional scoping scheme in which all blocks (code inside of { }) have a local scope rather than only functions, as is the case with JavaScript. So this convention makes it explicit where variables are available, and there is no confusion around the scoping of variables set inside of a `for` loop or `if` statement. This is not a convention adhered to strictly in this book, but it is a good thing to recognize.

Of the 42 lines in Listing 3.3, at least one-half of them (mostly at the beginning) describe a general but somewhat unclear implementation of classes and subclasses. In CoffeeScript compilation, the goal of creating easily, understandable JavaScript is not nearly as important as the CoffeeScript syntax. Fortunately, there is a native JavaScript method that accomplishes creating an object quite simply. Listing 3.4 shows the file after its transformation to use the `Object.create` method. Use the code in Listing 3.4 as the beginning of the game.js file.

**Listing 3.4**   Using Object.create for Inheritance for the game.js File

```
atom.input.bind(atom.key.LEFT_ARROW, 'left');
game = Object.create(Game.prototype);
game.update = function(dt) {
  if (atom.input.pressed('left')) {
```

```
    return console.log("player started moving left");
  } else if (atom.input.down('left')) {
    return console.log("player still moving left");
  }
};
game.draw = function() {
  atom.context.fillStyle = 'black';
  return atom.context.fillRect(0, 0, atom.width, atom.height);
};
window.onblur = function() {
  return game.stop();
};
window.onfocus = function() {
  return game.run();
};
game.run();
```

Here, you can reduce the amount of lines significantly. It's shorter and much clearer than the compiled version of the JavaScript. What is best is that all the complexity around creating an object from a template has become a single line with the `Object.create` method. There is one important thing to note about this function, however. The `Game` variable that atom.js makes available is the `constructor` of the game object that you want to inherit from. Although there are instances in which this is not strictly the case, the `prototype` and `constructor` properties conceptually operate in a nearly opposite fashion. The `prototype` of an object refers to its template object, whereas the `constructor` refers to the function that produces an object based on the `prototype`.

If you run your game, you see output to the console (Firebug or Chrome developer tools console) when you press the left arrow key. Assuming modern browsers, the create method works appropriately. The `constructor` of `game` is the function `Game`, which is responsible for producing games of the form of the `prototype` of `Game`.

## note

If you want to absorb what prototype and constructor mean, try running `game.constructor` in the console. Then follow that up with `game.constructor.prototype`. You can actually chain `.constructor.protoype.constructor.prototype`... to `game` indefinitely in this way, and it will always return the same two results: the function that describes the creation of the object (constructor) and the template that is created with the constructor (prototype).

This isn't a special case for `game` either. You can see this applied to normal JavaScript objects as well. Try `"myString".constructor.prototype` and `var obj = {}; obj.constructor.prototype` (along with primitives such as numbers and other custom objects) to see this effect in action.

If you're confused by all this inheritance stuff, it's okay. The important thing is that for the purpose of your game, `Object.create` is an adequate substitute for the inheritance implementation provided by compiled CoffeeScript. One thing to note here is that it is a relatively new method, unsupported by older browsers, so you may have to implement a "polyfill" to support this behavior. See modernizr in Appendix C, "Resources," if you're curious about polyfills.

## warning

**DIFFERENT BROWSERS DESCRIBE OBJECTS DIFFERENTLY**   When you are debugging in multiple browsers, you may notice that one console describes your object differently than another, for instance the __proto__ attribute, and what exists inside and outside of it. If you are confused by this, test the interface by running methods on the objects. Often, you find that the interface is acceptable across multiple browsers, even if the internal representation and description of that representation is inconsistent.

# Recipe: Drawing with Canvas

Currently, in addition to faithfully provides methods for update and draw, your game basically takes input from the keyboard and prints it to the console. So far in this book, you haven't dealt with the canvas, which is arguably the most important part of HTML5 in HTML5 games. You use the canvas in this recipe to draw a background for your game.

atom.js provides a good first exposure to working with the canvas, simply because it does as little as possible. Other game frameworks tend to override drawing methods and abstract away what is at its core, a fairly simple API. Listing 3.5 from the atom.js file shows how atom handles working with the canvas. This doesn't require any changes, as you can observe.

**Listing 3.5**   How canvas Is Accessed Through atom.js

```
atom.canvas = document.getElementsByTagName('canvas')[0];
atom.context = atom.canvas.getContext('2d');
```

These two lines are the most important part of any canvas-based approach. The first finds the first `canvas` element (in the html file) and assigns it to `atom.canvas`. The second line defines the interface describing it as two-dimensional. The other option is `experimental-webgl`, which is 3-D context. The remaining lines bind mouse events.

> ## note
>
> The 3-D context is significantly more complex and would require a book (or two) of its own to describe analogous techniques that you can achieve in 2-D context. When all is said and done, 2-D games are popular and do not require as broad of a programming/graphical skill set to create. 2-D games certainly cover a lot of ground, including all the genres in this book, but franchises such as Paper Mario, Super Smash Brothers, and Street Fighter prove 2-D techniques to be valuable for major modern titles as well. If you're interested in 3-D, see Appendix C for an idea of where to start.

So now, armed with hooks into the canvas and its 2-D context, you can begin drawing. Replace the `draw` method in game.js with the code in Listing 3.6.

**Listing 3.6**   Drawing a Background

```
game.draw = function() {
  atom.context.beginPath();
  atom.context.fillStyle = '#34e';
  atom.context.fillRect(0, 0, atom.width, atom.height/2);
  atom.context.fillStyle = '#ee3';
  atom.context.arc(140, atom.height/2 -30, 90, Math.PI*2, 0);
  atom.context.fill();
  atom.context.fillStyle = '#2e2';
  atom.context.fillRect(0, atom.height/2, atom.width, atom.height/2);
};
```

First, you use the `beginPath` function to indicate a new path is being drawn. It is good to lead drawing functions with this. If it is not there, you may see unexpected results due to old styles from previous renderings sticking around. After that set the `fillStyle` attribute of the context to blue. In the next line, fill in the top half of the canvas with the `fillRect` method. The parameters for this method are starting x position, starting y position, width, and height. Next, change the color again (to yellow) with the `fillStyle` method, in preparation of drawing the sun. In the `arc` method, describe the circle by defining the x-position (140 pixels to the right), y position (a bit above center), radius of the circle (90 pixels), the beginning angle (360 degrees in radians is 2*pi), and the ending angle (0). To actually draw the circle described by `arc`, also use the `fill` method. The last two lines draw the ground in a similar way to drawing the sky. Keep in mind that as shapes are drawn, they cover previously drawn shapes. Use this to your advantage in drawing the ground over the sun rather than rending a more complex shape of a partial circle.

> ### note
> Many libraries and game engines (such as easel.js in Chapter 4, "Puzzle") implement their own convenience methods so that you can more easily express your interest in say, drawing a circle, and just defining the radius, height, and width coordinates. In addition to that, they frequently obviate the need for calling the shape description and rendering code in two separate steps. More high-level ways of drawing is covered in later chapters.

After updating the draw method to draw the background, loading index.html gives you something like Figure 3.1.

**Figure 3.1** The background drawn

# Recipe: Drawing Holes

Now you have a simple backdrop for your whack-a-mole-type game. The next step is giving the moles somewhere to come out of. We'll call these "holes," and deal with drawing them in a minute. First, to keep your `draw` method simple, do a bit of cleanup to the drawing code you have in Listing 3.7.

**Listing 3.7** Keeping the draw Method Simple

```
game.draw = function() {
  this.drawBackground();
};
game.drawBackground = function(){
  atom.context.beginPath();
  atom.context.fillStyle = '#34e';
  atom.context.fillRect(0, 0, atom.width, atom.height/2);
  atom.context.fillStyle = '#ee3';
  atom.context.arc(140, atom.height/2 -30, 90, Math.PI*2, 0);
  atom.context.fill();
  atom.context.fillStyle = '#2e2';
  atom.context.fillRect(0, atom.height/2, atom.width, atom.height/2);
};
```

Here, move all the code you had before into a `game.drawBackground` method. Then call this method in the `draw` function. If you started this book without much JavaScript knowledge, the `this` keyword might still be confusing in the draw method. In that context, `this` refers to `game`, so saying `this.drawBackground()` is the same as saying `game.drawBackground()`. As always, whenever you're confused, adding a `console.log(thingIAmConfusedAbout);` line to things can be helpful. For more on what to do when you're stuck, see Appendix B, "Quality Control. "

> ## tip
>
> The process of moving code around without changing functionality is known as *refactoring*. It is impossible to plan programs perfectly. As you build, taking time to reorganize the code can help to prevent it from becoming a jumbled mess. Refactoring is a rather large topic, with many approaches. In general though, look out for functions that are too long, files that are too long, functions with nondescriptive names, setting too many variables, and using too much conditional logic (if statements). All these things present barriers to maintainability and collaboration for your games, so it is good to eliminate them when possible.

Next, add some code for drawing the holes in Listing 3.8. This means adding a new method called `drawHoles`, which draws four circles for holes and the text of the letter keys that can be used later for bopping the moles. You can also call that method from the `draw` function.

**Listing 3.8**  Drawing Holes

```
game.draw = function() {
  this.drawBackground();
  this.drawHoles(['A', 'S', 'D', 'F'], 145, 85);
};
game.drawHoles = function(holeLabels, xOffset, yOffset){
  for(i = 0; i < holeLabels.length; i++){
    atom.context.fillStyle = game.hole.color;
    var holeLocation = [xOffset + game.hole.spacing*i, yOffset];
    game.hole.draw(holeLocation, holeLabels[i]);
  }
};
game.hole = {
  size: 40,
  spacing: 280,
  color: '#311',
  labelOffset: 140,
  labelColor: '#000',
  labelFont: "130px monospace",
  draw: function(holeLocation, holeLabel){
    atom.context.beginPath();
    atom.context.arc(holeLocation[0], atom.height/2+holeLocation[1],
➥this.size, 0, Math.PI*2, false);
    atom.context.fill();
    atom.context.fillStyle = this.labelColor;
    atom.context.font = this.labelFont;
    atom.context.fillText(holeLabel, holeLocation[0] -
➥this.size, atom.height/2+holeLocation[1] + this.labelOffset);
  }
};
game.drawBackground = function(){
...
```

Trusting that all the code inside of the draw function will be executed every frame of the game loop (one of the major utilities of atom.js), we know that all we need to do is place the drawing code inside of the draw function somehow. To that end, add a call to the drawHoles function that takes three parameters. The first is an array of letters that you want to be in each hole. The second and third parameters are the x offset and y offset of all the holes. Keep in mind that, unlike what you might see typically in graphs with coordinate 0, 0 being at the bottom-left corner, when drawing on the canvas, the y-axis begins at the top, so 0, 0 would be at the top-left corner.

When you call the `drawHoles` function, it loops through the array of hole labels, determines the location of the hole, and draws each hole by calling the `draw` function of the `hole` object, which you define next. In the `game.hole` object, you define properties, strings, numbers, and the `draw` function. The strings and numbers are referenced internally in the `draw` function, by calling `this.propertyName`, which is simple enough. Most of the code in the `draw` function of `game.hole` should be familiar because it behaves similarly to how you drew the sun before; the exceptions are the last two full lines of code. The first sets the size and font for the text with the `context.font` method. The second draws the text with the `context.fillText` method, which takes three parameters here: the text to display, the x position, and the y position.

With the holes in place, after opening the index.html file in a browser, you should now see something like Figure 3.2.

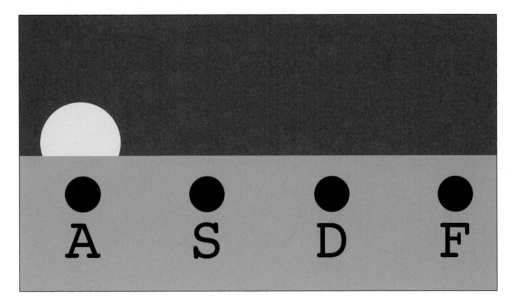

**Figure 3.2** Holes in place

# Recipe: Drawing a Mole

The holes are taken care of, completing the environment. Now you need the antagonist in the story (the mole) to make an appearance. You're just testing rendering the mole, so any place is as good as the next. For now, augment your draw function to make the mole appear in the top-left corner with the bolded line in Listing 3.9.

**Listing 3.9**   Drawing a Mole in the Main draw Function

```
game.draw = function() {
  this.drawBackground();
  this.drawHoles(['A', 'S', 'D', 'F'], 145, 85);
  this.mole.draw(100, 100);
};
```

You don't actually have a `game.mole` object. For the code to work, you need one of those, along with a `draw` method. Now add that with the code in Listing 3.10. This can be anywhere in game.js as long as it is not within another function or object.

**Listing 3.10**   A Mole Object with a draw Method

```
game.mole = {
  size: 40,
  color: '#557',
  noseSize: 8,
  noseColor: "#c55",
  eyeSize: 5,
  eyeOffset: 10,
  eyeColor: "#000",
  draw: function(xPosition, yPosition){
    this.drawHead(xPosition, yPosition);
    this.drawEyes(xPosition, yPosition);
    this.drawNose(xPosition, yPosition);
    this.drawWhiskers(xPosition, yPosition);
  },
  drawHead: function(xPosition, yPosition){
    atom.context.beginPath();
    atom.context.fillStyle = this.color;
    atom.context.arc(xPosition, yPosition, this.size, 0, Math.PI*2);
    atom.context.fill();
  },
  drawNose: function(xPosition, yPosition){
    atom.context.beginPath();
    atom.context.fillStyle = this.noseColor;
    atom.context.arc(xPosition, yPosition, this.noseSize, 0,
➥Math.PI*2);
    atom.context.fill();
  },
  drawEyes: function(xPosition, yPosition){
    atom.context.beginPath();
    atom.context.fillStyle = this.eyeColor;
    atom.context.arc(xPosition + this.eyeOffset, yPosition -
➥this.eyeOffset, this.eyeSize, 0, Math.PI*2);
```

```
      atom.context.fill();
      atom.context.beginPath();
      atom.context.fillStyle = this.eyeColor;
      atom.context.arc(xPosition - this.eyeOffset, yPosition -
➡this.eyeOffset, this.eyeSize, 0, Math.PI*2);
      atom.context.fill();
    },
    drawWhiskers: function(xPosition, yPosition){
      atom.context.beginPath();
      atom.context.moveTo(xPosition - 10, yPosition);
      atom.context.lineTo(xPosition - 30, yPosition);
      atom.context.moveTo(xPosition + 10, yPosition);
      atom.context.lineTo(xPosition + 30, yPosition);
      atom.context.moveTo(xPosition - 10, yPosition + 5);
      atom.context.lineTo(xPosition - 30, yPosition + 10);
      atom.context.moveTo(xPosition + 10, yPosition + 5);
      atom.context.lineTo(xPosition + 30, yPosition + 10);
      atom.context.stroke();
    }
  }
```

First, define simple integer and string properties to be used later in the function. Next, define the `draw` function for the `mole` object that you call in the main `draw` function. This function takes parameters for the mole's position and delegates the actual drawing to specific functions that draw each part (head, nose, eyes, and whiskers). Because they draw circles as you are experts with now, the head, nose, and head drawing functions should make sense, but the `drawWhiskers` function has three new functions that you should address.

Conceptually, think of the `moveTo` function as saying "put the pen here," and the `lineTo` function as "drag the pen from where it is to here." But these pen strokes are in invisible ink. That's where the `stroke` method comes in. It says "make the invisible ink that you drew appear now."

The list of properties in the mole object might seem a bit long. You could break it up into smaller pieces, but for the remainder of the game, you treat a mole as a singular unit. You have some nearly identical code in a few places (such as `drawWhiskers`) where you could conceivably condense it a bit. By all means do this if you feel compelled, but beware of making the code smaller by writing for overly prescribed circumstances or obscuring the meaning of the code. Making code short to be understandable is great, but often, you won't see the perfect way of how to shorten it until it becomes more complex.

After implementing the mole object and calling its draw method, you should see something that looks like Figure 3.3 by opening index.html in the browser.

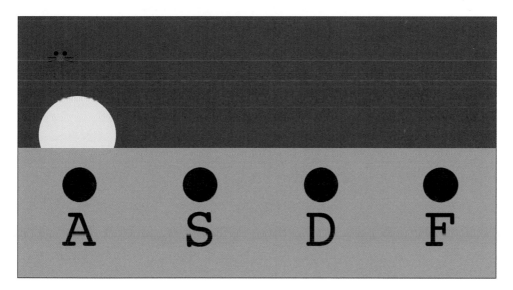

**Figure 3.3** The mole drawn in the upper-left corner

# Recipe: Putting the Moles in the Holes

For this recipe, you need to rework the code for holes significantly. Right now, all you have for holes is a function that asks that some holes be drawn to the screen. For mole bopping, you need some kind of logic to say when a mole has been bopped. There are a few possibilities here. You could add a "bopped" attribute to the mole object and keep track of which hole it is in, but if you think about a physical version of the game, a mole is simply a chunk of plastic that decorates the hole. You don't want more complex entities than you need, so take that approach and leave the mole as a decoration that appears or disappears depending on whether a hole is active.

The first change in Listing 3.11 is at the bottom of the game.js file, just before the `run` function is called.

**Listing 3.11**   Calling the makeHoles Function

```
window.onfocus = function() {
  return game.run();
};
game.makeHoles(['A', 'S', 'D', 'F'], 145, atom.height/2 + 85);
game.run();
```

The bolded line is new here. You still want to draw holes on every loop of the main `draw` function, but you want to construct the objects only once. That is why this function call exists outside of the `draw`, `update`, or `run` functions.  Now take a look at this function in Listing 3.12, which can be placed right after the `game.draw` function.

**Listing 3.12**   The makeHoles Function Definition

```
game.makeHoles = function(labels, xOffset, yOffset){
  game.holes = [];
  for(var i = 0; i < labels.length; i++){
    var newHole = Object.create(game.hole);
    newHole.holeLocation = [xOffset + game.hole.spacing*i, yOffset];
    newHole.label = labels[i];
    newHole.active = true;
    game.holes.push(newHole);
  };
};
```

In this function, you create a `game.holes` array that can store each hole as a newly constructed object. You set a few properties on each hole and then add it to the array. Because you draw each one individually, you can delete the `drawHoles` function now.

You have quite a bit to add to your `game.hole` object in Listing 3.13. It is no longer just a wrapper for a `draw` method, but actually contains important logic for drawing label, hole, and mole entities to the screen.

**Listing 3.13**   The Hole with More Drawing Responsibilities

```
game.hole = {
  size: 40,
  spacing: 280,
  color: '#311',
  labelOffset: 140,
  labelColor: '#000',
  labelFont: "130px monospace",
  moleOffset: 20,
  draw: function(){
    this.drawHole();
    this.drawLabel();
    if (this.active === true){
      this.drawMole(this.holeLocation[0], this.holeLocation[1] -
➡this.moleOffset);
    };
  },
  drawHole: function(){
    atom.context.fillStyle = this.color;
    atom.context.beginPath();
    atom.context.arc(this.holeLocation[0], this.holeLocation[1],
➡this.size, 0, Math.PI*2, false);
    atom.context.fill();
  },
  drawLabel: function(){
    atom.context.fillStyle = this.labelColor;
    atom.context.font = this.labelFont;
    atom.context.fillText(this.label, this.holeLocation[0] - this.size,
➡ "this.holeLocation[1] + this.labelOffset);
  },
  drawMole: function(xPosition, yPosition){
    game.mole.draw(xPosition, yPosition);
  }
};
```

The first change is that you have a `moleOffset` that you use later to place the mole slightly above the hole. Next, in a similar way to how you split up the task of drawing the mole into its component features earlier, you now do the same by splitting out drawing the hole, the label, and the mole. The mole is drawn only if the hole is `active`, aka having a mole peeking out of it. The code for drawing the mole contains a lot of details, so we still let the `game.mole` object do the heavy lifting by passing the function off to it. Nothing has changed within the mole's `draw` method.

The last change that you need to make for this recipe is in the main `game.draw` function, which you can see in Listing 3.14.

**Listing 3.14** The New draw Method

```
game.draw = function() {
  this.drawBackground();
  for (var i = 0; i < game.holes.length; i++){
    game.holes[i].draw();
  }
};
```

We still draw the background as before, but now loop through each hole, calling its `draw` method, rather than calling functions to draw holes and moles here.

If all went according to plan, you should end up with all the holes as active, meaning there are moles peeking out of every hole, as shown in Figure 3.4. You can view this by opening index.html in your browser.

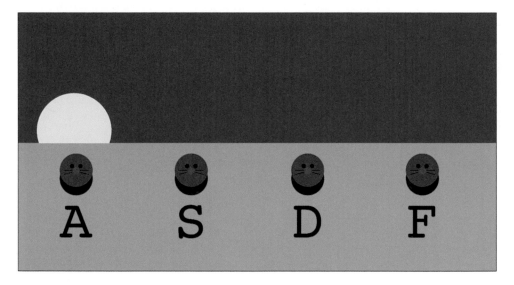

**Figure 3.4** The moles all peeking out

Now that the drawing is taken care of, you have a lovely image of some moles in front of a sunset, but it's not a game yet. Let's get closer in the next recipe by adding some dynamic mole peeking.

# Recipe: Dynamic Mole Peeking

Right now, you are setting all the holes as active. In this recipe, you set them as active one at a time, for a couple of seconds each before switching which hole is active. First, adjust your `update` function in game.js, and set some variables required for `update` beforehand with the code in Listing 3.15.

**Listing 3.15**  Making the Update Function Work

```
atom.currentMoleTime = 0;
atom.tillNewMole = 2;
game.update = function(dt) {
  atom.currentMoleTime = atom.currentMoleTime + dt;
  if (atom.currentMoleTime > atom.tillNewMole){
    game.activeMole = Math.floor(Math.random()*4);
    atom.currentMoleTime = 0;
  };
},
```

In `currentMoleTime`, you store the amount of time that a given hole has been active. The next line stores the number of total number of seconds before making a new hole active. If you want the mole to stick around longer, increase this number. Inside of the `update` function, you can replace the code from the sample "moving left" game, and you can finally take advantage of the `dt` parameter, which stores the length of time, in seconds (with a floating point number such as 0.017) since the last execution of the `update` function. We add these subsecond values to the `currentMoleTime`. When it has been more than 2 seconds since the last mole displayed, activate a new hole at random, and reset the counter to zero.

The main `draw` function largely stays the same, but you need to set the active state of each hole. Listing 3.16 shows how to do this.

**Listing 3.16**   Setting the Active State of Holes

```
game.draw = function() {
  this.drawBackground();
  for (var i = 0; i < game.holes.length; i++){
    if (i === game.activeMole){
      game.holes[i].active = true;
    }
    else{
      game.holes[i].active = false;
    };
    game.holes[i].draw();
  }
};
```

Only the lines setting the active state in bold have changed. Because you now set this property here, you no longer need to set the state to active as you did for each hole in the last recipe. Now that you set the `active` property in the `draw` function, remove the following line from the `game.makeHoles` function:

```
newHole.active = true;
```

Now if you load up index.html in a browser, you see a mole moving around from hole to hole.

# Recipe: Bopping Moles

Now the moles are getting out of control. You finally use the hole labels (ASDF) for something other than strange decoration. The first change to make comes from a recognition that you need to reference the array literal `['A', 'S', 'D', 'F']` more than once. Listing 3.17 shows the changes you need to make to the beginning and end of the file.

**Listing 3.17**   game.keys in Action

```
//Delete this line: atom.input.bind(atom.key.LEFT_ARROW, 'left');
game = Object.create(Game.prototype);
game.keys = ['A', 'S', 'D', 'F'];
for (var i = 0; i < game.keys.length; i++){
  atom.input.bind(atom.key[game.keys[i]], game.keys[i]);
```

```
};
...
game.makeHoles(game.keys, 145, atom.height/2 + 85);
game.run();
```

Actually, you never used this first line since the sample game was first imported. It binds the left arrow key to a nickname called `left`. Inside of the loop, bind each of these keys, getting them, so that you can detect key-press events later. At the end of the file, change the call to the `game.makeHoles` function to take `game.keys` as the first parameter instead of the array literal that you used before.

> ## note
>
> You might wonder why you used `game.keys[i]`, instead of `game.keys.i`. Both the bracket syntax and dot syntax refer to properties of an object, but there are reasons to use one and not the other. The dot syntax is clear and short. It has been established as preferable when it is possible to use it. The bracket syntax is used when you need to allow for characters that would cause an error with the dot syntax, for example, `["myProperty" + "1"]` or if, as in this case, you need to use a variable name rather than the literal name of the property.

Next, introduce a `bop` object that contains logic to handle moles bopping. This code in Listing 3.18 can go after the update function.

**Listing 3.18** The game.bop Object

```
game.bop = {
  bopped: true,
  total:0,
  draw: function(){
    atom.context.fillStyle = '#000';
    atom.context.font = '130px monospace';
    atom.context.fillText('Score: ' + this.total, 300, 200);
  },
  with_key: function(key){
    if (!!(game.activeMole + 1) === true && key ===
➥game.holes[game.activeMole].label){
      this.total = this.total+1;
      game.activeMole = -1;
      this.bopped = true;
    }
    else{
```

```
        this.total = this.total-1;
      }
    }
  }
```

You can put this code right before the `game.draw` function. Because the code you write later will subtract from the score when it draws a mole if `bopped` is `false`, you set the state of `bopped` to `true` so that you won't take a penalty to your `total` on the first mole drawing. Next set the total of moles bopped to zero. Then you define a `draw` function that draws the total to the screen. The `with_key` function is called indirectly when a key that you had registered is pressed. If the `key` that is pressed matches the label of the `activeMole` (this is the second part of the conditional), the `total` is incremented; set `activeMole` to `-1` and `bopped` to `true`. In the case of a miss, decrement the total. You can see the bopped checker in action as part of the revised `game.update` method in Listing 3.19.

> ## note
>
> The first half of the conditional check in `with_key` is a bit unintuitive. The whole reason for the first half of the conditional is so that you will not run the second half and cause an error when `game.activeMole` is `undefined`. This technique is known as a *guard*. You could set a default value somewhere, but there is a simple way to handle this situation. It does require some explanation, however.
>
> In JavaScript, `0` evaluates to `false` in a conditional check such as `if (0)...` Note that `!!(value)` performs this type of check inline to reveal the "truthiness" of an object. Because of that, your possible range of values for `game.active-Mole` (0, 1, 2, or 3) could present a problem when checking to see if something has been assigned to `game.activeMole` yet because `!!(undefined)` and `!!(0)` both evaluate to `false`. When `activeMole` refers to the first hole (at index 0), you would like it to evaluate to `true`. You also want to support the case in which there is no active mole after it has been bopped and disappears. You could manually set a value to undefined, but that approach could be fairly confusing later. So what you do to check for existence in this case is add 1. 0-3 ends up as 1-4, and all of them will appropriately evaluate to `true`. -1 (the state of `activeMole` post-bopping), will become 0 and appropriately evaluate to `false`. When `activeMole` is `undefined`, it receives the value of `NaN` (not a number). When 1 is added to it, it will evaluate to false, which is what you want for this case as well.
>
> That is a brief tour of existence checks, null guards, and truthiness in JavaScript. There are many edge cases, and the language demands that you think a little too hard sometimes when you want to support them all.

**Listing 3.19**  Checking for Bopped Moles

```
game.update = function(dt) {
  atom.currentMoleTime = atom.currentMoleTime + dt;
  if (atom.currentMoleTime > atom.tillNewMole){
    game.activeMole = Math.floor(Math.random()*4);
    atom.currentMoleTime = 0;
    if(game.bop.bopped === false){
      game.bop.total = game.bop.total-1;
    }
    else{
      game.bop.bopped = false;
    }
  };
  for (var i = 0; i < game.keys.length; i++){
    if (atom.input.pressed(game.keys[i])){
      game.bop.with_key(game.keys[i]);
    }
  };
};
```

The first part of the new code in bold shows what happens if you don't bop the mole by the time it's time to draw a new one. The score is reduced. The else condition is for a hit. In that case, bopped is reset to false for the next mole emergence. The for loop cycles through the keys that you registered and calls the game.bop.with_key method when any of them are pressed.

The last change you need to make is to draw the bop total in your main draw function, making it look like Listing 3.20.

**Listing 3.20**  An Updated draw Function

```
game.draw = function() {
  this.drawBackground();
  for (var i = 0; i < game.holes.length; i++){
    if (i === game.activeMole){
      game.holes[i].active = true;
    }
    else{
      game.holes[i].active = false;
    };
    game.holes[i].draw();
  }
  this.bop.draw();
};
```

Wonderful. The game is now complete. If everything went according to plan, and you played the game for a while, you might see something like what is in Figure 3.5.

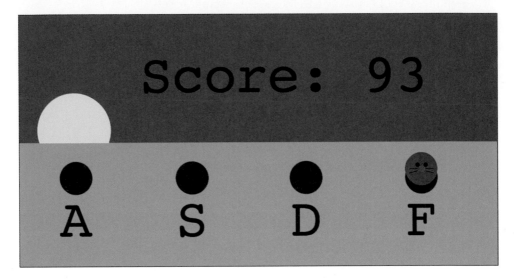

**Figure 3.5** A great score for a great game

You're almost all set. Before you close this chapter though, spend some time considering how you would turn this from a "party" game into a "rhythm" game.

# Wallowing in Despair with HTML5's \<audio> tag

I would like to say that audio is easy in HTML5 and JavaScript. I would like to say that it is as easy to play a sound as it is to display graphics, using something like `audiocontext.play(noteOrFrequency)`. I would like to say that browsers old and modern, mobile and desktop, and even native mobile clients support audio in a reasonable way. I would like to say that the web offers a simple way to make the sound you want come out of your speakers, and whether you compose, mix beats, or play an instrument, you will have a ton of fun exploring your musical talents in a new context. For the sake of this chapter, I would love to say that you could make something like *Rock Band* just by adding licensing, more graphics, more levels, and a more precise scoring system.

None of this is true as of this writing. Browser groups have varying opinions about which codecs to support, mostly based on open-source/closed-source leanings, which means even for playing an audio file, you need two versions of the file (.ogg and .mp3). In addition, at the low-level of creating (rather than just playing) sounds, there is also a lack of agreement. Mozilla's latest efforts center around something called the Audio API Extension, which is now deprecated. Chrome works with the standard known as Web Audio that is being developed by the W3C (http://www.w3.org/TR/webaudio/). Firefox announced plans to support this in the future, but as of this writing, there is no single API that is supported by both Chrome and Firefox.

There are additional problems. Attempting to load multiple sounds in mobile devices can crash your game. If you are looking for transparency of what browsers are capable of, you will also be disappointed. Take a look at Listing 3.21.

**Listing 3.21**   Capability of Playing Media in Browsers

```
<audio id="myAudio"></audio>
<script>
  var myAudio = document.getElementById("myAudio");
  myAudio.canPlayType('audio/ogg; codecs="vorbis"');
</script>
```

Feature detection is problematic. When you apply the `canPlayType` function to an HTML MediaElement such as `myAudio`, you might expect a straight answer such as `true` or `false`. Instead, you will be greeted by one of three possible return values that read more like prom rejections than expected and reasonable responses from a computer. They are `"probably"`, `"maybe"`, or `""`.

The last thing that I would like to say is that it's getting better for audio in the browser. I hope that this is true, but it is hard to say. There have been significant changes in the past couple years, but it is still much the Wild West.

> ## note
>
> Don't look so glum! With this chapter, I wanted to explain some of the low-level issues with audio in the browser, but hope is on the way. Check out the resources in Appendix C. Some people are doing amazing things with audio. But cross-browser issues are difficult, and audio is nowhere near as fully featured as graphics are in HTML5.
>
> Using high-level tools, you can usually load background music and sound effects. Keep in mind that in many cases, this means using flash as a fallback in circumstances where audio is unsupported otherwise. Also keep in mind that this does not solve the problem of dynamically generated audio.

If you want to make a *Rock Band*-style game out of the mole-bopping game you have, you have two main options for audio. You can either create the audio dynamically, creating it on-the-fly with either of the low-level Firefox or Chrome-specific APIs, or you can use a premade audio. With the latter option, this means creating the audio (or using someone else's audio with appropriate licensing), tagging each subsecond audio snippet, and adding hooks for each snippet mapped to the appropriate button and point in time. To keep the code in this book extensible and sustainable, neither one of these options is satisfactory.

## Summary

This chapter covered a lot of ground. You explored what it is like to work with the minimalist game engine atom.js; used the canvas API without the benefit of abstractions you find in other game engines; learned a little bit about the pros and cons of CoffeeScript; and discussed some of the more confusing parts of the object model in JavaScript including `prototype`, `constructor`, and how to mitigate this confusion with the `Object.create` function. We topped it all off with the current state of audio in the browser.

Excluding mouse event bindings, you used all the main parts of atom.js in your game. Learning more about atom.js would likely mean learning more about CoffeeScript or plain old JavaScript to add functionality or trying to make an even smaller game engine.

If you want improve the mole game, you have plenty of options. You can increase the difficulty level by adding multiple moles at a time or adjusting the amount of time for new moles to appear. You can add a high-score counter. You can add a concept of "game over" complete with a "Play Again" button. You can change the input mechanism to use the mouse instead of the keyboard. You can even use css to change the cursor to an image of a hammer for bopping or an earthworm (what moles eat) if you want to give the player a more benevolent role.

# CHAPTER 4

# PUZZLE

In games such as *Bejeweled*, *Snood*, and *Tetris Attack*, the player's goal is to match up blocks of color as quickly as possible using simple mechanisms to add, remove, move, and switch blocks. This genre is a popular format for casual web games but appears in other places as well.

One unique feature of these games is that they are relatively easy to build. Beyond simplifying their development as standalone games, this also uniquely positions them as puzzles or embeddable minigames in larger form games. On the Super Nintendo console system, *Lufia 2* is especially notable for making heavy use of dungeon puzzles involving pushing around colored blocks. A more familiar example might be the *Legend of Zelda* series, which consistently employs puzzles of this type to unlock doors and treasure chests, and generally advance through the game.

In a nondigital context, the *15 Puzzle* is a good example of this type of game. By ratcheting up the complexity of the rules of what the "blocks" are capable of, adding some winning, losing, and tie conditions, you can get games such as *tick tac toe*, *go*, and *chess* (For chess, you would also need some general medieval theming.)

In this chapter, you build *Memory*, a common children's game with a simple object: Click two identical pictures to remove them until they all disappear. For this game, use the JavaScript game engine easel.js.

In programming, we sometimes refer to high-level and low-level abstractions. This simply means taking care of many of the small details yourself (low level) or leaving it to the library, language, or in your case, JavaScript game engine to take care of the details for you (high level). Engines covered in this book tend toward the high-level side, but easel.js is more low level, that is to say that it is less of a game engine and more of a convenient, general interface to the canvas rendering API. It is particularly appropriate for this chapter because the *Memory* game is fairly simple, and by using this low-level engine, you can drill down into some of the details that you won't be able to in other chapters.

To start, you have an index.html file like in Listing 4.1 in the puzzle/initial directory. This sets the doctype, loads the easel.js engine, and creates the canvas element that you interact with throughout this chapter.

**Listing 4.1**   Starter HTML File

```
<!DOCTYPE html>
<html>
  <head>
    <title>Recipe: Drawing a square</title>
    <script src="easel.js"></script>
</head>
<body>
  <canvas id="myCanvas" width="960" height="600"></canvas>
</body>
</html>
```

If you open this file in Firefox or Chrome, you won't see anything going on yet. Let's get our first taste of working with easel.js to render something to the screen.

# Recipe: Rendering with easel.js

Traditionally, the basis of knowing that a program is working is to demonstrate the program's capability to announce something such as "Hello World!". easel.js is a rendering graphics rendering engine, so let's try rendering something simple by making a square with a random color.

You need some way to kick off the JavaScript. There are a few options here, and we will be exploring even more throughout the book. You could just have a `<script>` tag that runs each line of JavaScript. One potential problem with this approach is that the JavaScript may run before all the elements are fully rendered, which could leave you with a broken script. The second option is to bind a JavaScript event to the `window` using a script like in Listing 4.2. You won't be doing this, but the sample is here for illustration.

**Listing 4.2**   Binding the init Function to the Window

```
<script>
  function init(){
    //start our square rendering code
  }
  window.onload = init;
</script>
```

For this chapter, you take a simpler, but less elegant, approach of binding the JavaScript directly to the `body` tag's `onload` attribute, as shown in Listing 4.3. Make this change in index.html.

**Listing 4.3**   Obtrusive JavaScript Style of Loading Code

```
//simply change this:
<body>
//to this
<body onload="init()">
```

Web purists may recoil here at the use of what is pejoratively referred to as "obtrusive JavaScript." The ideal behind that thinking is completely sound. To maintain extensible web code bases, it is best to characterize each bit of code as content (HTML), presentation (CSS), and behavior (JavaScript), keeping them as separate as possible for maximum flexibility and elegance. There is a time for that, and if you are interested, you should search for "unobtrusive JavaScript" and "JavaScript patterns." The rabbit hole can go deep here though, so it's also good to know when to pursue elegance, and when quick and dirty will suffice. Coding for scale, extensibility, and robustness can at times come in conflict with the YAGNI (Ya Ain't Gonna Need It) principle, so for now, keep in mind that there are different ways to do things. After all, most features that have survived the HTML spec to this point, such as the `onload` (and its other JavaScript triggering companions `onclick()`, `onMouseover()`, and more), have their place, so it's good to know about them.

With that out of the way, it's back to square one. Assuming the obtrusive, quick-and-dirty method of attaching the `onload()`, you need an `init()` function. Now add a new `<script>` tag just below the `<script>` tag that loads the easel.js library and simply alerts "hello world" when it loads (see Listing 4.4).

**Listing 4.4**   Adding a New script Tag with Your init Function

```
<script src="easel.js"></script>

<script type="text/javascript">
  function init() {
    alert("hello world");
  }
</script>
```

You still have a bit of work to do before you can show your square. You can see your `init()` function a little more fleshed out in Listing 4.5. This can replace your "hello world" that we used earlier to make sure everything was working.

**Listing 4.5**   init Function with More Detail

```
<script type="text/javascript">
  var canvas;
  var stage;
  function init() {
    canvas = document.getElementById('myCanvas');
    stage = new Stage(canvas);
    var square = drawSquare();
    stage.addChild(square);
    stage.update();
  }
</script>
```

This might be a lot to take in.  Let's take it line by line to try to make sense of it. First, declare the variables `canvas` and `stage`, which will, respectively, refer to your `canvas` HTML element, and an instance of the `Stage` Object defined by easel.js. Inside of your function, the `canvas` variable is assigned to the `canvas` element with the `id` of `myCanvas` via the native (browser-defined, not easel.js-defined) JavaScript method `getElementById()`. Next, the `stage` variable is assigned to a new `Stage` object, which wraps the `canvas` variable (which maps to the `canvas` element). The next line assigns a variable `square` to the result of the `drawSquare()` method, which you have yet to define. Assuming that you have a proper square from your `drawSquare()` method, the next line simply adds that `square` to the `stage` through the `addChild()` method. Once it is "there" though, it will not actually be rendered until the `stage.update()` method is called, to show your square.

Simple enough? Okay. Moving on to your `drawSquare()` method, you need something like Listing 4.6. You can add this code right before the closing `<script>` tag.

**Listing 4.6**  drawSquare Method

```
function drawSquare() {
  var shape = new Shape();
  var graphics = shape.graphics;
  graphics.setStrokeStyle(5);
  graphics.beginStroke(Graphics.getRGB(20, 20, 20));

  graphics.beginFill(Graphics.getRGB(20, 20, 20));
  graphics.rect(5, 5, 70, 70);

  return shape;
}
```

The methods for drawing shapes as defined by easel.js are still fairly low level but should be easy enough to follow. You are manipulating a `shape` object here, specifically its `graphics`. `setStrokeStyle()` lets you define the thickness of the line; `beginStroke()` lets you define a color parameter. `beginFill()` lets you define the color of the interior of the `shape`. `rect()` takes parameters for x position, y position, width, and height of the `shape`. Finally, you can return your `shape` object back where it will be assigned as `square` and rendered in the `init()` function.

Now if you run the code by opening index.html in the browser, you see a gray square, as shown in Figure 4.1.

Gray squares are nice, but now add a little color and make it change every time the page is reloaded. You need to make some slight changes to your `drawSquare()` function and add a `randomColor()` function (see Listing 4.7).

# Recipe 1

**Figure 4.1**  Rendering a gray square

**Listing 4.7**  Creating Random Colors on Page Load

```
function drawSquare() {
  var shape = new Shape();
  var graphics = shape.graphics;
  var color = randomColor();
  graphics.setStrokeStyle(5);
  graphics.beginStroke(Graphics.getRGB(20, 20, 20));
  graphics.beginFill(color);
  graphics.rect(5, 5, 70, 70);
  return shape;
}
function randomColor(){
  var color = Math.floor(Math.random()*255);
  var color2 = Math.floor(Math.random()*255);
  var color3 = Math.floor(Math.random()*255);
  return Graphics.getRGB(color, color2, color3)
}
```

In your `drawSquare()` function, you need to add a call to the `randomColor()` function. Inside the `randomColor()` function, you are simply generating random rgb values between 0 and 255 and returning them to be used in the `graphics.beginFill()` function. `Math.floor` rounds numbers down so that you have integers instead of floats. Now with every page reload, you can see a different random-colored square (see Figure 4.2).

> ## tip
>
> Before moving on, if you are a bit confused about what is a native JavaScript function, and what belongs to the easel.js API, don't be too stressed about it. There are only three possibilities for where names of variables and functions are coming from. First, you defined it yourself, so you should find it somewhere in your code. Second, it is a native method or object, in which case, https://developer.mozilla.org/ would be an excellent resource. The third possibility is that it is something defined by a library that you've included (such as easel.js). In this case, you can usually find

the documentation or example code quite easily by searching for things such as **library-name docs**, **library-name documentation**, **library-name API**, or **variable-or-function-name library-name**. For more information on the different types of APIs you will encounter while working with JavaScript, see Appendix A, "JavaScript Basics."

## Recipe 1

**Figure 4.2** Nongray box

# Recipe: Rendering More Than One Thing

Rendering a square is not a game, even a simple one. You're still setting up the basic rendering, and there's still a little more to do before you can introduce any kind of goal for the player. First, clean up the code a bit by creating a few variables that you'll be using in various functions for this recipe. Add the bold lines in Listing 4.8.

**Listing 4.8**  Declaring Variables for Making Squares

```
<script type="text/javascript">
  var canvas;
  var stage;
  var squareSide = 70;
  var squareOutline = 5;
  var max_rgb_color_value = 255;
  var gray = Graphics.getRGB(20, 20, 20);
  function init() {
```

There's nothing too exotic here. You're just assigning some variables. `squareSide` represents the length and width of a square. `squareOutline` is the thickness of the border of the square. `max_rgb_color_value` is a value that you pass to the random number generator that generates rgb values with 0-255. `gray` gets a color object from the `Graphics` object of easel.js. You use that color for the outline of your squares.

Next, add the bolded lines in Listing 4.9 to the `init()` function, which follows the code in Listing 4.8.

**Listing 4.9**   Declaring Variables for the init() Function

```
function init() {
  var rows = 5;
  var columns = 6;
  var squarePadding = 10;
  canvas = document.getElementById('myCanvas');
  stage = new Stage(canvas);
  //removed var square = drawSquare();
  //removed stage.addChild(square);
  //removed stage.update();
}
```

Again, you just assign variables here to be used later. `rows` and `columns` will be used to say how many squares you want. Given these values, you end up with 36 squares. `squarePadding` is the space between the squares. You also removed the code that actually drew your original square. It's comparatively complicated, so it is introduced a bit later in this section.

Depending on your level of coding experience, you might be wondering why you're creating variables here instead of including the numbers inline. This is done for organizational reasons. As things get more complicated, it is difficult to know what numbers mean, so setting them to variables helps you understand the code better when you read it later. Also, for variables that are reused, it is much easier to tweak values when you have to change them only in one place. You may also wonder why some variables are declared outside of the function and some are declared inside. The reason for this is that the variables declared outside of the function are available to every function inside of the script, and the ones declared inside are only visible to the function itself.

> ## note
>
> With JavaScript in general, but especially in games with high-performance requirements, one trade-off that you may face is that structure can sometimes be at odds with optimizing for speed. One particularly popular JavaScript optimization technique is to work with code in a development-friendly way (descriptive variable and function names, whitespace for readability, comments, and so on), but deploy a "minified" version that is less readable for humans, but much smaller and faster for a browser to download and interpret.

Next up, tweak your `drawSquare` function by adding the bolded lines in Listing 4.10.

**Listing 4.10** drawSquare Function

```
function drawSquare() {
  var shape = new Shape();
  var graphics = shape.graphics;
  var color = randomColor();
  graphics.setStrokeStyle(squareOutline);
  graphics.beginStroke(gray);
  graphics.beginFill(color);
  graphics.rect(squareOutline, squareOutline, squareSide, squareSide);
  return shape;
}
```

Not much has changed here other than how you use the variables previously set up as parameters to various functions.

The `randomColor` function is updated to use a new variable as well (see Listing 4.11).

**Listing 4.11** Adding the randomColor Function

```
function randomColor(){
  var color = Math.floor(Math.random()*max_rgb_color_number);
  var color2 = Math.floor(Math.random()*max_rgb_color_number);
  var color3 = Math.floor(Math.random()*max_rgb_color_number);
  return Graphics.getRGB(color, color2, color3)
}
</script>
```

Last up for this recipe is adding a `for` loop to the `init()` function. Add the bold lines in Listing 4.12 to the init function.

**Listing 4.12** full init() Function for Rendering Squares

```
function init() {
  var rows = 5;
  var columns = 6;
  var squarePadding = 10;
  canvas = document.getElementById('myCanvas');
  stage = new Stage(canvas);
  for(var i=0;i<rows*columns;i++){
    var square = drawSquare();
    square.x = (squareSide+squarePadding) * (i % columns);
    square.y = (squareSide+squarePadding) * Math.floor(i / columns);
```

```
        stage.addChild(square);
        stage.update();
    }
}
```

There is a lot going on here if you haven't dealt much with `for` loops before. In the first line, a variable `i` is created, which keeps track of the loop counter. After the semicolon, the `i<rows*columns` part sets the loop to happen only when `i` is less than the number of squares you want to display. The last part of the first line (after the second semicolon) says to increment the loop counter after each loop iteration.

The x coordinate is set by multiplying the total width of the square (`squareSide+squarePadding`) by the row position of the square. If you haven't seen the `%` operator before, you can just think of it as the remainder after dividing the first number by the second. For y position, we multiply the total height of the square (also `squareSide+squarePadding`) by the integer portion of the loop counter divided by the number of columns.

If you successfully implemented these changes, you should see a rendering similar to Figure 4.3.

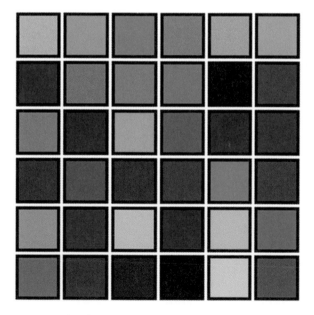

**Figure 4.3** Many squares rendered

# Recipe: Creating Pairs

So far, every tile has been generated with a random color, and the odds that you get a single pair is actually very improbable. We'll need to ensure that we actually have pairs of tiles to match before adding the logic for click handling.

We need pairs of random colors to appear in random positions. First, let's build a `placement Array` that is the same size as the number of tiles we want to place. Add the following bold lines (shown in Listing 4.13) to your code.

**Listing 4.13**   Building a placementArray

```
. . .
var gray = Graphics.getRGB(20, 20, 20);
var placementArray = [];

function init() {
  var rows = 5;
  var columns = 6;
  var squarePadding = 10;
  canvas = document.getElementById('myCanvas');
  stage = new Stage(canvas);

  var numberOfTiles = rows*columns;
  setPlacementArray(numberOfTiles);
. . .
```

All you're doing here is declaring an empty array and then calling a function that will build the array you want. You also add a `numberOfTiles` variable because with your additions in this recipe, you'll be referencing the value of `rows*columns` more than once. Beyond the benefits mentioned in the last recipe, performing a calculation more than necessary slows down your code.

Next, add the `setPlacementArray()` function that you're calling here (see Listing 4.14). This can go just above your closing `</script>` tag.

**Listing 4.14**   setPlacementArray Function

```
function setPlacementArray(numberOfTiles){
  for(var i = 0;i< numberOfTiles;i++){
    placementArray.push(i);
  }
}
```

In this function, you create an array that is the size of `numberOfTiles`, with each element of the array equaling its index. The `push()` function simply tacks on each index to the end of the array. This means that you end up with an array that looks like this: `[0, 1, 2, 3, ...,` `numberOfTiles]`.

With that out of the way, we have some slight adjustments that need to be made to the loop in the `init()` function with the bold lines in Listing 4.15.

**Listing 4.15**   init() Function Loop Adjustments

```
for(var i=0;i<numberOfTiles;i++){
  var placement = getRandomPlacement(placementArray);
  if (i % 2 === 0){
    var color = randomColor();
  }
  var square = drawSquare(color);
  square.x = (squareSide + squarePadding) * (placement % columns);
  square.y = (squareSide + squarePadding) * Math.floor(placement /
columns);
  stage.addChild(square);
  stage.update();
}
```

Other than using `numberOfTiles` rather than `row * column` directly as your termination condition for your loop, there are two more changes to note. First, you are now relying on the `placement`, rather than the index `i` of the loop, to determine the coordinates of the square. Second, you are assigning a new `randomColor` at every even loop index and passing that to the `drawSquare()` function to achieve pairs of colors.

Let's adjust the `drawSquare()` function as shown in Listing 4.16 so that it takes a parameter color and relies on that for `beginFill()` instead of `randomColor()`.

**Listing 4.16**   The New drawSquare() Function

```
function drawSquare(color) {
  var shape = new Shape();
  var graphics = shape.graphics;
//remove this line: var color = randomColor();
  graphics.setStrokeStyle(squareOutline);
  graphics.beginStroke(gray);
  graphics.beginFill(color);
  graphics.rect(squareOutline, squareOutline, squareSide, squareSide);
  return shape;
}
```

Now you can implement the `getRandomPlacement()` function with the code in Listing 4.17, which can be put just above the closing `</script>` tag.

**Listing 4.17** getRandomPlacement

```
function getRandomPlacement(placementArray){
    randomNumber = Math.floor(Math.random()*placementArray.length);
    return placementArray.splice(randomNumber, 1)[0];
}
```

This function does a few things. First, it gets a random element from the `placementArray`. Then, it removes that element from the array and returns it to be set as `placement` in the `init()` function. `getRandomPlacement()` will be executed with each loop, giving one less element to randomly select each time.

Now you have pairs of tiles in random locations, producing something like Figure 4.4.

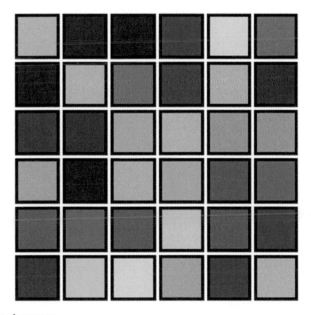

**Figure 4.4** Pairs of squares

# Recipe: Matching and Removing Pairs

Next, you want to match and remove pairs of tiles. This involves a few tweaks to your setup and a new function for handling click events. Take a look at the simple tweaks first in Listing 4.18.

**Listing 4.18** Set Up Tweaks for Clicking, Matching, and Removing

```
var placementArray = [];
var highlight = Graphics.getRGB(255, 255, 0);
var tileClicked;
function init() {
...
for(var i=0;i<numberOfTiles;i++){
  ...
  var square = drawSquare(color);
  square.color = color;
  square.x = (squareSide+squarePadding) * (placement%columns);
  square.y = (squareSide+squarePadding) *
➥Math.floor(placement/columns);
  stage.addChild(square);
  square.onPress = handleOnPress;
  stage.update();
```

First, we create a highlight color and initialize a variable `tileClicked` to store the value of the first tile that is clicked. The last bold line sets a click handler function to each square that is added to the stage. We will define that function in a minute, but first, let's take a closer look at the second bold line, `square.color = color;`.

This is among the author's favorite features of JavaScript. If you have a JavaScript object like `square`, you can define a property of it with this short syntax, and the property can be a number, an object, or even a function. Many languages would require you to define a new method for getting and setting this property. JavaScript does not, and that's awesome. On the not so awesome side, be aware that if square already had a `color` property defined, it would be overwritten by an assignment like this. Also be aware that, although it is namespaced in a fairly safe way because you have to reference it through the object, this property `color` has the same scope as `square`.

Now, to implement the `handleOnPress()` function, put the following code (shown in Listing 4.19) just above the closing `</script>` tag.

**Listing 4.19** The handleOnPress Function

```
function handleOnPress(event){
  var tile = event.target;
  if(!!tileClicked === false){
      tile.graphics.setStrokeStyle(squareOutline).beginStroke
➥(highlight).rect(squareOutline, squareOutline, squareSide,
➥squareSide);
```

```
      tileClicked = tile;
    }else{
      if(tileClicked.color === tile.color && tileClicked !== tile){
        tileClicked.visible = false;
        tile.visible = false;
      }else{
          tileClicked.graphics.setStrokeStyle(squareOutline)
  .beginStroke(gray).rect(squareOutline, squareOutline, squareSide,
  ➥squareSide);
      }
      tileClicked = null;
    }
    stage.update();
  }
```

In this function, there are two main objects to keep track of. First is the `tile` object, which represents the tile that was just clicked, and the `tileClicked` object, which refers to a tile that was clicked before `tile`. Initially, the previously clicked tile is `undefined` because there is no value set to it. Your conditional check here may seem a little strange. You could have said `if (tileClicked === undefined)`, but this would fail later after setting the variable to `null`. Admittedly, you can set the variable to `undefined` with `tileClicked = undefined`, but defining something as `undefined` is strange and could lead to confusion. Your strategy here is to account for the cases in which the variable is set to either an object (which should evaluate to true) or `undefined/null` (which should evaluate to false). The `!!` operator first says "give me the negative of the 'truthy' value of what comes after the '!'," and then it says that again. The effect is that the "truthy" value of what follows `!!` is returned. If you're confused, try experimenting in a console a bit or spending some time with Appendix A. For your purposes, this conditional could be read simply as, "if `tileClicked` is undefined or `null`." So what happens in that case?

First, the tile receives a highlighted border. Next, the `tileClicked` variable is set to `tile`. That means that the next time a tile is clicked, it follows the `else` path of this conditional. The conditional checks to see if the two tiles clicked were a match. It does this strictly by checking the color property of the tiles. There is a second condition after the `&&` that ensures that clicking the same tile twice does not count as a match. When a match occurs, the visibility of both tiles is set to `false`, which hides them. If there is no match, the highlight is removed from the tile that was clicked first. In both cases, `tileClicked` is set to `null` so that the next time `if (!!tileClicked === false)` evaluates to `true`, starting the cycle over again.

After opening index.html up, and clicking some of the pairs, you should see something like Figure 4.5.

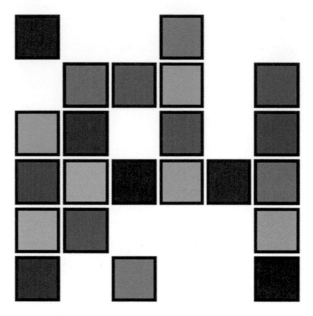

**Figure 4.5** Some matched tiles removed

# Recipe: Hiding and Flipping the Pictures

This is pretty good. It feels more like a game now, but we've made *Memory* a little too easy. Part of the fun in *Memory* is not knowing what to do until you learn where the matches are located. There is a surprise and challenge that comes along with remembering things that the game doesn't have right now (so it's not actually "memory" yet). Let's hide the pictures, and make them flippable.

First, when we call the `drawSquare()` method, let's make the initial color look gray instead of whatever color it is deep-down inside. We'll still store the color as a property, but make the following change to the call (see Listing 4.20).

**Listing 4.20** Hiding the Tiles' True Colors

```
// this needs to be changed: var square = drawSquare(color);
var square = drawSquare(gray);
square.color = color;
```

Next, you no longer use the `highlight` variable, so feel free to get rid of it with the code in Listing 4.21.

**Listing 4.21**  Remove the Highlight Variable

```
var gray = Graphics.getRGB(20, 20, 20);
// var highlight = Graphics.getRGB(255, 255, 0); //Remove this line
var placementArray = [];
```

The last thing you need to do for this recipe is adjust the `handleOnPress()` function with the code in Listing 4.22.

**Listing 4.22**  handleOnPress Changes

```
function handleOnPress(event){
  var tile = event.target;
  tile.graphics.beginFill(tile.color).rect(squareOutline,
squareOutline, squareSide, squareSide);
  if(!!tileClicked === false || tileClicked === tile){
    tileClicked = tile;
  }else{
    if(tileClicked.color === tile.color && tileClicked !== tile){
      tileClicked.visible = false;
      tile.visible = false;
    }else{
      tileClicked.graphics.beginFill(gray).rect(squareOutline,
squareOutline, squareSide, squareSide);
    }
    tileClicked = tile;
  }
  stage.update();
}
```

There are a few deletions as well as insertions here, so it might be better to just copy and paste over the original code or type it all rather than trying to inject the new lines. This code first exposes the color of the tile clicked. Next, it checks to see if either this is the first tile clicked, or if it is the same as the previously clicked tile. If it fulfills either of these conditions, you simply need to update the `tileClicked` variable and update the stage.

If those conditions are not met, there are two more code branches that are possible. The first, (the `if` inside of the `else`) works as before, checking for a matching pair and removes them. The condition for "no match" updates the previously clicked tile (two clicks ago) to make it gray. In either of these two branches, the `tileClicked` and `stage` variables are updated.

With everything working correctly, you should have something similar to Figure 4.6 after finding a few matches.

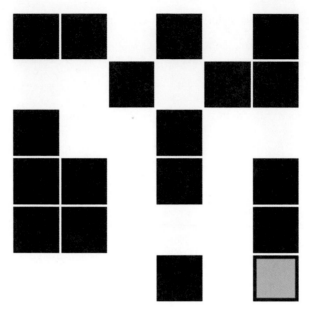

**Figure 4.6**   Hidden tiles after a few matches

# Recipe: Winning and Losing

Now the game plays like *Memory*, and you've almost achieved what you set out to accomplish. Let's create a way to win and lose. First, you need some new variables to keep track of the maximum time allowable, the matches possible and found, a few text areas to keep the player updated, and an array of squares to store references to the tiles when the player loses. You can do this with the code in Listing 4.23.

**Listing 4.23**   New Variables After <script> Tag

```
<script>
...
  var timeAllowable;
  var totalMatchesPossible;
  var matchesFound;
  var txt;
  var matchesFoundText;
  var squares;
```

Next, you need to set these variables and their attributes inside of the `init()` function. See Listing 4.24.

**Listing 4.24**   Setting the New Variables Inside of the init() Function

```
function init() {
...
  matchesFound = 0;
  timeAllowable = 200;
  txt = new Text(timeAllowable, "30px Monospace", "#000");
  txt.textBaseline = "top"; // draw text relative to the top of the em
➟box.
  txt.x = 500;
  txt.y = 0;
  stage.addChild(txt);
  squares = [];
  totalMatchesPossible = numberOfTiles/2;
  matchesFoundText = new Text("Pairs Found: "+matchesFound+"/
➟"+totalMatchesPossible, "30px Monospace", "#000");
  matchesFoundText.textBaseline = "top"; // draw text relative to the
➟top of the em box.
  matchesFoundText.x = 500;
  matchesFoundText.y = 40;
  stage.addChild(matchesFoundText);
```

Next, you need a `Ticker` object to help keep track of your time. You should also add each square to your `squares` array inside of the `for` loop in Listing 4.25. This beginning of this code can immediately follow Listing 4.24, with the other bolded line, appearing right after `square.y` is set.

**Listing 4.25**   The Rest of the init Function

```
Ticker.init();
  Ticker.addListener(window);
  Ticker.setPaused(false);

  setPlacementArray(numberOfTiles);

  for(var i=0;i<numberOfTiles;i++){
    var placement = getRandomPlacement(placementArray);
    ...
    square.y = (squareSide+squarePadding) *
➟Math.floor(placement/columns);
    squares.push(square);
    ...
  }
}
```

Now implement your `tick()` function next. You can add the code in Listing 4.26 just above the closing `</script>` tag.

**Listing 4.26** The tick() Function

```
function tick() {
  secondsLeft = Math.floor((timeAllowable-Ticker.getTime()/1000));
  txt.text = secondsLeft;
  if (secondsLeft <= 0){
    gameOver(false);
  }
  stage.update();
}
```

This function calculates the seconds that are left in play, updates the stage with that information, and calls the `gameOver()` function when the timer hits zero. Because there are certain cases where it could become negative (for example, the `tick` function does not execute when the page doesn't have focus), you do not just want to check for `secondsLeft === 0`, so check for anything less than or equal to 0. Let's implement the `gameOver()` function, as shown in Listing 4.27. This can appear after the `tick` function.

**Listing 4.27** The gameOver() Function

```
function gameOver(win){
  Ticker.setPaused(true);
  for(var i=0;i<squares.length;i++){
    squares[i].graphics.beginFill(squares[i].color).rect(5, 5, 70, 70);
    squares[i].onPress = null;
  }
  var replayParagraph = document.getElementById("replay");
  replayParagraph.innerHTML = "<a href='#' onclick='replay();'>Play
➥Again?</a>";

  if (win === true){
    matchesFoundText.text = "You win!"
  }else{
    txt.text = secondsLeft + "... Game Over";
  }
}
```

So now we see why we passed `false` to the function for a loss. That parameter determines whether to change the text to You win! or Game Over. In either case, you can reveal the squares that were not matched before losing and disable the click handler. (This is why you needed the squares array earlier.) Then pause the ticker, and update a `replay` element to allow a player to start over.

To implement the replay option fully, you need two things: a `div` with `id` of `replay` and a `replay` function that is called through `onClick` of that element. You can do this with the code in Listing 4.28.

**Listing 4.28**  Defining the replay Function for Starting Over

```
    function replay(){
      init();
    }
  </script>
</head>
<body onload="init()">
  <header id="header">
    <p id="replay"></p>
  </header>
  <canvas id="myCanvas" width="960" height="500"></canvas>
</body>
```

The last change you need to make for this recipe is to create a winning condition. You do this in the `handleOnPress()` function, incrementing the `matchesFound` counter and calling `gameOver(true)` in the case in which a player clicks the last remaining match (see Listing 4.29).

**Listing 4.29**  Determining if the Player Won

```
function handleOnPress(event){
  var tile = event.target;
  tile.graphics.beginFill(tile.color).rect(squareOutline,
➥squareOutline, squareSide, squareSide);
  if(!!tileClicked === false || tileClicked === tile){
    tileClicked = tile;
  }else{
    if(tileClicked.color === tile.color && tileClicked !== tile){
      tileClicked.visible = false;
      tile.visible = false;
      matchesFound++;
      matchesFoundText.text = "Pairs Found: "+matchesFound+"/
➥""+totalMatchesPossible;
      if (matchesFound===totalMatchesPossible){
        gameOver(true);
      }
```

In this recipe, you set up logic for winning and losing the game. In the next one, you will get into some possibilities for optimization.

# Recipe: Caching and Performance

You may have heard of a technique called *caching*. At its core, the basic idea is that you make the access to particular information less computationally expensive. You can think of it as storing food in your fridge rather than having to go to the grocery store every time you need something to eat. easel.js comes with its own caching mechanism that you can explore in just a couple of lines of code. First though, let's talk about the good and bad with caching.

The good news is that caching done well can boost your performance. As it applies to graphics in games, this means either having to redraw only of the screen instead of the whole thing, or drawing less frequently. If you have a mostly static screen with one element that moves around, it makes sense to update only the part where the element is (and has been), right?

There are some serious drawbacks, though. First , you will need to think about when to cache, when to update the cache, and when the cache no longer serves a purpose. *Cache invalidation* can be tricky. Debugging a system that uses caching is more difficult. This is because the objects that you are caching have two possible states now: the "truth" assuming no caching is in place, and the "fast almost truth." Adding to the complexity, cached objects are sometimes explicitly invalidated or recached explicitly by code, but other times the cache is set to expire after a certain period of time. Bringing back the metaphor, yes, you have food in your fridge and don't have to run to the store, which is great. But you have to know when food goes bad and plan new trips to the store so that you don't eat spoiled food. When you ask your house-mate to procure an apple, you have no idea where he's getting it from, how long it will take, and whether it's spoiled unless you make your instructions explicit or watch him carefully as it happens.

To complicate things further, browsers have their own internal caching mechanisms that don't all behave consistently. It's like having friends over for a meal and sometimes they like to bring their own food, fresh from the store. The table (your available memory) gets cluttered, and the conversation about what everyone is eating can become a burden. As of this writing, easel.js's demo code for caching performs better in Firefox with caching on and better in Chrome when caching is off. So when you have a party, you have to remember who is invited and what they will do if you try to serve them leftovers.

Performance on any given platform can vary for a variety of reasons, so the best thing you can do is target specific platforms and test their performance. Using a tool such as jsperf.com is a popular way to gain insight into this, and Appendixes B and C offer more suggestions. For simple cases of testing particular functions, a search for benchmarking JavaScript can reveal some common libraries for doing this. As it pertains to games, your main concern will be the frame rate of your game, which is typically measured in frames per second. (Sixty and above is generally considered good.)

With that weighty disclaimer out of the way, we now see how to use easel.js's caching in your *Memory* game, ignoring whether it actually helps or hurts performance. First, in the main `for` loop in the `init()` function, let's cache every square. Listing 4.30 shows where this appears.

**Listing 4.30**  Initializing the Cache

```
stage.addChild(square);
square.cache(0, 0, squareSide + squarePadding, squareSide +
➥squarePadding);
square.onPress = handleOnPress;
```

Next, you need to update the cache in your `handleOnPress()` function so that when an element is supposed to change color, the cache is updated to reflect the changes. Without these lines, the tiles stays gray when you click them. The `source-overlay` parameter is one option among several for how to blend the newly cached piece of the canvas with whatever is underneath it (see Listing 4.31).

**Listing 4.31**  Updating the Cache

```
function handleOnPress(event){
  var tile = event.target;
  tile.graphics.beginFill(tile.color).rect(squareOutline,
squareOutline, squareSide, squareSide);
  if(!!tileClicked === false || tileClicked === tile){
    tileClicked = tile;
    tileClicked.updateCache("source-overlay");
  }else{
    if(tileClicked.color === tile.color && tileClicked !== tile){
      tileClicked.visible = false;
      tile.visible = false;
      matchesFound++;
      matchesFoundText.text = "Pairs Found: "+matchesFound+"/
➥"+totalMatchesPossible;
      if (matchesFound===totalMatchesPossible){
        gameOver(true);
      }
```

```
    }else{
      tileClicked.graphics.beginFill(gray).rect(squareOutline,
➥squareOutline, squareSide, squareSide);
    }
    tileClicked.updateCache("source-overlay");
    tile.updateCache("source-overlay");
```

The last change you need to make here is to remove caching on the squares when a player loses so that you can show the squares that were missed (see Listing 4.32).

**Listing 4.32**  Removing Caching

```
function gameOver(win){
  Ticker.setPaused(true);
  for(var i=0;i<squares.length;i++){
    squares[i].graphics.beginFill(squares[i].color).rect(5, 5, 70, 70);
    squares[i].onPress = null;
    if (win === false){
      squares[i].uncache();
    }
  }
}
```

As one final (and unfortunate) bit of cleanup, the uncache function does not accomplish all that you need it to regarding setting the game up again. Regardless of your uncache call, the cache ids are still used on the next play through. If you click any of the squares, it attempts to update the cache of both the current square that is displayed and that of the square that was there before. This is curious behavior given that the unique id from the old squares are reused for the fresh batch, but rather than fight against this, you can just do the simple thing and refresh the page when "replay" is clicked, as shown in Listing 4.33.

**Listing 4.33**  Change the Call to Replay to Reload the Page

```
var replayParagraph = document.getElementById("replay");
replayParagraph.innerHTML = "<a href='#'
➥onClick='history.go(0);'>Play Again?</a>";
```

This makes use of the new JavaScript History API to go to the current page.

# Recipe: Matching Pairs Instead of Duplicates

How could you make memory more interesting? You could add more complex rules for how to manipulate tiles and create something like *Bejeweled*, but the game can also be completely transformed into something different.

You don't need to necessarily match identical tiles; you can also organize tiles into pairs. For example, you can match the picture of a square with the word "square." These types of mappings might be nice for kids just learning how to read. You can also match words with definitions, synonyms, or translations into other languages.

Let's try making a flashcard system for learning the most basic font set in Japanese, hiragana. A lot has to change in this script, so take it from the top with the code in Listing 4.34.

**Listing 4.34**   The Beginning of the New Script

```
<script type="text/javascript">
  var canvas;
  var stage;
  var placementArray = [];
  var tileClicked;
  var timeAllowable;
  var totalMatchesPossible;
  var matchesFound;
  var txt;
  var matchesFoundText;
  var tileHeight = 30;
  var tileWidth = 45;
  var border = 1;
  var globalPadding = 10;
  var margin = 10;
  var padding = 5;
  var numberOfTiles;
  var textTiles;
```

First, we define a few new variables that we need for positional reasons, and get rid of some of the former positional and dimensional elements, such as `squareSide`. We also no longer have a use for the `gray` or `max_rgb_color_number` variables because we simply render the colors inline this time. We also change the name of our array of objects called `squares` to the new variable called `textiles`. This is the full list of variables that we define before the `init` function definition, except for one that we define in Listing 4.35.

For the most important change in the program, we introduce an array called flashcards that stores all of our mappings between the Japanese characters and their phonetic sounds mapped onto English characters (known as romaji). You can find this Listing at http://unicode.org/charts/PDF/U3040.pdf. Generally you can discover mappings like this at http://unicode.org/charts/. Add the flashcards array with the code in Listing 4.35 immediately following the code in Listing 4.34 and just before the init function definition.

**Listing 4.35** The Flashcard Array

```
var flashcards = [
["a", "\u3042"],["i", "\u3044"],["u", "\u3046"],["e", "\u3048"],["o",
➡"\u304A"],
["ka", "\u304B"],["ki", "\u304D"],["ku", "\u304F"],["ke",
➡"\u3051"],["ko", "\u3053"],
["sa", "\u3055"],["shi", "\u3057"],["su", "\u3059"],["se",
➡"\u305B"],["so", "\u305D"],
["ta", "\u305F"],["chi", "\u3061"],["tsu","\u3064"],["te", "\u3066"],
➡ ["to", "\u3068"],
["na", "\u306A"],["ni", "\u306B"],["nu", "\u306C"],["ne",
➡"\u306D"],["no","\u306E"],
["ha", "\u306F"],["hi", "\u3072"],["fu", "\u3075"],["he",
➡"\u3078"],["ho", "\u307B"],
["ma", "\u307E"],["mi", "\u307F"],["mu", "\u3080"],["me",
➡"\u3081"],["mo", "\u3082"],
["ya", "\u3084"],["yu", "\u3086"],["yo", "\u3088"],
["ra", "\u3089"],["ri", "\u308A"],["ru", "\u308B"],["re",
➡"\u308C"],["ro", "\u308D"],
["wa", "\u308F"], ["wo", "\u3092"], ["n", "\u3093"]
];
```

In our init() function, things become more complicated than before because we are rendering pairs instead of duplicates (see Listing 4.36).

**Listing 4.36** First Part of the init() Function

```
function init() {
  canvas = document.getElementById('myCanvas');
  stage = new Stage(canvas);
  totalMatchesPossible = flashcards.length;
  var numberOfTiles = totalMatchesPossible * 2;
  matchesFound = 0;
  var columns = 12;
  timeAllowable = 500;
  txt = new Text(timeAllowable, "30px Monospace", "#000");
  txt.textBaseline = "top";
```

```
    txt.x = 700;
    txt.y = 0;
    stage.addChild(txt);
    textTiles = [];
    matchesFoundText = new Text(matchesFound+"/"+totalMatchesPossible,
➥"30px Monospace", "#000");
    matchesFoundText.textBaseline = "top";
    matchesFoundText.x = 700;
    matchesFoundText.y = 40;
    stage.addChild(matchesFoundText);
    Ticker.init();
    Ticker.addListener(window);
    Ticker.setPaused(false);
    setPlacementArray(numberOfTiles);
```

Many of these updates have to do with new spacing concerns and ensuring that our interface
for indexing the tiles still behaves as expected. Let's give ourselves 500 seconds because Japanese is difficult compared to matching colors. Again, squares has been renamed textTiles.
You also change the text to be smaller to fit on the screen. The most prominent change is necessary because you have a known, fixed number of elements. We also now concern ourselves
only with how many columns should be used, rather than insisting on a number of rows as well.

Next, let's deal with the for loop in our init() function. It has quite a few changes (see Listing 4.37).

**Listing 4.37**  The Main for Loop

```
    for(var i=0;i<numberOfTiles;i++){
        var placement = getRandomPlacement(placementArray);
        var pairIndex = Math.floor(i/2);
        text = flashcards[pairIndex][i%2];
        var textTile = drawTextTile(text, pairIndex);
        textTile.x = (tileWidth+margin) * (placement%columns) +
➥globalPadding;
        textTile.y = (tileHeight+margin) * Math.floor(placement/columns)
➥+ globalPadding;
        stage.addChild(textTile);
        background = new Shape();
        background.x = textTile.x-padding;
        background.y = textTile.y-padding;
        background.graphics.setStrokeStyle(border).beginStroke("#000")
➥.beginFill('#eee').drawRect(0, 0, tileWidth, tileHeight);
        textTiles.push(background);
        stage.addChildAt(background);
        background.text = textTile;
```

```
    background.onPress = handleOnPress;
    stage.update();
  }
} //don't forget this closing brace to the init function
```

There are a lot of changes here. We dropped our old way of pairing by switching the color every time. Now, explicitly pass in the `pairIndex` (a reference to which pair the Japanese or pronunciation belongs to) to the `drawTextTile()` function. We will see how this is used in a minute, but first notice that we are treating the flashcard array as one dimensional by looping through every subelement; grabbing the higher level index of the flashcards by dividing by 2 (and dropping the fractional part); and getting the text by using that `pairIndex` with a % check of the index to see if the element is 0 or 1. Then we set the positioning for the textTile and add it to the stage. There is a new `shape` called `background` that we use for each `textTile` to provide color behind the text. We use a new easel.js function `addChildAt()` so that the text appears in front. The background gets the `onPress` handler assigned, and we update the `stage`.

The `drawTextTile` function is a bit simpler than the `drawSquare` function from before but has the same goal (see Listing 4.38). You can replace the `drawSquare` function with the `draw-TextTile` function.

**Listing 4.38**   drawTextTile Function

```
function drawTextTile(text, pairIndex) {
  textTile = new Text(text, "20px Monospace", "#000");
  textTile.pairIndex = pairIndex;
  textTile.textBaseline = "top";
  return textTile;
}
```

This function should look familiar as it is similar to how you have been rendering the text for matches found and the timer. One notable difference between that text rendering is how you add the `pairIndex` attribute to `textTile`. You did this before with a `color` attribute, and as before, you use it in a similar way when you check for matches.

The `setPlacementArray()` and `getRandomPlacement()` functions in Listing 4.39 work exactly as they did before.

**Listing 4.39**   setPlacementArray

```
function setPlacementArray(numberOfTiles){
  for(var i = 0;i< numberOfTiles;i++){
    placementArray.push(i);
  }
```

```
}
function getRandomPlacement(placementArray){
  randomNumber = Math.floor(Math.random()*placementArray.length);
  return placementArray.splice(randomNumber, 1)[0];
}
```

The `handleOnPress()` function works similarly to how it did before you started hiding tiles. But for continuity's sake, let's see what it looks like now in Listing 4.40, with bolded portions illustrating what's new compared to the last recipe.

**Listing 4.40**  The handleOnPress Function

```
function handleOnPress(event){
  var tile = event.target;
  if(!!tileClicked === false || tileClicked === tile){
    tileClicked = tile;
  }else{
    tileClicked.graphics.beginFill('#eee').drawRect(0, 0, tileWidth,
➥ tileHeight);
    tile.graphics.beginFill('#aae').drawRect(0, 0, tileWidth,
➥ tileHeight);
    if(tileClicked.text.pairIndex === tile.text.pairIndex &&
➥ tileClicked.id != tile.id){
      tileClicked.visible = false;
      tile.visible = false;
      matchesFound++;
      matchesFoundText.text = matchesFound+"/"+totalMatchesPossible;
      if (matchesFound===totalMatchesPossible){
        gameOver(true);
      }
    }
    tileClicked = tile;
  }
  stage.update();
}
```

Now, you fill in the `background` (still called `tile` here) to indicate which tiles you are trying to match, and removing the `background` when there is a match. The code for detecting a match now relies on your `pairIndex` attribute, rather than `color`. There is also a change to make the `matchesFoundText` shorter than in the last recipe because you're more constrained on space than in the last recipe.

The for loop in your `gameOver()` function has been simplified by no longer using caching. See the full function in Listing 4.41.

**Listing 4.41** The gameOver Function

```
function gameOver(win){
  Ticker.setPaused(true);
  var replayParagraph = document.getElementById("replay");
  replayParagraph.innerHTML = "<a href='#' onclick='replay();'>Play
➡ Again?</a>";
  for(var i=0;i<textTiles.length;i++){
    textTiles[i].onPress = null;
  }
  if (win === true){
    matchesFoundText.text = "You win!"
  }else{
    txt.text = secondsLeft + "... Game Over";
  }
  stage.update();
}
```

Finally, your `tick()` and `replay()` functions stay exactly as they were in the recipe prior to caching (see Listing 4.42).

**Listing 4.42** tick and replay Functions

```
function tick() {
  secondsLeft = Math.floor((timeAllowable-Ticker.getTime()/1000));
  txt.text = secondsLeft;
  if (secondsLeft === 0){
    gameOver(false);
  }
  stage.update();
}
function replay(){
  init();
}
```

Phew! That's it. If you have everything right, after opening index.html in the browser, you should end up with something like Figure 4.7.

## Recipe 8: Making a Flashcard System

Figure 4.7  A flashcard system with a few matches

# Summary

For such a simple game, we definitely covered a good bit of ground. We covered easel.js, obtrusive event handlers in HTML, adding dynamic attributes to JavaScript, performance, and caching. While we were at it, we implemented the classic card game *Memory* and created a flashcard-style trainer for Japanese.

There are a lot of places you could take these games next. You could adjust the timer on each won or lost game to provide a consistent challenge. You could keep track of high scores, color ranges, or Japanese characters that cause the player the most difficulty. As for the flashcard system specifically, you could create smaller or larger sets of flashcards, keep them hidden at first, provide hints at the right answer, or use the same system to memorize country capitals, your friends' and relatives' birthdays, or even more Japanese characters if that's your cup of お茶.

As for easel.js, you took advantage of much of what it has to offer. If you are looking for more, its documentation at http://createjs.com/Docs/EaselJS/ might interest you. As for high-value things that weren't covered you can look into the Bitmap/BitmapAnimation classes along with the SpriteSheets.

For simple games like this, taking more control by using something lower-level such as easel.js is great. You could even try to remake memory or the hiragana trainer using the canvas API directly if you're feeling adventurous. Chapter 3, "Party," uses the canvas API directly if you need a reference. If nothing else, it will give you an appreciation for the utilities and abstractions that even this low-level game library affords.

# CHAPTER 5

# PLATFORMER

When we think about games, *Super Mario Brothers*, the canonical platformer originally released on the Nintendo Entertainment System in 1985, frequently comes to mind. This game illustrates a classic genre that has maintained relevance for decades, and continues to be innovated upon today, both in big production houses and in the indie games scene. It may be obvious, but games like this are called "platformers" because they usually involve jumping from one platform to another. These games are frequently created for the web as well as the console, so HTML5 is a perfect fit.

# Getting Started with melon.js

For building this chapter's game, we're going to be using melonJS. This engine has a simple API for developing games that is straightforward and easy to code against. It even contains prebuilt functions to manage jumping and walking in a side view type environment, which is perfect as you build your platformer. Not only does it make common development tasks very easy, but this engine also provides a ton of functionality to support more complex game behavior.

One feature of melonJS that newcomers to game making can appreciate is its integration with a tilemap editor called Tiled. Tilemap editors are incredibly useful, not only for generating level maps, but also for seeing at a glance what layers and objects are going into the game. In the other games in this book, you form your maps from simpler structures such as arrays. Tiled creates a map in a .tmx format (a type of XML).

If you look in the platformers/initial directory of this book's project files, you will not see a tmx file. You can either copy it from a later recipe's directory or create a new one by going to mapeditor.org, downloading Tiled, and following the first recipe, "Creating a Tiled Map."

# Recipe: Creating a Tiled Map

Open Tiled and select File, New. You will see a box that allows you to enter values for Orientation, Map size, and Tile size. Fill out the box as in Figure 5.1 by selecting the following values: Orientation: Orthogonal, Width: 40 tiles, Height: 30 tiles, Width: 16px, and Height: 16px.

**Figure 5.1** Creating a New Map with Tiled

On the right side, you will see a tile layer called Tile Layer 1. Rename this "foreground" so that it represents what it is a little better.

Next, you'll need to import a tileset, often called a spritesheet in other contexts and chapters. For this game, the sprites are included in the platformers/initial directory. These might be good for starters, but you can draw your own if you're so inclined (see the "Art Creation/Finding" section of Appendix C, "Resources"). Wherever you get your sprites, the most important thing here is that they are 16-pixels wide and 16-pixels high and have no margins between the sprites.

To start, in Tiled, go to Map ...New Tileset and you will see the New Tileset dialog box. Fill it out as in Figure 5.2 and click OK. Note that if your levelSprites image lives somewhere other than in the platformers/after_recipe1 directory, you should pull it from there instead.

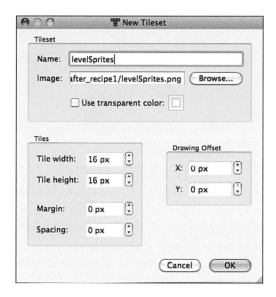

**Figure 5.2**  Creating a New Tileset in Tiled

Now you can edit the map. This is the fun part. Select the sprites on the right side of the Tiled window, and place them on the big, gray box in the middle wherever you want. Ground, water, lava, sky, and item boxes have been included. You might end up with something like Figure 5.3. If you are less sadistic, you might have placed the item box somewhere other than directly over the lava.

Next, you want to save your map in a format that melonJS will understand. If you go to Tiled, Preferences, there is a select box next to Store Tile Layer Data As with five different options. melonJS can use the formats XML, Base64 (uncompressed), and CSV. It cannot work with the Base64 compressed formats. Base64 (uncompressed) produces the smallest file that melonJS can work with, so it's best to use that.

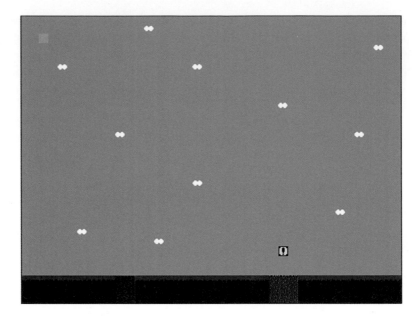

**Figure 5.3** Creating a New Level with Tiled

Saving as CSV is an interesting option for another reason, however, because you can more easily see which sprites are where (and edit the map file directly). For further options on saving the map data, try looking into export as. Normally, Tiled will save as a tmx file, but there are other options available (for example, json) for working with other game creation software or game engines. Also good to keep in mind is that Tiled has many options for opening different types of map files.

Save your file as level1.tmx in the same directory as index.html.

## Recipe: Starting the Game

Now that we've created the map, let's get it running in a browser. We'll need the .tmx file that we created earlier, along with a copy of the melonJS engine. First, let's flesh out the index.html file in Listing 5.1.

**Listing 5.1** HTML Document Loading JavaScript Files

```
<!DOCTYPE html>
<html>
<head>
  <title>Guy's Adventure</title>
```

```
  </head>
  <body>
<div id="wrapper" style="width: 640px; text-align: center;
➥margin-left:auto; margin-right:auto;">
    <div id="jsapp">
      <script type="text/javascript" src="melon.js"></script>
      <script type="text/javascript" src="resources.js"></script>
      <script type="text/javascript" src="screens.js"></script>
      <script type="text/javascript" src="main.js"></script>
    </div>
  </div>
</body>
</html>
```

I called my game Guy's Adventure (my niece named it actually), so I've set that as the title. Next, we add some slightly prettier styling to contain the game screen. Now for the tricky part. We make a div with `id="jsapp"` and inside of it include the melonJS library, a resources.js file, a main.js file, and a screens.js file. We'll be referring to this div in just a moment.

These files could all be combined into one file, as is the case with other games in this book. That said, it's useful to know a few different ways to do things, such as how we don't use a separate JavaScript file in Chapter 4, "Puzzle." We're headed in the opposite direction here. So what's in these files?

The melon.js file is the game engine. We'll be using a good section of its API in this chapter, but the documentation at http://www.melonjs.org/docs/index.html is absolutely worth a look if you want to have a reference as you're building. Note that all of the game engine project pages are listed in Appendix C, "Resources." In case you're curious, you won't be making any changes to the engine itself, but like all the engines covered in this book, it is open source. That means if you see some feature missing or a bug you'd like to fix, you can implement it and help make the engine better for yourself and everyone else.

The resources.js file is where you store all your information about what images, audio, and level files (created in Tiled) you need. For now, this file can be simple. All you need is the code in Listing 5.2 to add the resources for the level and sprites you used to build it. Save this as a file called resources.js.

**Listing 5.2**   Adding a Resources.js File

```
var resources = [{
  name: "levelSprites",
  type: "image",
  src: "levelSprites.png"
},
```

```
{
  name: "level1",
  type: "tmx",
  src: "level1.tmx"
}];
```

The screens.js file is also simple. Think of "screens" as mapping to large game states such as Play, Menu, and GameOver. For now, all you need to do is create a new `PlayScreen` that inherits from `me.ScreenObject` and says to load `level1` whenever entering the state of being on this screen. Add the code from Listing 5.3 and save it as screens.js.

**Listing 5.3**    Adding a PlayScreen Object to screens.js

```
var PlayScreen = me.ScreenObject.extend({
  onResetEvent: function() {
    me.levelDirector.loadLevel("level1");
  }
});
```

If you wonder what "me" is, it stands for Melon Engine and provides a namespace for every object in melonJS. Most code that you write and use will not have an object called `levelDirector`, but for more common words, namespaces are useful to ensure that a name refers to only one object. This is also a good reason to make sure to declare variables using the `var` keyword. In JavaScript, declaring variables without `var` creates them in the "global" namespace, meaning that they are accessible from everywhere.

Let's get back to the code. In Listing 5.4, the main.js file contains your high-level logic and is a bit more complex. First, we create a variable called `jsApp`. We are using the object pattern here to create two functions. The `onload` function runs when the `window` is loaded. Inside of this function, the `div` with the `id` of `jsapp` is declared to be the canvas object you'll be manipulating throughout the game. It takes four additional parameters for width, height, double buffering, and scale. Because you are using 16x16 sprites, your game is set at a 2.0 scale (zoomed in) compared to the default expectation of melonJS. Because we are using scale, we need to set double buffering to `true`.

Next, the `me.loader.onload` function sets the `loaded` function as the callback function for when the `onload` function completes. `bind(this)` ensures that the callback function will have the context of `jsApp`. The `preload` function preloads your images and level map from the resources file.

The `loaded` callback function associates the `PlayScreen` object that you created in screens.js with the built-in state `PLAY` (with the `game.set` function) and then changes the state of the game to `PLAY` with the `state.change` function. Finally, the `window.onReady()` call runs the code `jsApp.onload()` when the `window` is loaded.

**Listing 5.4**   Initializing the App and Loading Assets

```
var jsApp = {
  onload: function() {
    if (!me.video.init('jsapp', 320, 240, true, 2.0)) {
      alert("html 5 canvas is not supported by this browser.");
      return;
    }
    me.loader.onload = this.loaded.bind(this);
    me.loader.preload(resources);
    me.state.change(me.state.LOADING);
  },
  loaded: function() {
    me.state.set(me.state.PLAY, new PlayScreen());
    me.state.change(me.state.PLAY);
  }
};
window.onReady(function() {
  jsApp.onload();
});
```

If you open index.html now, you should see a screen similar to Figure 5.4. It's a portion of the map that you made. It's not a game yet, though. What else do we need? Let's find out in the next recipe.

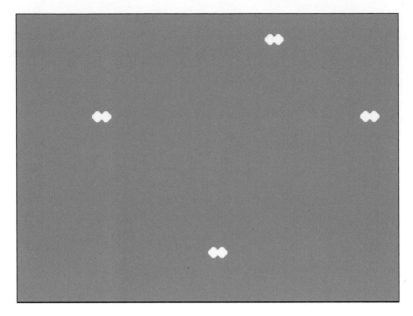

**Figure 5.4** Our map loaded in a browser

# Recipe: Adding a Character

Let's bring a character into the game. We'll call him Guy. He's the one who will be doing the adventuring. First, you need to use Tiled again to set a starting position. To do this, you need to add an object layer. Go to Layer, Add Object Layer. In the Layers pane on the right side (if for some reason you can't see your layers, go to View… Layers), and rename this object layer player. Also, as you did before, by following the Map… Add Tileset instructions, add the player.png image with the tileset name player.

You can place Guy somewhere safe-looking near the ground. To do this, click the insert object icon (see Figure 5.5) or press O and then click somewhere on the map to place him. Note that unlike the foreground sprites, you won't actually see him. Then, right-click the gray box that has been added, and select Object Properties… You need to fill out the Name field with player. You also need to set two new properties in the bottom of the box. They should be named image and spritewidth, with values of player and 16, respectively (see Figure 5.6).

**Figure 5.5** The add object button

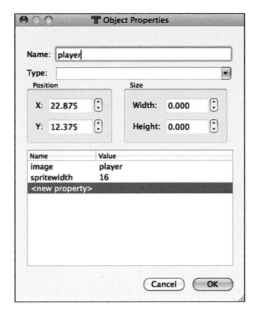

**Figure 5.6** The player object

If you tried to load your game now, you wouldn't have much luck. You still have a bit of work to properly integrate Guy into his new world. First, you need to add his image to your array in resources.js with the code in Listing 5.5. Remember to watch your commas.

**Listing 5.5** Adding Your Player to resources.js

```
{
  name: "player",
  type: "image",
  src: "player.png"
}
```

Next, add him to the melonJS entity pool in the `loaded` function of main.js with the code in Listing 5.6.

**Listing 5.6** Adding Your Player to the Entity Pool of main.js

```
me.entityPool.add("player", PlayerEntity);
```

You also need to create the last file you'll use for this tutorial, entities.js. With game development, it is common to refer to important objects as entities. Sometimes, these are enemies, the player, or projectiles. Unlike in traditional object-oriented programming, an entity-based system is typically supported by a less strict hierarchy. This paradigm can take a bit of getting used to, and we'll explore it more in Chapter 10, "RTS." It's a good start just to think of entities as being composed of logical units that describe properties such as their movement capabilities and what happens when they hit each other. In addition, it is worth considering that these are not just objects "in the code," but also objects "in the game." So if you say "the player entity," you are referring both to the lines of code representing the player and the notion of a "thing" that exists in the game world.

You need to add entities.js to your index.html file near all the other included JavaScript files with the code in Listing 5.7.

**Listing 5.7**   Loading the entities.js File in index.html

```
<script type="text/javascript" src="entities.js"></script>
```

The code in Listing 5.8 is fairly straightforward. You create the entities.js file, initialize a `PlayerEntity` variable that inherits from `ObjectEntity`, and set the `viewport` to follow the character around. Next, set an `update` function to handle updating the animation when the player moves.

**Listing 5.8**   Adding the PlayerEntity Object

```
var PlayerEntity = me.ObjectEntity.extend({
  init: function(x, y, settings) {
    this.parent(x, y, settings);
    me.game.viewport.follow(this.pos, me.game.viewport.AXIS.BOTH);
  },
  update: function() {
    this.updateMovement();
    if (this.vel.x!=0 || this.vel.y!=0) {
      this.parent(this);
      return true;
    }
    return false;
  }
});
```

If you load the game now, you'll see something encouraging for us but fairly drastic for our hero. He starts in the position we set him to in Tiled (great), but he then immediately falls off the screen. What's going on? We never created any solid ground for him to stand on.

# Recipe: Building a Collision Map

Let's add a new tile layer. As before (see Figure 5.2), go to Layer… Add Tile Layer. Then name this layer collision. Some tile layers can be arbitrarily named, but melonJS will not recognize a collision layer unless it contains the word "collision." Next go to Map… New Tileset, import collision.png, and as before do not include margins and use 16x16 tiles. Next, right-click the first tile of the collision tileset on the right. (If you cannot see the tileset toolbar, go to View, Tilesets.) To do this, you may have to select the collision tileset. Add a property of "type" with a value of "solid."

On the collision tile layer, paint the ground with the tile you called "solid." You should see something similar to Figure 5.7 where the black tiles are the solid collision tiles that you just added. You see the collision layer because it is on top, but you can reorder, filter, and change the opacity of your layers on the layers toolbar on the right to see different visual representations of your map.

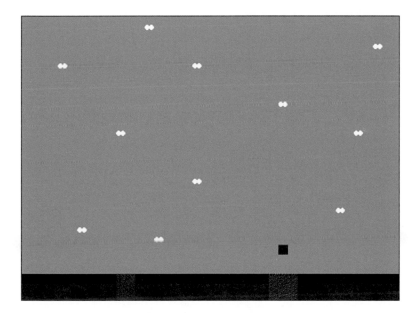

**Figure 5.7**  Collision layer over foreground

Save and reload index.html to see Guy successfully standing on the ground. This is quite an accomplishment. Perhaps "just standing there" games are going be big in the future, but we have little evidence of this. Let's stick with the platformer ideal and make him a little more adventure-capable.

# Recipe: Walking and Jumping

To enable walking and jumping, we'll have to make two changes. First, we'll want to bind the jump, left, and right buttons to keys on the keyboard. If we alter the screens.js file so that we can do that, we will arrive at something like the code in Listing 5.9.

**Listing 5.9**  Binding Keys to Move

```
var PlayScreen = me.ScreenObject.extend({
  onResetEvent: function() {
    me.levelDirector.loadLevel("level1");
    me.input.bindKey(me.input.KEY.LEFT, "left");
    me.input.bindKey(me.input.KEY.RIGHT, "right");
    me.input.bindKey(me.input.KEY.SPACE, "jump");
  }
});
```

Then, the `init` and `update` functions of the `PlayerEntity` must be altered in your entities.js file. In your `init` function, you need to set the default walking and jumping speed, and in the `update` function, you need to handle updating the movement based on input, as well as checking for collisions. The code needed for these tasks is in Listing 5.10.

**Listing 5.10**  Handling Player Movement

```
init: function(x, y, settings) {
  this.parent(x, y, settings);
  me.game.viewport.follow(this.pos, me.game.viewport.AXIS.BOTH);
  this.setVelocity(3, 12);
},
update: function() {
  if (me.input.isKeyPressed('left')) { this.doWalk(true); }
  else if (me.input.isKeyPressed('right')) { this.doWalk(false); }
  else { this.vel.x = 0; };
  if (me.input.isKeyPressed('jump')) { this.doJump(); }
  me.game.collide(this);
  this.updateMovement();
  if (this.vel.x!=0 || this.vel.y!=0) {
    this.parent(this);
    return true;
  }
  return false;
}
```

melonJS comes with these handy convenience functions of doJump() and doWalk(), which are useful for getting started. Keep in mind that hand-crafting acceleration envelopes, although more challenging, can provide a different character for a game. Sonic the Hedgehog is a notable example, owing much of its popularity to the unique slow acceleration and high maximum velocity of the title character. In fact, there is even an HTML5 game engine created entirely to explore his movement in a three-dimensional space.

If you load the index.html file, you may notice that the arrow keys and spacebar can now be used to control Guy! You're well on your way. You may have also noticed that Guy's feet move when he walks. melonJS did that for you. All you had to do was load the player.png spritesheet with two sprites, and it knew what you wanted. Fantastic!

What's next? Despite your best efforts, Guy will occasionally fall in a hole. Then, you should expect the player to refresh the browser every time, right? Nope. Let's reset the game when things go awry.

# Recipe: Title Screen

First, you need the TitleScreen object that you'll show players when they start the game or when Guy falls into a hole. Let's add the code in Listing 5.11 to the bottom of the screens.js file.

**Listing 5.11**   Creating a TitleScreen Object

```
var TitleScreen = me.ScreenObject.extend({
  init: function() {
    this.parent(true);
    me.input.bindKey(me.input.KEY.SPACE, "jump", true);
  },
  onResetEvent: function() {
    if (this.title == null) {
      this.title = me.loader.getImage("titleScreen");
    }
  },
  update: function() {
    if (me.input.isKeyPressed('jump')) {
      me.state.change(me.state.PLAY);
    }
    return true;
  },
  draw: function(context){
    context.drawImage(this.title, 50, 50);
  }
});
```

Let's look at what this code in Figure 5.11 does. First, you create the variable `TitleScreen` to inherit from `me.ScreenObject`. Then in the `init` function, you call `this.parent(true)` to set the `TitleScreen` as visible and ensure that the `update` and `draw` functions work. You also bind the spacebar to the `jump` key.

In the `onResetEvent` function, you load the `titleScreen` image if it has not already been set. The `update` function waits for the spacebar to be pressed and goes to the main game loop if it has.

The `draw` function draws the image (first parameter) at the specified pixel offsets (second and third parameters). If you haven't been through any of the other chapters with games that use canvas-based engines, you may wonder what `context`, the parameter in the `draw` function, refers to. This is the Canvas Rendering Context. melonJS declared it for you. In this case, it is the 2-D canvas, but the API that declared this as `canvas.getContext('2d')`, can also be used to initialize a `webgl` (3d) context.

As one last bit of cleanup, there's no sense in binding the `jump` key twice, so while you're in the screens.js file, take out this line from the `PlayScreen` object: `me.input.bindKey(me.input.KEY.SPACE, "jump", true);`.

Next, load the screen image to resources.js as in Listing 5.12.

**Listing 5.12** Loading the Screen Image as a Resource

```
{ name: "titleScreen", type: "image",
  src: "titleScreen.png"
}
```

Next, you need to make three changes to your `loaded` function in main.js. First, you need to assign your `TitleScreen` object to the predefined `MENU` state. Then, you need to change the state that is loaded at the beginning of the game from `PLAY` to `MENU`. Last, you can define a `transition` effect between screens. It should now look like Listing 5.13.

**Listing 5.13** Working with the MENU State

```
loaded: function() {
  me.entityPool.add("player", PlayerEntity);
  me.state.set(me.state.PLAY, new PlayScreen());
  me.state.set(me.state.MENU, new TitleScreen());
  me.state.transition("fade", "#2FA2C2", 250);
  me.state.change(me.state.MENU);
}
```

We're almost there; our title screen boots up quite nicely at the beginning, but we still haven't enabled automatic resetting after falling into a hole. To do this, we'll make a few minor adjustments to our `PlayerEntity` object in the entities.js file.

Add the `gameOver` function after the update function in the `PlayerEntity` object with the code in Listing 5.14. This can go just above the last line in the file. Make sure to add the comma to the curly brace above the `gameOver` function. Don't add a new curly brace there. Just the comma.

**Listing 5.14**   The gameOver Function in entities.js

```
}, // Don't forget to add this comma here
gameOver: function() {
  me.state.change(me.state.MENU);
}
}); // This is the end of the file (not new)
```

You also need some condition to trigger the `gameOver` function, as shown in Listing 5.15. Depending on how you set up your map, you may want to do it differently, but a basic "fell in the hole" type condition is to check the position of Guy along the y-axis. If he's too low, it's game over. This can directly follow the call to `updateMovement`.

**Listing 5.15**   Game Over if Guy Falls in a Hole

```
this.updateMovement();
if (this.bottom > 490){ this.gameOver(); }
```

Now players see the title screen when they lose, which is a much better experience than having to reload the page after every mishap. That's great, but we still have a problem. Right now, the only "adventure" that Guy is on is the "adventure of trying not to fall in holes." How about we give him a better reason for leaving home?

# Recipe: Adding Collectables

What does every platform adventurer love? That's right—metal objects as big as they are, to collect and carry around while they try to run and jump.

Let's start by editing the map again in Tiled. Add a new object layer (Layer... Add Object Layer) called coin. After adding the layer, add a new tileset for the coins (Map... New Tileset) and call the tileset coin as well. See Figure 5.5 to recall how to add objects to the screen.

For each coin added to the screen, be sure to right-click (Object Properties...) to set the name as coin, as well as the attributes image:coin and spritewidth:16. You can right-click to duplicate this object, and choose the selector tool to move it around. Note that it will create the clone directly above the original, so you may not initially realize that there are stacked objects until you move one.

Now we have quite a bit of code to add. Let's start simply by adding coins to the entity pool in the `loaded` function of main.js, as in Listing 5.16, directly following where the `PlayerEntity` is added.

**Listing 5.16**   Adding Coins to the entityPool

```
me.entityPool.add("player", PlayerEntity);
me.entityPool.add("coin", CoinEntity);
```

Next, in Listing 5.17, add the coin file as an image resource within resources.js.

**Listing 5.17**   Adding the Coin Sprite to resources.js

```
}, // Reminder: Add these commas to preceding objects as you go!
{ name: "coin",
  type: "image",
  src: "coin.png"
}
```

Now, in Listing 5.18, create the `CoinEntity` at the end of the entities.js file.

**Listing 5.18**   Creating the CoinEntity

```
var CoinEntity = me.CollectableEntity.extend({
  init: function(x, y, settings) {
    this.parent(x, y, settings);
  },
  onCollision : function (res, obj) {
    this.collidable = false;
    me.game.remove(this);
  }
});
```

Here, we start by declaring the `CoinEntity` as inheriting from `CollectableEntity` (which itself inherits from `ObjectEntity`). We then call the `parent` constructor to enable certain methods to be accessible. Last, we add some logic for collisions with the coin so that it cannot be collected twice.

Load index.html and notice how far we've come. Guy can now collect coins to pay for all his adventuring needs. Life might seem a little too good for Guy right now, though. Let's add a little more conflict.

# Recipe: Enemies

First, create a new object layer in Tiled (Layer… Add Object Layer) and call it EnemyEntities. Then add a new object (no new tileset required) to the map, and right click to name it Enemy-Entity. Here is the tricky part. You can be more precise in declaring the X and Y positions of the baddie, but you can also specify width and height. With all these numbers, the assumption is made to multiply by 16, which means that for any whole integer value of X and Y, the enemy will be placed on your grid. The height should be set to 1 assuming your bad guy is 16-pixels tall. The cool part is that when you set the width, you are not indicating the width of sprite, but rather, the horizontal area that the enemy can walk back and forth.

Next, you need to add your enemy to the entity pool in main.js, as shown in Listing 5.19. This can directly follow your `CoinEntity` code.

**Listing 5.19**  Adding the EnemyEntity to the entityPool

```
me.entityPool.add("coin", CoinEntity);
me.entityPool.add("EnemyEntity", EnemyEntity);
```

Then add the `badGuy` to the resources.js file, as shown in Listing 5.20. Again, remember to watch your commas.

**Listing 5.20**  Adding the badGuy Image to resources.js

```
{ name: "badGuy",
  type: "image",
  src: "badGuy.png"
}
```

By now, you might have guessed that you need to define `EnemyEntity` in entities.js. This is a fairly complex entity, but the overall structure of the code should be starting to look familiar at this point. One big change is that you are defining some of the properties (settings) for the `EnemyEntity` object directly in melonJS (Listing 5.21) instead of Tiled. Also notice how the path is indicated with the `settings.width`. The last important thing to notice is that you now have a new Game Over condition for when Guy touches the bad guy. The code in Listing 5.21 can go at the end of the entities.js file.

**Listing 5.21**  Creating the EnemyEntity

```
var EnemyEntity = me.ObjectEntity.extend({
  init: function(x, y, settings) {
    settings.image = "badguy";
    settings.spritewidth = 16;
    this.parent(x, y, settings);
    this.startX = x;
    this.endX = x + settings.width - settings.spritewidth;
    this.pos.x = this.endX;
    this.walkLeft = true;
    this.setVelocity(2);
    this.collidable = true;
  },
  onCollision: function(res, obj) {
    obj.gameOver();
  },
  update: function() {
    if (!this.visible){
      return false;
    }
    if (this.alive) {
      if (this.walkLeft && this.pos.x <= this.startX) {
        this.walkLeft = false;
      }
      else if (!this.walkLeft && this.pos.x >= this.endX){
        this.walkLeft = true;
      }
      this.doWalk(this.walkLeft);
    }
    else { this.vel.x = 0; }
    this.updateMovement();
    if (this.vel.x!=0 || this.vel.y!=0) {
      this.parent(this);
      return true;
    }
    return false;
  }
});
```

Guy has a lot to deal with now, and if you were cruel and created a lava and bad guy-filled wasteland for a map, he could be having a rough time. Let's make sure Guy can still get the upper hand.

# Recipe: Powerups

Did you put any coins out of Guy's reach? Let's give him some winged boots to help him jump higher. In Tiled, you need to add an object layer called boots. Then add objects in the same way as with coins before, declaring the name to be boots with image:boots and spritewidth:16. First, add `boots` to the resources.js file in Listing 5.22. Remember to watch your commas between each object in the array.

**Listing 5.22**   Adding the boots Image

```
{
  name: "boots",
  type: "image",
  src: "boots.png"
}
```

Next, add the boots to the entity pool in main.js, as shown in Listing 5.23.

**Listing 5.23**   Adding the boots to the entityPool

```
me.entityPool.add("EnemyEntity", EnemyEntity);
me.entityPool.add("boots", BootsEntity);
```

Then declare the BootsEntity at the bottom of entity.js, as shown in Listing 5.24.

**Listing 5.24**   Creating the BootsEntity

```
var BootsEntity = me.CollectableEntity.extend({
  init: function(x, y, settings) {
    this.parent(x, y, settings);
  },
  onCollision : function (res, obj) {
    this.collidable = false;
    me.game.remove(this);
    obj.gravity = obj.gravity/4;
  }
});
```

This should all look incredibly familiar because it's basically the same as the `CoinEntity`, with one notable exception. On the last line is the powerup part. When the player gets these boots, Guy will experience one-fourth the gravity. He should have no problem reaching any coins in the sky now!

The game is now complete. For one last recipe though, let's take a look at how we might improve the presentation of the game a bit.

# Recipe: Losing, Winning, and Information

Sometimes people like to be a little bit confused. Puzzles can be fun. However, "what button do I press to jump?" and "did I win?" are not terribly interesting puzzles. Yes, you could make a game where there was a puzzle about which button to press to jump. It might be clever or artfully done. But we're not doing anything so bold or groundbreaking in this chapter. We're making a no-nonsense platformer, so we should present the game to players as clearly as possible.

Let's add some containers for our messages to our index.html file, as shown in Listing 5.25, after the closing `</div>` of the jsapp.

**Listing 5.25**   Adding Some Containers for Messages and Instructions

```
</div>
<div id="info" style="text-align:left; margin-top:20px;">
  <div>
    <div style ="font-size: 14px; font-family: Courier New">
       <div id="game_state"></div>
       <div id="instructions"></div>
    </div>
  </div>
</div>
```

In the screens.js file, let's add the bolded lines in Listing 5.26 to the onResetEvent function of the PlayScreen object with some basic instructions for the player.

**Listing 5.26**   Tell the Player How to Move

```
me.input.bindKey(me.input.KEY.RIGHT, "right");
document.getElementById('game_state').innerHTML = "Collect all of the
➥coins!";
document.getElementById('instructions').innerHTML = "Arrows to move and
➥Space to jump.";
```

In that same file, let's clean up those messages in onResetEvent for the TitleScreen object, as shown in Listing 5.27.

**Listing 5.27**   Clear Out Old Messages

```
this.title = me.loader.getImage("titleScreen");
document.getElementById('game_state').innerHTML = "";
document.getElementById('instructions').innerHTML = "";
```

Then, in your entities.js file, let's add a bit to the `gameOver` function so that it looks like Listing 5.28.

**Listing 5.28**   Create the gameOver State

```
gameOver: function() {
  me.state.change(me.state.MENU);
  document.getElementById('game_state').innerHTML = "Game Over";
  document.getElementById('instructions').innerHTML = "";
}
```

Now that we've extended our `gameOver` function, it's making the game look a little bleak for Guy. He should be able to win, not just lose. Let's add a winning state that looks like Listing 5.29 after `gameOver`. Don't forget to add a comma to the end of the `gameOver` function.

**Listing 5.29**   Create the youWin State

```
}, // This is at the end of the gameOver function.  The brace needs a
comma now.
youWin: function() {
  me.state.change(me.state.MENU);
  document.getElementById('game_state').innerHTML = "You Win!";
  document.getElementById('instructions').innerHTML = "";
}
```

Say that you can enter this winning state by getting all the coins on the level. How do you do that? Add `coins` and `totalCoins` to the `onload` function of the `jsApp` variable in main.js, as shown in Listing 5.30.

**Listing 5.30**   Add Coins and Total Coins

```
me.gamestat.add("coins", 0);
me.gamestat.add("totalCoins", 2);
```

Note that you might have a different number for `totalCoins` depending on how you created your level in Tiled.

Next, add the code from Listing 5.31 to add an `onDestroyEvent` function to the `PlayScreen` object in screens.js to reset the coins collected. Put this before `onResetEvent`, and be careful with your commas.

**Listing 5.31** Reset Coins When Game Ends

```
onDestroyEvent: function() {
  me.gamestat.reset("coins");
},
```

Next, we'll need to add the bolded code in Listing 5.32 to our `CoinEntity` inside of entities.js. It should increment the coin value when collected and check to see if all the coins are collected. If they all are collected, the player sees the "You win" message.

**Listing 5.32** Create a Way to Win if All the Coins Are Collected

```
var CoinEntity = me.CollectableEntity.extend({
  init: function(x, y, settings) {
    this.parent(x, y, settings);
  },
  onCollision : function (res, obj) {
    me.gamestat.updateValue("coins", 1);
    this.collidable = false;
    me.game.remove(this);
    if(me.gamestat.getItemValue("coins")
➥=== me.gamestat.getItemValue("totalCoins")){
      obj.youWin();
    }
  }
});
```

Naturally, there are other ways to handle winning and losing other than simply printing text below the game. You could even create an entire new screen for each case.

# Summary

I hope you enjoyed building a platformer with melonJS and Tiled. Using these tools, we were able to create a basic game with powerups, enemies, coins, as well as winning and losing states in a short amount of time. There are some ways of extending the game you've created: Fireballs, enemy/player health, enemy AI, animations for death and jumping, more levels, a countdown timer, saving, high scores…the list goes on and on. And if you're looking to explore more features of melonJS, there's plenty to choose from, including timers, audio, parallax scrolling, heads up displays, and bitmap font rendering.

In this chapter, we took advantage of some low-tech, standard JavaScript methods to display information to players. Don't forget that you are creating games on the web, so techniques such as standard DOM manipulation, pulling in content from other sites, and even redirecting players to other URLs are not only possible, but also rather easy and potentially surprising for players.

# CHAPTER 6

# FIGHTING

Relative to interactive fiction and shooters, fighting games are a new genre, but as longstanding franchises like *Street Fighter* indicate, they are not going away anytime soon. Whether you're on the professional circuit or in your living room, 30 seconds to kick, punch, and fireball your opponent can be a pretty intense experience. To that end, in this chapter, we use the game.js engine to make our first two-player game.

# Recipe: Getting Started with game.js

game.js is based on the Python game-making library pygame. If you have some familiarity with that engine, many of the methods and classes will be familiar to you, but it would be difficult to say that knowing one would make you an expert in the other. Even if you feel that JavaScript differs from Python in mostly superficial and syntactic ways, that stance will afford little to a beginner to one or both languages, to which those differences matter the most. Moreover, the environments are radically different. Whereas with pygame the goal is to create games that function as native applications for major platforms (Windows, OSX, and Linux), with game.js, as with the rest of this book, the target platform is the web browser.

In this chapter, you create a simple, two-player fighting game. Let's start by introducing the index.html file in Listing 6.1.

**Listing 6.1**   Starter index.html File

```
<!DOCTYPE html>
<html>
  <head>
    <title>Fighting</title>
    <script src="le.js"></script>
    <script src="game.js"></script>
    <script>
      require.setModuleRoot('./');
      require.run('main')
    </script>
  </head>
  <body>
    <div id="gjs-loader">
      Loading...
    </div>
    <canvas id="gjs-canvas"></canvas>
  </body>
</html>
```

Most of this should be familiar. Starting from the bottom, unlike some engines, you declare the canvas element explicitly and give it the id gjs-canvas. In the div above that, add Loading... as the text in a div with the id of gjs-loader. This is the text that displays before your game fully loads. It could just as easily be an image or a loading screen complete with a progress bar to let players know that they must wait a second, and good things are on their way. Depending on what they use for preloading assets and other files, some engines come with progress bars built in. Moving up to the last <script> tag block, these two lines load your main.js file as a "module." We have looked at the module pattern in a previous chapter, but here, yabble.js, which is included in the first script tag, takes modularity to a whole new level. With game engines we have looked at so far, it has been typical to be able to access the major overarching namespace object for the engine through the console while the game is running. An example of this is "me" for "melon engine" that we used in the last chapter. On the plus side, this means that we don't have to worry about overwriting function and variable names as much. On the negative side, we will need to rely on inserting debugging statements into the code (for example, `console.log(thingIWantToLookAt)`) instead of, as with global variables, typing `thingIWantToLookAt` into the console while the program runs.

Next let's introduce our basic JavaScript file, main.js in Listing 6.2. In most of the games in this book, you have a game.js file that acts as the main JavaScript file that you write to. That name is taken by game.js the engine, so we'll use main.js instead to prevent confusion.

**Listing 6.2**   Starter main.js File

```
var gamejs = require('gamejs');
function main() {
  var display = gamejs.display.setMode([1200, 600]);
  var sprites = gamejs.image.load('sprites.png');
  display.blit(sprites);
};
gamejs.preload(['sprites.png']);
gamejs.ready(main);
```

The first line sets the `gamejs` variable to reference the game.js library loaded in index.html. The main function sets the width and height of the canvas element, and then loads and blits the sprites file. Keep in mind that the main function doesn't run until the last line here. Before that happens, the engine preloads the sprites file. The reason to load images ahead of time is so that you don't have disruptive, slow, unpredictable calls to load images when you need them. If you load index.html into a browser, you will see something like Figure 6.1.

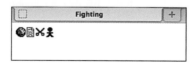

**Figure 6.1**   Sprites rendered

same as "rendering" or "showing" the image, because not every surface created will necessarily be displayed. If you come from a web background and are familiar with the z-index css property, you can think of it as a more powerful version of that, which enables you to lay elements on top of one another *and* do mathematical calculations on their pixel color values.

Outside of an html5 canvas, *blitting* could mean various things, but in this book, blitting can reliably be understood as an abstraction built on top of the canvas context's notion of "compositing," of which there are many options. You can find more information at http://dev.w3.org/html5/2dcontext/#compositing.

Seeing the sprites is a good start, but before we leave the first recipe, let's add the bold code in Listing 6.3 to main.js to make them a little bigger.

**Listing 6.3**  Scaling Up the Sprites

```
var gamejs = require('gamejs');
var screenWidth = 1200;
var screenHeight = 600;
var scale = 8;
var spriteSheetWidth = 64;
var spriteSheetHeight = 16;

function main() {
 var display = gamejs.display.setMode([screenWidth, screenHeight]);
  var sprites = gamejs.image.load('sprites.png');
  sprites = gamejs.transform.scale(sprites, [spriteSheetWidth*scale,
➥spriteSheetHeight*scale]);
  display.blit(sprites);
};
gamejs.preload(['sprites.png']);
gamejs.ready(main);
```

In preparation to use the values of the variables more than once later, start by renaming the hardcoded numbers. The third line of the main function is the only new piece of functionality introduced. It simply scales up the size of the images by a factor of 8. After scaling up, you should see something like Figure 6.2.

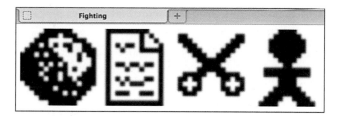

**Figure 6.2**  Scaled sprites

# Recipe: Accessing Individual Sprites from a Spritesheet

For this recipe, you want to gain access to each of your sprites individually. First, change some of your initial variables to reflect Listing 6.4 so that they are a little easier to work with.

**Listing 6.4**  Friendlier Variables

```
var gamejs = require('gamejs');
var screenWidth = 1200;
var screenHeight = 600;
var scale = 8;
var spriteSize - 16;
var numSprites = 4;
```

Next, in Listing 6.5, add a proper function to do the scaling, rather than doing the manipulation directly inline. This code can be added directly under those variables in Listing 6.4.

**Listing 6.5**  scaleUp Function

```
function scaleUp(image){
  return gamejs.transform.scale(image, [spriteSize*scale,
➥spriteSize*scale]);
};
```

The last thing that you need to change in order to reference sprites directly is your `main` function. It should be altered to look like Listing 6.6.

**Listing 6.6**  Individual Sprite Rendering main Function

```
function main() {
  var display = gamejs.display.setMode([screenWidth, screenHeight]);
  var sprites = gamejs.image.load('sprites.png');
  var surfaceCache = [];
  for (var i = 0; i < numSprites; i++){
    var surface = new gamejs.Surface([spriteSize, spriteSize]);
    var rect = new gamejs.Rect(spriteSize*i, 0, spriteSize,
➡spriteSize);
    var imgSize = new gamejs.Rect(0, 0, spriteSize, spriteSize);
    surface.blit(sprites, imgSize, rect);
    surfaceCache.push(surface);
  };
  for (var i=0; i < surfaceCache.length; i++) {
    var sprite = scaleUp(surfaceCache[i]);
    display.blit(sprite, [i*spriteSize*scale, spriteSize*i*scale]);
  };
};
```

First, initialize an empty array called surfaceCache. Then you have two loops that, ultimately, display the sprites diagonally. Certainly, you could have done this in two separate loops, but they perform different functions. The first prepares a sprite by creating a new surface, rect, and imgSize. All are the size of a sprite, with rect, having the special task of controlling the offset when the sprites are blitted onto the surface. The last step in the first loop is to add the surface as an element in the surfaceCache array. The second loop simply scales up the images and displays them diagonally.

> ## tip
>
> For the beginners out there: If you can easily identify the purpose of a loop or set of lines in your code, it can often be useful to abstract them out into a function. This can make your code more maintainable and modular. However, in early phases of a project, it is sometimes better to wait to create structure. Knowing the appropriate timing to restructure and refactor is a fantastic skill, and one that takes time to master. Just keep in mind that for questions concerning when to refactor, "always" and "never" are usually both bad answers on projects with anything important or long term.

Assuming all went well, if you open index.html in your browser, you should see something like Figure 6.3.

**Figure 6.3**   Diagonally presented individual sprites from a sheet

# Recipe: Handling Input from Two Players

So far there's no interaction in your game. This recipe handles that by introducing a `Player` object, which can press keys to change the sprite. Start by adding the code in Listing 6.7 to main.js. It can be added right after the `scaleUp` function.

**Listing 6.7**   The Player Object

```
function Player(placement, sprite){
  this.placement = placement;
  this.sprite = sprite;
};
Player.prototype.draw = function(display) {
  sprite = scaleUp(this.sprite);
  display.blit(sprite, [spriteSize+this.placement, spriteSize]);
};
```

There are two functions here. The first is a constructor function, as you can tell by the capitalization. This function initializes a new `Player` object later, when `new Player` is called. The `draw` method performs a more nuanced version of what the second `for` loop of Listing 6.6 handled.

> ## warning
>
> **STICK TO CONVENTIONS FOR OBJECT INHERITANCE**    If you name your constructor functions with lowercase letters, your browser will not complain. However, sticking to an uppercase convention for constructors is important to indicate to future developers, including yourself, that these functions have a special purpose. Also, you can call a constructor function without using the `new` keyword, but you will receive unexpected results (especially hazardous is that `this` will bind to the global context). It is, to some extent, for these gotcha reasons that some people prefer to use the `create` method for instantiating objects.

The `main` function has become quite large, so we will break it into four listings, starting with Listing 6.8 and ending with Listing 6.11. No code should appear in `main` that is not contained within these listings. Make sure to delete the second for loop that is in main as part of Listing 6.8.

**Listing 6.8**    Nicknames for Sprites

```
function main() {
  var display = gamejs.display.setMode([screenWidth, screenHeight]);
  var sprites = gamejs.image.load('sprites.png');
  var surfaceCache = [];
  for (var i = 0; i < numSprites; i++){
    var surface = new gamejs.Surface([spriteSize, spriteSize]);
    var rect = new gamejs.Rect(spriteSize*i, 0, spriteSize,
➥spriteSize);
    var imgSize = new gamejs.Rect(0, 0, spriteSize, spriteSize);
    surface.blit(sprites, imgSize, rect);
    surfaceCache.push(surface);
  };
// delete this  for (var i=0; i < surfaceCache.length; i++) {
// delete this    var sprite = scaleUp(surfaceCache[i]);
// delete this    display.blit(sprite, [i*spriteSize*scale,
➥spriteSize*i*scale]);
// delete this  };
  var rock = surfaceCache[0];
  var paper = surfaceCache[1];
  var scissors = surfaceCache[2];
  var person = surfaceCache[3];
```

The code that is bold is all that's new here. All we are doing is giving nicknames to each of the sprites in the `surfaceCache`. Listing 6.9 is still inside of the `main` function. Add the code in Listing 6.9 directly following Listing 6.8.

**Listing 6.9**  Handling Key Presses

```
function handleEvent(event) {
  if(gamejs.event.KEY_DOWN) {
    if(event.key === gamejs.event.K_UP) {
      player2.sprite = person;
    }else if(event.key === gamejs.event.K_DOWN) {
      player2.sprite = paper;
    }else if(event.key === gamejs.event.K_RIGHT) {
      player2.sprite = scissors;
    }else if(event.key === gamejs.event.K_LEFT) {
      player2.sprite = rock;
    }else if(event.key === gamejs.event.K_w) {
      player1.sprite = person;
    }else if(event.key === gamejs.event.K_a) {
      player1.sprite = rock;
    }else if(event.key === gamejs.event.K_s) {
      player1.sprite = paper;
    }else if(event.key === gamejs.event.K_d) {
      player1.sprite = scissors;
    }
  }
};
```

This code is all new but fairly straightforward. When this function is called and a key is pressed (this function executes many times per second, so it can catch it), depending on what the key is, the players' sprites (just the attributes, nothing is rendered here) will change to particular shapes. Listing 6.10 covers the last remaining function defined inside of `main`. This directly follows the code in Listing 6.9.

**Listing 6.10**  gameTick

```
function gameTick(msDuration) {
  gamejs.event.get().forEach(function(event) {
    handleEvent(event);
  });
  display.clear();
  player1.draw(display);
  player2.draw(display);
};
```

A `gameTick` function can go by various names depending on the engine, but the most important thing to remember is that for simple games, it can house anything that handles gathering input, updating objects, and updating display. Note what this excludes as well: loading assets, defining objects, initializing utility functions, and so on. A second important thing to remember about it is that it passes a parameter that exposes the milliseconds since the last execution. In this declaration of the `gameTick` function, we just handle key presses and update the player sprites accordingly. Finally, Listing 6.11 shows the last lines of code for the `main` function. This directly follows Listing 6.10 and is followed by the line: `gamejs.preload(['sprites.png']);`

**Listing 6.11**  Last Lines of the main Function

```
    var player1 = new Player(0, person);
    var player2 = new Player(200, person);
    gamejs.time.fpsCallback(gameTick, this, 60);
}; //the main function is closed here.
```

In these last lines, the player objects are initialized with their x offsets as the first parameter and initial sprite as the second parameter. The last full line kicks off the `gameTick` function in an infinite loop. The 60 indicates that the loop should attempt to run at a frame rate of 60 FPS (frames per second).

With that code in place, you should see something like Figure 6.4 by opening index.html with a browser and changing the sprites by pressing the keys indicated in Listing 6.9.

**Figure 6.4**  Changing sprites dynamically

What you have at this point is a keyboard interface to the traditional Rock, Paper, Scissors game. With the rest of the recipes in this chapter, we'll be turning it into a more standard fighting game, although it will still be based on Rock, Paper, Scissors.

# Recipe: Moving and Changing Forms

With this recipe, we'll allow players not just to change the sprite, but to move across the screen. For this, we'll introduce a new concept of forms that a player can take on, rather than using the old idea of sprites. Also, we'll be changing the interface slightly so that the right and left keys change direction, and the up and down keys cycle through these forms.

First, we'll want to render some text in this recipe, so we'll need to import the font module from game.js. You can do that by adding the bold line of code in Listing 6.12 near the top of main.js.

**Listing 6.12**   Making Text Possible

```
var gamejs = require('gamejs');
var font = require('gamejs/font');
```

Next, let's change the `Player` constructor function to reflect the code in Listing 6.13. We are now constructing a player based on forms rather than sprites.

**Listing 6.13**   Player with Forms Rather Than Sprites

```
function Player(placement, form, forms){
  this.placement = placement;
  this.form = form;
  this.forms = forms;
};
```

After that, we'll need to add the two functions in Listing 6.14 after the `Player` constructor of Listing 6.13. These enable you to cycle through the forms.

**Listing 6.14**   Form Changing Functions

```
Player.prototype.nextForm = function() {
  this.form = this.forms[this.form["next"]];
};
Player.prototype.previousForm = function() {
  this.form = this.forms[this.form["previous"]];
};
```

Next, you need to change the `Player` `draw` function to the code in Listing 6.15 to reference a form image instead of a sprite.

**Listing 6.15**   Updated Player draw Function

```
Player.prototype.draw = function(display) {
  sprite = scaleUp(this.form.image);
  display.blit(sprite, [spriteSize+this.placement, spriteSize]);
};
```

Next, you need to replace the sprite nicknames inside of the `main` function to be part of a `forms` object with the code in Listing 6.16.

**Listing 6.16**   Forms Object Instead of Sprite Nicknames

```
//delete the following four lines
//var rock = surfaceCache[0];
//var paper = surfaceCache[1];
//var scissors = surfaceCache[2];
//var person = surfaceCache[3];

var forms = {
  rock:
   {image: surfaceCache[0],
    next: 'paper',
    previous: 'scissors'},
  paper:
   {image: surfaceCache[1],
    next: 'scissors',
    previous: 'rock'},
  scissors:
   {image: surfaceCache[2],
    next: 'rock',
    previous: 'paper'},
  person:
   {image: surfaceCache[3],
    next: 'rock',
    previous: 'scissors'}
};
```

Next, replace the `handleEvent` function with the code in Listing 6.17. This enables cycling through forms with the up and down keys and moving the players with the left and right keys. The keys have remained the same, but as the bold lines indicate, the effect of pressing them has changed.

**Listing 6.17**   New Key Handling

```
function handleEvent(event) {
  if(gamejs.event.KEY_DOWN){
    if(event.key === gamejs.event.K_UP){
      player2.previousForm();
    }else if(event.key === gamejs.event.K_DOWN){
      player2.nextForm();
    }else if(event.key === gamejs.event.K_RIGHT){
      player2.placement = player2.placement + 25;
```

```
  }else if(event.key === gamejs.event.K_LEFT){
    player2.placement = player2.placement - 25;
  }else if(event.key === gamejs.event.K_w){
    player1.previousForm();
  }else if(event.key === gamejs.event.K_a){
    player1.placement = player1.placement - 25;
  }else if(event.key === gamejs.event.K_s){
    player1.nextForm();
  }else if(event.key === gamejs.event.K_d){
    player1.placement = player1.placement + 25;
  }
 }
};
```

Next, you need to make it so that the gameTick function draws some title text to the screen. For that, add the lines in bold from Listing 6.18.

### Listing 6.18   Adding Rendered Text to the Game

```
function gameTick(msDuration) {
  gamejs.event.get().forEach(function(event) {
    handleEvent(event);
  });
  display.clear(),
  var defaultFont = new font.Font("40px Arial");
  var textSurface = defaultFont.render("ROCK PAPER SCISSORS",
➡"#000000");
  display.blit(textSurface, [0, 160]);
  player1.draw(display);
  player2.draw(display);
};
```

Near the end of the main function, just before the callback to gameTick, we instantiate the player objects, passing in the x offset, beginning form, and forms variable as parameters to the Player constructor function with the code in Listing 6.19. The final curly brace "}" is included here to show that this is at the end of the main function.

### Listing 6.19   Calling the New Player Constructors

```
  var player1 = new Player(0, forms['person'], forms);
  var player2 = new Player(1000, forms['person'], forms);
  gamejs.time.fpsCallback(gameTick, this, 60);
};
```

After moving the players toward each other, and changing the left player to paper, you end up with something like Figure 6.5.

## ROCK PAPER SCISSORS

**Figure 6.5** Almost a fighting game

# Recipe: Nonblocking Input

The game is starting to shape up, and you might be already itching to add life bars, health, and special moves. There is one important piece of cleanup to handle before moving to more interesting elements of a fighting game. Right now, input from one player can block the other player. Granted, in some games, this might be a feature. Maybe in a dueling game, one player drawing and firing renders the other player frozen. Even in that case, what we have now for input handling is likely not an ideal implementation. In this recipe, we will separate out input (which must be as fast as possible) from updating the players (which can be time-consuming).

The first change that we'll need to make is storing the key presses on a registry inside of the `Player` object. Let's update the `Player` constructor function with the code in Listing 6.20 to store the new attributes that you'll need.

**Listing 6.20** Storing a Key Press Registry Inside of Player

```
function Player(placement, form, forms){
  this.placement = placement;
  this.form = form;
  this.forms = forms;
  this.up = false;
  this.down = false;
  this.left = false;
  this.right = false;
  this.canChange = true;
};
```

The new lines added in bold store the value for whether or not an up, down, left, or right key press has been registered. The `canChange` attribute may be a bit unexpected. This attribute stores whether or not a player can change forms. This prevents the endless cycling through forms that you may have noticed in the last recipe if you held down one of the form change keys.

To keep your function set small, you can reduce your previousForm and nextForm functions to one changeForm function, which takes the strings next or previous as a parameter. You can delete those two functions and replace them both with the changeForm function found in Listing 6.21.

**Listing 6.21**   Replacing previous and next with change

```
Player.prototype.changeForm = function(next_or_previous) {
  this.form = this.forms[this.form[next_or_previous]];
};
```

Next, we will create an update function for Player that reads from the up/down/left/right/canChange registries, and performs the relevant functions. The code to do this is in Listing 6.22 and can follow the changeForm function from Listing 6.21.

**Listing 6.22**   The Player update Function

```
Player.prototype.update = function(msDuration) {
  if(this.up){
    if (this.canChange) {
      this.changeForm('previous');
      this.canChange = false;
    }
  }
  if(this.down){
    if (this.canChange) {
      this.changeForm('next');
      this.canChange = false;
    }
  };
  if(this.left){
    this.placement = this.placement - 14;
  }else if(this.right){
    this.placement = this.placement + 14;
  }
};
```

You have two more changes to implement this recipe, and the first one is quite lengthy. Replace your current handleEvent function (in the main function) with Listing 6.23 to register input by setting boolean values on the player objects rather than interfering with the draw loop.

**Listing 6.23**  Registering Input on Player Objects

```
function handleEvent(event) {
  if(event.type === gamejs.event.KEY_DOWN){
    if(event.key === gamejs.event.K_UP){
      player2.up = true;
    }else if(event.key === gamejs.event.K_DOWN){
      player2.down = true;
    }else if(event.key === gamejs.event.K_RIGHT){
      player2.right = true;
      player2.left = false;
    }else if(event.key === gamejs.event.K_LEFT){
      player2.left = true;
      player2.right = false;
    }else if(event.key === gamejs.event.K_w){
      player1.up = true;
    }else if(event.key === gamejs.event.K_a){
      player1.left = true;
      player1.right = false;
    }else if(event.key === gamejs.event.K_s){
      player1.down = true;
    }else if(event.key === gamejs.event.K_d){
      player1.right = true;
      player1.left = false;
    }
  }else if(event.type === gamejs.event.KEY_UP){
    if(event.key === gamejs.event.K_UP){
      player2.up = false;
      player2.canChange = true;
    }else if(event.key === gamejs.event.K_DOWN){
      player2.down = false;
      player2.canChange = true;
    }else if(event.key === gamejs.event.K_RIGHT){
      player2.right = false;
    }else if(event.key === gamejs.event.K_LEFT){
      player2.left = false;
    }else if(event.key === gamejs.event.K_w){
      player1.up = false;
      player1.canChange = true;
    }else if(event.key === gamejs.event.K_a){
      player1.left = false;
    }else if(event.key === gamejs.event.K_s){
      player1.down = false;
      player1.canChange = true;
    }else if(event.key === gamejs.event.K_d){
      player1.right = false;
    }
  }
};
```

The most important thing to recognize here is that the event handler now recognizes key up and key down events. Generally speaking, with key down events, you set an attribute to true, and with key up events, you set the attribute as false. Left and right keys cancel the opposing attribute as well. Key up and key down events both set the `canChange` property to true for form changing keys. The reason to do this is so that, in combination with setting `canChange` to `false` after the `update` function runs, the effect is that a change event happens only once per key press.

The last change for this recipe is in Listing 6.24. Here you call the `update` function for each player before the `draw` function for each player in the `gameTick` function.

**Listing 6.24**   Calling update for Players

```
player1.update();
player2.update();
player1.draw(display);
player2.draw(display);
```

# Recipe: Implementing Bitmasks

In this recipe, you use a bitmask to handle some of your player attributes, rather than storing them as simple true or false values. If you are unfamiliar with bitwise operations or masks, this recipe may be somewhat confusing. Before addressing the changes you need to make to the code, let's talk about numbers a little bit. For readers with a traditional computer science background (either formally educated or self-taught), this will not be new information, but it is essential to understanding the techniques used in this recipe. Feel free to skip ahead and come back if you are confused.

Numbers (and all information) in a traditional computer architecture are represented as a series of 1s and 0s. You can represent any number in a binary (or base 2) system (0 or 1 per bit) just as well as you can in a decimal (or base 10) system (0-9 per "digit"). Because each number represents only multiplication by 2 rather than 10, the binary representation of a number is typically much longer than the decimal representation. In Table 6.1, you can see some binary numbers and their decimal equivalents.

**Table 6.1**   Binary and Decimal Number Equivalents

|  | Binary | Decimal |
| --- | --- | --- |
| Small Examples | 0, 1, 10, 11, 100, 101, 110, 111, 1000, 1001, 1010 | 0, 1, 2, 3, 4, 5, 6, 7, 8, 9, 10 |
| Large Example | 10000001 | 129 |

Okay, so that's how numbers are represented in binary. Why is that relevant to what you're doing? Well, say that you had four values to keep track of that could be true or false. Your first instinct might be to store them as variables (var1, var2, var3, and var4). Then, you could set them as true or false using the assignment operator "=" or check to see if they were true or false already by using the comparison operator "===". Where these concepts come together is that you can also represent those same four boolean values in four bits by substituting true for 1 and false for zero. For example, if the variables were set to true, false, false, and true, they could be represented as 1001 binary (9 in decimal).

What you're left with is the problem of querying and setting each bit. In a roundabout way, you could somehow rely on the = and === operators, but that is not consistent with this approach. Instead, we'll have to use boolean arithmetic for these operations. See Table 6.2 for examples.

**Table 6.2**  Boolean Arithmetic Needed in This Recipe

| Object | Variable-Based Approach | Bitwise Approach |
|---|---|---|
| Setting to true | `var1 = true` | `mask |= var1` |
| Setting to false | `var1 = false` | `mask &= ~var1` |
| Determining true or false (truthiness) | `if (var1){}` | `if(var1 & mask){}` |

For this bitwise approach to work, we would update mask as the integer container of true/false (0 and 1) values. var1 would be some number that is 2 to the bit place power. So if you decide that the first bit (all the way on the right) represents the "left" property of a player, you can store var1 as 1 ($2^0$). The next bit would be $2^1$ (2), then $2^2$ (4), and so on.

> **note**
>
> If this is your first exposure to bitwise operators, you might still wonder whether thinking about all this is worth it. Well, that depends on your goals. This is one case in which you give up a bit of code clarity in favor of potential performance gains. Programs are bound by space and time. The bitwise approach has advantages for each. As for space (memory), storing bits in an integer can be more efficient than storing many boolean variables. As for time, performing bitwise comparisons and potentially not declaring variables instead of declaring and checking booleans can be faster.
>
> As with anything in JavaScript, performance can differ significantly between browser versions. If you're unsure about what is faster, test it on the browsers you care about the most.

Now let's move on to the code. The first change is that we will set the convenience variables for each bit inside of the mask. Add the bold line in Listing 6.25. Notice this new syntax of using commas to declare variables. They still all act as though they have the `var` keyword applied.

**Listing 6.25**   Adding the Convenience Variables

```
var screenWidth = 1200;
var screenHeight = 600;
var scale = 8;
var spriteSize = 16;
var numSprites = 4;
var up = 1, down = 2, left = 4, right = 8, canChange = 16;
```

Next, you can cut some of the attributes in the `Player` object and add the `mask` attribute. It should now look like Listing 6.26. The reason that we set the `mask` to 16 is because we want it to be equal to the sum of all the convenience variables that are true. For our purposes, this is only `canChange`, which has a value of 16. If no variables were true, we would want the mask to be 0. If `down` and `left` were true, this value would be 6.

**Listing 6.26**   Player Object with mask Attribute

```
function Player(placement, form, forms){
  this.placement = placement;
  this.form = form;
  this.forms = forms;
  this.mask = 16;
};
```

Next, we'll change the update method of Player so that we can use our new way of checking and updating the player mask attribute. Replace the update method with the code in Listing 6.27.

**Listing 6.27**   A bitwise update Method

```
Player.prototype.update = function() {
  if(this.mask & up){
    if (this.mask & canChange) {
      this.changeForm('previous');
      this.mask &= ~canChange;
    }
  }
  if(this.mask & down){
    if (this.mask & canChange) {
      this.changeForm('next');
```

```
        this.mask &= ~canChange;
      }
    };
    if(this.mask & left){
      this.placement = this.placement - 14;
    }else if(this.mask & right){
      this.placement = this.placement + 14;
    }
  };
```

The last change you need to make for this recipe is to update your `handleEvent` function to set the bits of the mask. For this, you can use the code in Listing 6.28.

**Listing 6.28**  Event Handling Using the mask

```
function handleEvent(event) {
  if(event.type === gamejs.event.KEY_DOWN){
    if(event.key === gamejs.event.K_UP){
      player2.mask |= up;
    }else if(event.key === gamejs.event.K_DOWN){
      player2.mask |= down;
    }else if(event.key === gamejs.event.K_LEFT){
      player2.mask |= left;
      player2.mask &= ~right;
    }else if(event.key === gamejs.event.K_RIGHT){
      player2.mask |= right;
      player2.mask &= ~left;
    }else if(event.key === gamejs.event.K_w){
      player1.mask |= up;
    }else if(event.key === gamejs.event.K_s){
      player1.mask |= down;
    }else if(event.key === gamejs.event.K_a){
      player1.mask |= left;
      player1.mask &= ~right;
    }else if(event.key === gamejs.event.K_d){
      player1.mask |= right;
      player1.mask &= ~left;
    }
  } else if(event.type === gamejs.event.KEY_UP){
    if(event.key === gamejs.event.K_UP){
      player2.mask &= ~up;
      player2.mask |= canChange;
    }else if(event.key === gamejs.event.K_DOWN){
      player2.mask &= ~down;
      player2.mask |= canChange;
    }else if(event.key === gamejs.event.K_RIGHT){
```

```
      player2.mask &= ~right;
    }else if(event.key === gamejs.event.K_LEFT){
      player2.mask &= ~left;
    }else if(event.key === gamejs.event.K_w){
      player1.mask &= ~up;
      player1.mask |= canChange;
    }else if(event.key === gamejs.event.K_a){
      player1.mask &= ~left;
    }else if(event.key === gamejs.event.K_s){
      player1.mask &= ~down;
      player1.mask |= canChange;
    }else if(event.key === gamejs.event.K_d){
      player1.mask &= ~right;
    }
  }
};
```

After implementing this recipe, your game should be exactly the same as it was before.

# Recipe: Masking Collisions

If you still wonder what masks are good for, this recipe has an answer for you. Some engines detect collisions between objects based on the overlap of the rectangular or elliptical areas (hitboxes) around the object. game.js is special because it provides a mask library to detect collisions based on the color value of the sprites associated with an object. Interestingly, game.js stores this pixel information as true and false values rather than as integers where each of the 1s and 0s within are relied upon for collision information.

To correctly do collisions, you have two main challenges. First, because when images are scaled they can have a haloing effect, resulting in imprecise color values that collision detection relies upon, you should scale up your images somehow to create a bigger version of each sprite. You could do this by meticulously re-creating the image and coloring in more small pixels or stretching the image. You could also decide to keep your game small. Taking the scaling approach, it is necessary to clean up the edges after the fact. If you're using Gimp (http://www.gimp.org), the tool you want to use to find edges between colors is the *magic wand*. For your convenience, the sprites.png files in fighting/after_recipe7 and fighting/final have been scaled and called sprites_big.png.

After you scale your image, you no longer have any need for the scale variable or the scaleUp function. If you made the sprite 8 times wider and 8 times taller in keeping with the sprite ratio defined by scale before, you want to change the spriteSize variable to be 128 instead of 16. For total clarity, this line is in Listing 6.29.

**Listing 6.29** Altering the Size of the Sprite

```
var screenWidth = 1200;
var screenHeight = 600;
var spriteSize = 128;
var numSprites = 4;
```

You also need to simplify the code in the `Player`'s `draw` method because it no longer requires scaling. The new draw method code is in Listing 6.30.

**Listing 6.30** A draw Method Without Scaling

```
Player.prototype.draw = function(display) {
  display.blit(this.form.image, [this.placement, 0]);
};
```

Next, replace the parameter passed in to the load and reload functions with the name of your new sprite. In this case, it is called `sprites_big.png`. Listing 6.31 shows this change.

**Listing 6.31** load and preload Should Reference New Sprite

```
function main() {
  var display = gamejs.display.setMode([screenWidth, screenHeight]);
//replace sprites with sprites_big
//  var sprites = gamejs.image.load('sprites.png');
  var sprites = gamejs.image.load('sprites_big.png');
. . .
//replace sprites with sprites_big
//gamejs.preload(['sprites.png']);
gamejs.preload(['sprites_big.png']);
gamejs.ready(main);
```

Next, you need a `maskCache` array to store your sprites. Start by including the mask library near the top of the file, as shown in Listing 6.32. By default, requiring game.js does not load all its utilities. So similarly to the font utility, you add it explicitly.

**Listing 6.32** Including the mask Utility

```
var gamejs = require('gamejs');
var font = require('gamejs/font');
var mask = require('gamejs/mask');
```

After requiring the utility, build up your `maskCache` array inside of your `main` function and add the `maskCache` element as a property of `form`, which itself becomes a property of `Player` later. The code to make this adjustment is in Listing 6.33. The most important thing to notice here is that you use the `mask.fromSurface` function in reference to the mask variable that is not associated with a player.

**Listing 6.33**  Building a maskCache Array

```
function main() {
  var display = gamejs.display.setMode([screenWidth, screenHeight]);
  var sprites = gamejs.image.load('sprites_big.png');
  var surfaceCache = [];
  var maskCache = [];
  for (var i = 0; i < numSprites; i++){
    var surface = new gamejs.Surface([spriteSize, spriteSize]);

    var rect = new gamejs.Rect(spriteSize*i, 0, spriteSize,
spriteSize);
    var imgSize = new gamejs.Rect(0, 0, spriteSize, spriteSize);
    surface.blit(sprites, imgSize, rect);
    surfaceCache.push(surface);

    var maskCacheElement = mask.fromSurface(surface);
    maskCache.push(maskCacheElement);
  };

  var forms = {
    rock:
      {image: surfaceCache[0],
      mask: maskCache[0],
      next: 'paper',
      previous: 'scissors'},
    paper:
      {image: surfaceCache[1],
      mask: maskCache[1],
      next: 'scissors',
      previous: 'rock'},
    scissors:
      {image: surfaceCache[2],
      mask: maskCache[2],
      next: 'rock',
      previous: 'paper'},
```

```
person:
  {image: surfaceCache[3],
   mask: maskCache[3],
   next: 'rock',
   previous: 'scissors'}
};
```

The last change that you need to make to your file to get masking working is to add the code in Listing 6.34 just before the end of the gameTick function. This code will check for a collision, and if one is found, print to the console.

**Listing 6.34** Altering the End of the gameTick Function

```
player1.draw(display);
player2.draw(display);
var hasMaskOverlap = player1.form.mask.overlap(player2.form.mask,
[player1.placement - player2.placement, 0]);
if (hasMaskOverlap) {
  console.log(hasMaskOverlap);
}
```

Now you have collision detection in place, but you're not doing anything interesting with it. Let's address that in the final recipe.

# Recipe: Giving and Taking Damage

We now know how to move players, change forms, and hit each other. In this recipe, we'll do what we need to make this a genuine fighting game.

For starters, we're going to need some new variables. Add them just below the mask values near the top of the file, as shown in Listing 6.35.

**Listing 6.35** Some New Variables

```
var up = 1, down = 2, left = 4, right = 8, canChange = 16;
var forms = [];
var timeBetweenHits = 300;
var timeSinceHit = 0;
var activeGame = true;
var defaultFont = new font.Font("40px Arial");
```

Next, replace your Player constructor function with the code in Listing 6.36. Now you're keeping track of the forms outside of the player object, tracking health, hit, and basing the form on a `formIndex` parameter, rather than the form itself.

**Listing 6.36**  Storing More Information of Player

```
function Player(placement, formIndex){
  this.placement = placement;
  this.form = forms[formIndex];
  this.mask = 16;
  this.hit = false;
  this.health = 30;
};
```

Based on the name `formIndex`, you may have guessed that you are now using a numerically keyed array for forms, rather than an array with string-based keys. We are making this change to simplify the combat interactions, but as a nice side effect, it shortens your `changeForm` code to one simple line, which you can see in Listing 6.37.

**Listing 6.37**  An Updated changeForm Function

```
Player.prototype.changeForm = function(index) {
  this.form = forms[index];
};
```

Next, you need a `registerHit` function for the player. Add the code from Listing 6.38 for this function. It can be added directly after the `changeForm` function. With this function, you can determine, based on the form index, which player is being hit. Rock beats scissors, scissors beats paper, and paper beats rock. Everything beats the initial stick-person form, including the person form itself. (Health will be deducted from both players.)

**Listing 6.38**  Registering Hits

```
Player.registerHit = function(player1, player2){
  player1Index = player1.form.index;
  player2Index = player2.form.index;
  if(player1Index === 0){
    if (player2Index === 1) {
      player1.hit = true;
    }else if (player2Index === 2) {
      player2.hit = true;
    };
  }else if (player1Index === 1){
    if (player2Index === 0) {
```

```
        player2.hit = true;
      }else if (player2Index === 2) {
        player1.hit = true;
      };
    }else if (player1Index === 2){
      if (player2Index === 0) {
        player1.hit = true;
      }else if (player2Index === 1) {
        player2.hit = true;
      };
    }else{
      player1.hit = true;
    }
    if(player2Index === 3){
      player2.hit = true;
    }
    if(player2Index !== player1Index || player1Index === 3){
      timeSinceHit = 0;
    };
};
```

> ## note
>
> Because it is a boolean, you could have added hit to the mask. Because hit begins as false, this would not affect the initial mask value of 16. You would just need to update the value checking and setting to use bitwise operators instead of the = and === methods
>
> Another important thing to keep in mind is that there is a limit to how many booleans you can pack into an integer. On the latest Firefox and Chrome, this is 32 bits. You may never want to store more than that, but it is nice to occasionally try something wacky that you don't need and hit a limit in architecture. It builds character.

Next, let's take a look at the player update function in Listing 6.39. There are three important changes here. One is that we change the form by passing in a numerical value relative to the current form. Two is that at the end of the function, you update the player health. Three is that you check the placement of the players so that they can't go past the edge of the screen.

**Listing 6.39**  Player update Function

```
Player.prototype.update = function(msDuration) {
  if(this.mask & up){
    if (this.mask & canChange) {
      this.changeForm((this.form.index+3-1)%3);
```

```
      this.mask &= ~canChange;
    }
  }
  if(this.mask & down){
    if (this.mask & canChange) {
      this.changeForm((this.form.index+1)%3);
      this.mask &= ~canChange;
    }
  };
  if(this.mask & left){
    if(this.placement > 0){
      this.placement = this.placement - 14;
    }
  }else if(this.mask & right){
    if(this.placement < 1000){
      this.placement = this.placement + 14;
    }
  }
  if(this.hit===true){
    this.health = this.health -3;
    this.hit = false;
  };
};
```

In the draw function, we have a tiny update (see Listing 6.40) to leave room for the game title at the top by moving the players down.

**Listing 6.40**   Bump Players Down

```
Player.prototype.draw = function(display) {
  //display.blit(this.form.image, [this.placement, 0]);
  display.blit(this.form.image, [this.placement, 80]);
};
```

As for your forms definition, you can replace the original implementation with the (numerical index based) array found in Listing 6.41.

**Listing 6.41**   forms as a Normal Array

```
//non-bold lines provide for context
  var maskCacheElement = mask.fromSurface(surface);
  maskCache.push(maskCacheElement);
};
forms = [
  {index: 0,
```

```
      image: surfaceCache[0],
      mask: maskCache[0]},
   {index: 1,
      image: surfaceCache[1],
      mask: maskCache[1]},
   {index: 2,
      image: surfaceCache[2],
      mask: maskCache[2]},
   {index: 3,
      image: surfaceCache[3],
      mask: maskCache[3]}
];
```

The gameTick function has changed quite a bit. Listing 6.42 shows the entire thing. It's not so bad when you just look at the bold lines. The activeGame variable tracks whether or not a game has finished. When it does, it does not run the contents of the gameTick function. The second bold chunk of code determines whether it has been long enough since the last hit and if there has been a hit, and calls registerHit when necessary. The Player update calls now take a duration in milliseconds as a parameter. There is a good amount more text that is drawn to the screen. Finally, if a player has health at 0, the game is over, activeGame is set to false, and a "defeated" message comes up for the defeated player.

**Listing 6.42** Updates to gameTick

```
function gameTick(msDuration) {
  if(activeGame){
    gamejs.event.get().forEach(function(event) {
      handleEvent(event);
    });
    display.clear();
    if(timeSinceHit > timeBetweenHits){
      var hasMaskOverlap = player1.form.mask.overlap(player2.form.mask,
➡[player1.placement - player2.placement, 0]);
      if (hasMaskOverlap) {
        Player.registerHit(player1, player2);
      };
    }else{
      timeSinceHit +=msDuration;
    };
    player1.update(msDuration);
    player2.update(msDuration);

    display.blit(defaultFont.render("ROCK PAPER SCISSORS", "#000000"),
➡[300, 0]);
```

```
    display.blit(defaultFont.render("Player 1: ", "#000000"),
➡ [0, 240]);
    display.blit(defaultFont.render(player1.health, "#000000"),
➡ [170, 240]);
    display.blit(defaultFont.render("Controls: W A S D", "#000000"),
➡ [0, 280]);
    display.blit(defaultFont.render("Player 2: ", "#000000"), [600,
➡ 240]);
    display.blit(defaultFont.render(player2.health, "#000000"), [770,
➡ 240]);
    display.blit(defaultFont.render("Controls: \u2191 \u2193 \u2190
➡\u2192", "#000000"), [600, 280]);

    player1.draw(display);
    player2.draw(display);
    if(player1.health === 0 || player2.health === 0){
      activeGame = false;
      if (player1.health === 0){
        display.blit(defaultFont.render("Player 1 Defeated",
➡ "#000000"), [0, 320]);
      }
      if (player2.health === 0){
        display.blit(defaultFont.render("Player 2 Defeated",
➡ "#000000"), [600, 320]);
      }
    };
  };
};
```

The last bit of code in this recipe is that when a player is created, it now passes in a numerical form id, rather than a form object. You can see this change in Listing 6.43.

**Listing 6.43**  Players Called with Form id 3 (Stick Person)

```
var player1 = new Player(0, 3);
var player2 = new Player(1000, 3);
gamejs.time.fpsCallback(gameTick, this, 60);
```

If all went according to plan, you now have a simple two-player fighting game that, due to drawing from the popular folk game concept of rock, paper, scissors, most people will understand easily. If you open up index.html in a browser, you should see something like Figure 6.6 at the end of a match.

**ROCK PAPER SCISSORS**

Player 1: 6
Controls: W A S D

Player 2: 0
Controls: ↑ ↓ ← →
Player 2 Defeated

**Figure 6.6** After a match

## Summary

Congratulations. You just made a 2-D fighting game using game.js. In this chapter, you also had a chance to cover spritesheets, bit masks, nonblocking input, and pixel-perfect collisions. You tackled a good amount of the game.js library. If you want to learn more about it, check out the astar pathfinding library, or if you're REALLY looking for a challenge, see if you can use python with pygame to "port" this game to a native desktop platform.

As for other things that could be done in this game, there are many possibilities. Maybe you want to experiment with drawing only the playing portion of the canvas most of the time to improve performance. Maybe you want to add punches, kicks, and special moves such as fireballs, as modifications of the stick person sprite, rather than having a rock-, paper-, scissors-based game. Maybe you want to add blocking or jumping. On the UI side, a "health bar" is more interesting and common than a numerical health value, and a "timer" might add some sense of urgency during play.

# CHAPTER 7

# SHOOTER

Possibly inspired by pinball games, shooters employ a similar mechanic of "Using stuff to shoot stuff." But despite the theming that pinball machines can achieve through artwork on and inside the cabinet, the interface's innerworkings are exposed. Whereas in pinball, you might say "hit the 'ball' into the 'bumper,'" in a videogame shooter, it is more likely to hear something like "'shoot' a 'missile' at the 'enemy plane.'" This distinction may seem subtle, but this abstraction gives you freedom to do something a bit unique; your enemies become numbers, and your weapons become mathematical functions.

# Some Background Info on Rendering

gameQuery is unlike the game engines we have covered so far in two ways. First, it relies on jQuery's capability to select and manipulate elements of the DOM. The second major difference is a consequence of the first: gameQuery is DOM-rendering-based and does not rely on the canvas element.

This has real implications for the internals of the engine, as well as your interface to it as a game developer. The reason is that the canvas knows only about its pixels. You tell it to render shapes and lines and images, and it dutifully draws what you say. And then it forgets. It has no memory of all that work it did. You have to keep references to all your old objects and draw them again. You can select pieces of the canvas to redraw or cache, but if you inspect the DOM element for the canvas, you can see that it knows nothing about itself. It's all wrapped up in the JavaScript interface to the context of the canvas. With a regular HTML page (or DOM-based game), all the elements know their styling information like the location and background-color and what is inside, whether that is text or nested elements. With absolute positioning, you can tell these elements where to go to, and they stick around between renderings.

But isn't canvas what makes modern games work?

There are many ways to make games on the web. Canvas-based rendering is a popular option right now, but depending on what types of rendering your game requires (and on what browsers), you should consider any of the following rendering options: canvas with a 3-D (WebGL) context, canvas with a 2D - context, DOM, CSS3, and SVG. Also, keep in mind that you may want a combination of technologies. You should be familiar in general with the strengths and weaknesses of each (see Table 7.1), but keep in mind that whenever a new browser version hits the market, you may want to test the performance of each technology all over again. This information changes really fast.

**Table 7.1**  Rendering Options for Games

| Rendering Type | Strengths | Weaknesses |
|---|---|---|
| Canvas 2-D context | Pixel-level interface with a simple x and y grid. Fast compared to DOM rendering for many elements. | Any objects that you create are fully up to you to maintain. |
| Canvas 3-D context | IT IS IN 3-D! Also three.js provides a simpler (but by no means simple) interface to working with WebGL. | Complexity! You need to know about cameras, shaders, polygons, textures, and some math and physics. |

| Rendering Type | Strengths | Weaknesses |
|---|---|---|
| SVG (Scalable Vector Graphics) | Good for scrolling around and no pixilation when zooming in or zooming out (think maps). Can create these images programmatically through JavaScript (try Raphael.js) or through image editors like svg-edit and Inkscape. Consistent interface to sprites regardless of where you are in the rendering cycle. | Not great performance with dynamic creation/destruction of many objects. (Don't try a "bullet hell" style shooting game.) No support for IE versions prior to 9. (You can use Raphael to create the analogous VML files.) |
| DOM (Document Object Model) | You can easily reference and update DOM elements with traditional JavaScript APIs and frameworks like jQuery. Although potentially much more dynamic, game objects resemble other elements on an HTML page, so you only need to understand one primary interface. Using the z-index allows easy overlapping of elements compared to canvas. | Similar performance implications of SVG when manipulating large amounts of elements. Complexity in layouts and cross-browser subtleties. Default styling (for example, padding and margin) of elements without resetting the CSS. |
| CSS (Cascading Style Sheets) | Generally faster than JavaScript for rendering simple changes. Relatively small API compared to JavaScript that provides a descriptive interface of styling. Browser automatically chooses when to draw changes, so you don't have to explicitly manage things like the framerate. Rendering can (at least conceptually and literally at times when CSS3 transitions are hardware-accelerated and offloaded to the GPU) take place outside of a JavaScript game loop. | Limited to visual effects mostly, so the heavy lifting in a game will still likely happen through JavaScript (without seriously crazy uses of radio buttons and describing every possible game state in the code). Default styling and cross-browser issues apply here as well. Code reuse is difficult without smart use of class and id names and a framework like SASS or LESS for namespacing and variables. |

**tip**

There are many debates about what technology should be used when and why. The smartest people don't argue about what is better. They build things using each and gather data.

As it relates to browser-rendering technologies, you can find examples of this type of behavior in projects such as Pascal Rettig's "Quintus" game engine, which exposes rendering APIs for DOM, canvas, and SVG, and Paul Bakaus's "domvas," which enables you to render an arbitrary piece of the DOM in a canvas element using an SVG image as the conduit.

# Recipe: Getting Started with gameQuery

Sorry for the digression. You didn't open this chapter to learn about browser-rendering. You are here to make games, right? Let's get back to getting a game going in gameQuery. We'll be creating a side-scrolling space shooter with a twist: Instead of ships and missiles, we'll be using numbers and functions. Listing 7.1 shows what is needed from the HTML side of things.

**Listing 7.1**   Starter HTML

```html
<html>
  <head>
    <title>Shooter</title>
  </head>
  <body>
    <div id="playground" style="width: 700px; height: 250px;
➥background: black;"></div>
    <script type="text/javascript" src="jquery.js"></script>
    <script type="text/javascript" src="jquery.gamequery.js"></script>
    <script type="text/javascript" src="game.js"></script>
  </body>
</html>
```

This should look familiar by now. You load the script files and add a title. But what is that `div` at the top of the `body` for? It's a `div` element called `playground` that you add all your DOM elements on top of. You have seen before where an initial `canvas` element fills the game container role. Just like with canvas-based rendering, most of the complexity is not in the HTML, but rather the JavaScript. Start the game.js file next with the code in Listing 7.2.

**Listing 7.2**   Setting Up the Background of the Game

```javascript
var PLAYGROUND_WIDTH = 700;
var PLAYGROUND_HEIGHT = 250;
var REFRESH_RATE = 15;
var farParallaxSpeed = 1;
var closeParallaxSpeed = 3;

var background1 = new $.gQ.Animation({imageURL: "background1.png"});
var background2 = new $.gQ.Animation({imageURL: "background2.png"});
var background3 = new $.gQ.Animation({imageURL: "background3.png"});
var background4 = new $.gQ.Animation({imageURL: "background4.png"});
```

```
$("#playground").playground({height: PLAYGROUND_HEIGHT, width:
➡PLAYGROUND_WIDTH, keyTracker: true});

$.playground().addGroup("background", {width: PLAYGROUND_WIDTH, height:
PLAYGROUND_HEIGHT})
.addSprite("background1", {animation: background1, width: PLAYGROUND_
WIDTH, height: PLAYGROUND_HEIGHT})
.addSprite("background2", {animation: background2, width: PLAYGROUND_
WIDTH, height: PLAYGROUND_HEIGHT, posx: PLAYGROUND_WIDTH})
.addSprite("background3", {animation: background3, width: PLAYGROUND_
WIDTH, height: PLAYGROUND_HEIGHT})
.addSprite("background4", {animation: background4, width: PLAYGROUND_
WIDTH, height: PLAYGROUND_HEIGHT, posx: PLAYGROUND_WIDTH})

$.playground().registerCallback(function(){
   $("#background1").x(($("#background1").x() - farParallaxSpeed -
PLAYGROUND_WIDTH) % (-2 * PLAYGROUND_WIDTH) + PLAYGROUND_WIDTH);
   $("#background2").x(($("#background2").x() - farParallaxSpeed -
PLAYGROUND_WIDTH) % (-2 * PLAYGROUND_WIDTH) + PLAYGROUND_WIDTH);
   $("#background3").x(($("#background3").x() - closeParallaxSpeed -
PLAYGROUND_WIDTH) % (-2 * PLAYGROUND_WIDTH) + PLAYGROUND_WIDTH);
   $("#background4").x(($("#background4").x() - closeParallaxSpeed -
PLAYGROUND_WIDTH) % (-2 * PLAYGROUND_WIDTH) + PLAYGROUND_WIDTH);
}, REFRESH_RATE);

$.playground().startGame();
```

We start out setting the height and width of the "playground," which corresponds with the size of the background images. Next, we set the refresh rate, which is the number of milliseconds between each refresh of the main game loop. The parallax speeds indicate how fast the backgrounds will scroll. Next, we assign the backgrounds to variables as if they are "animations," even though in actuality, there will be no animation at this level. If you did want an animated background, rather than a scrolling one, you would describe those animations in these variable declaration statements.

Following that, you initialize the playground as the element with the id of playground. After the playground is initialized, you follow up with the addGroup and addSprite methods, which, respectively, set up a new layer and add sprites to that layer.

In the next block of code, you use the `registerCallback` function to update the positions of the scrolling backgrounds. This runs a loop every 15 milliseconds per the REFRESH_RATE variable. To determine the frame rate, you first divide the milliseconds per frame by 1000, giving you 0.015 seconds per frame. Then you take the inverse of this, which is 1 divided by 0.015, giving you a frame rate of 66.667 frames per second.

The last thing to do is run the `startGame` function on `playground`, which reveals an outer-space scene with mathematical functional symbols for stars when you load the html file. If you open the index.html file in a browser, you should see something like Figure 7.1, with the larger (closer) symbols moving more quickly than the smaller (further away) symbols.

**Figure 7.1** Math space

# Recipe: Adding "Enemies"

The scrolling background is great for this kind of space shooter game, but under normal circumstances, most players won't be entertained by this alone. You can add some "enemies" to make it a little more interesting. Let's add the enemy constructor function and some new variables with the bold lines in Listing 7.3. This will be near the top of game.js.

**Listing 7.3**  Enemy Constructor and New Variables

```
var closeParallaxSpeed = 3;
var enemyHeight = 30;
var enemyWidth = 60;
var enemySpawnRate = 1000;
function Enemy(node, value){
  this.value = value;
  this.speed = 5;
  this.node = node;
  this.update = function(){
    this.node.x(-this.speed, true);
  };
};
```

Just under the variables that we added at the top of Listing 7.2, we add `enemyHeight` and `enemyWidth`. The `enemySpawnRate` is how many milliseconds between each new enemy appearing. After that, we add the `Enemy` constructor function. The `value` will store what in a traditional shooter might be "hit points" or "life." The `speed` describes how fast the enemy will move. The `node` property stores the `div` (wrapped in a jQuery object) that contains typical DOM information about the `enemy`. The `update` function subtracts the `speed` (moves the node left). Note that using the gameQuery-defined positional functions such as `x` without the second parameter of `true` makes the function behave in a completely different way. See the docs at gamequeryjs.com/documentation/api/ for details.

Next, we'll have to add a second layer for the enemies that sits on top of your background images. We can achieve that by adding the bold lines of code in Listing 7.4.

**Listing 7.4**  Adding Another Layer

```
.addSprite("background4", {animation: background4, width:
➥PLAYGROUND_WIDTH, height: PLAYGROUND_HEIGHT, posx: PLAYGROUND_WIDTH})
.end()
.addGroup("enemies", {width: PLAYGROUND_WIDTH, height:
➥PLAYGROUND_HEIGHT})

$.playground().registerCallback(function(){
...
  $("#background4").x(($("#background4").x() - closeParallaxSpeed -
➥PLAYGROUND_WIDTH) % (-2 * PLAYGROUND_WIDTH) + PLAYGROUND_WIDTH);
  $(".enemy").each(function(){
    this.enemy.update();
    if(($(this).x()+ enemyWidth) < 0){
```

```
        $(this).remove();
    }
  });
}, REFRESH_RATE);
```

With the first bolded line of code, you add a group (layer) called "enemies" to the playground. The `end` function ensures that this layer is added to the playground base layer rather than the background layer. Literally, this is adding a `div` that will contain sprites inside of it when you add them later. Unlike the `background` layer, the enemy sprites will be added dynamically, so you don't do it here. In the other bolded lines from this Listing (which exist inside of your main game loop), you loop through the enemies, and update their position with the `update` function. Then, check to see if it is too far to the left of the screen to be visible. If so, you remove it from the DOM.

> ## note
>
> You may wonder what the `addGroup` and `addSprite` methods are being called on throughout the section where they are used. This pattern used here is called "chaining" in jQuery, wherein, because a function's return value is still a jQuery object, you can apply another jQuery function to the return value. It is a little like applying multiple additions inline like this: $3 + 2 + 6$.
>
> Be warned that although you may still get a jQuery object, it may not be the exact same one. If you end up traversing with a `find` or `addGroup` function, to refer to the original object again, you need to call `end` function first.
>
> Why do things this way? Tracking down DOM elements is expensive, and creating variables to store the results that you want again can clutter up your code. So, this way of updating various aspects of the same jQuery object is handy and fast.
>
> For more information on traversal in jQuery, see the documentation at http://api.jquery.com/category/traversing/.

Now, you need to register another callback function for the slower loop to add the enemies. You need the code in Listing 7.5, added directly following the code in Listing 7.4.

**Listing 7.5**  Adding the Enemies Dynamically

```
$.playground().registerCallback(function(){
  var enemyValue = Math.ceil(Math.random()*21) - 11;
  var name = "enemy_"+(new Date).getTime();
```

```
$("#enemies").addSprite(name, {animation: '', posx: PLAYGROUND_WIDTH,
➡posy: Math.random()*PLAYGROUND_HEIGHT*0.9,width: enemyWidth, height:
➡enemyHeight});
    var enemyElement = $("#"+name);
    enemyElement.addClass("enemy");
    enemyElement[0].enemy = new Enemy(enemyElement, enemyValue);
    enemyElement.text(enemyValue);
}, enemySpawnRate);
```

The first and last lines are important here. You are declaring a secondary loop that adds enemies every 1000 milliseconds, per the enemySpawnRate variable. Easily setting independent game loops this way is a strong feature of this engine and should not be overlooked.

As for the body of this loop, first the enemyValue is set with a value from –10 to 10. Next, set the name of the enemy to be unique by virtue of containing the number of the milliseconds since the first second of 1970. (It might seem arbitrary, but there is no fighting how important that date is to "UNIX time," which measures the milliseconds elapsed since 1 January 1970.)

Next, you add to the enemy sprite to the enemies layer. For your first parameter, you pass in the name that will become the id of the element. You can set the animation to an empty string because you won't be using an image. You set its starting x position to the right side of the screen, the height to be some random value along the y-axis (the 0.9 helps to ensure that you don't go too low and have only the very top of the enemy appear on screen), and the width and height to be enemyWidth and enemyHeight.

Following that, you add the enemy class. Because jQuery selectors always return an array-like object, to add the enemy attribute, you have to get specific by grabbing the first element with [0]. You assign this attribute to a new Enemy object initializing it with the node equal to its jQuery-selected node and value assigned to the random value created earlier. Consider that here you are doing things a little topsy-turvy from how you would in a canvas-based engine. Rather than storing all positional information within the JavaScript object, you offload this to the DOM object, and refer to it through the JavaScript object. Depending on your viewpoint, this could be considered more or less convenient, but either way it is worth noting.

The last bit of this listing sets the enemy's value to the enemy's text node with the jQuery text function. To style this, you have two more small changes to make. First, create a game.css file and add the code in Listing 7.6 to it. Second, add the following line in the <head> section of index.html: <link rel="stylesheet" type="text/css" href="game.css">.

**Listing 7.6** Styling the Enemy Ship

```
.enemy{
  color:red;
  background-color: black;
  font-size:22px;
  border:1px solid red;
  text-align:center;
};
```

If all went according to plan, you should end up with something like Figure 7.2.

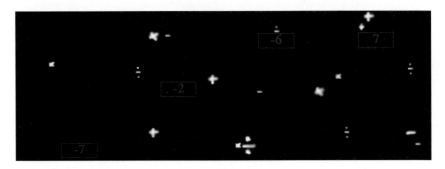

**Figure 7.2** Numbered enemies

# Recipe: Making Your Ship

Now that you've created some enemies, you'll probably want some way to deal with them. To kick things off, let's declare the player variables we need in Listing 7.7. This code can directly follow the last line of the Enemy function.

**Listing 7.7** Creating Your Ship Variables

```
var playerHeight = 60;
var playerWidth = 120;

function Player(){
  this.value = 10;
  this.number = 1;
};
```

There's nothing tricky here. You're just declaring the height, width, and a couple of defaults in the Player constructor function.

> **tip**
> You could place these height and width attributes inside of the `Player` constructor function, but because they will not change, you can leave them outside. That way, you won't have to dig into the object later. As far as code architecture goes, you can choose how complex to make your objects and how to reveal values through scope. Sometimes, you want to hide information deeply, and sometimes you want it constantly available without making potentially expensive traversals through your objects.

Next, we will want to add a layer and a sprite to our playground. You can achieve that by adding the bolded lines of Listing 7.8.

**Listing 7.8**   Adding Player to the Playground

```
.addGroup("enemies", {width: PLAYGROUND_WIDTH, height:
PLAYGROUND_HEIGHT})
.end()
.addGroup("player", {posx: 0, posy: PLAYGROUND_HEIGHT/2, width:
playerWidth, height: playerHeight})
.addSprite("playerBody",{animation: '', posx: 0, posy: 0, width:
playerWidth, height: playerHeight})

$("#player")[0].player = new Player();
$("#playerBody").html("<span class='value'>"+$("#player")[0].player.
➥value+"</span><br /><span class='number'>"+$("#player")[0].player.
➥number+"</span>");

$.playground().registerCallback(function(){
```

First, we chain the end function so that when we add the `player` layer, it is not nested inside of the `enemies` layer. When you add the player layer, you set the initial position on the left and halfway down. Then you add the sprite, and, as with the enemy sprites, you add a blank string for the animation because you're not using a sprite or animation here.

You may notice that the player layer is a little more specific than the enemy layer. With a few exceptions, you will mostly interact with the `player` element, rather than the `playerBody` element for the rest of this chapter.

Next, initialize a new player object, and assign it to an attribute referenced by the first element of the result of jQuery selector for `"#player"`. The last bit is just html for styling the `playerBody` element and the text that appears inside. No surprises there. You have a bit of styling information to add to game.css. You can do this with the bolded code in Listing 7.9.

**Listing 7.9** Styling the Ship

```
.enemy{
  color:red;
  background-color: black;
  font-size:24px;
  border:1px solid red;
  text-align:center;
}
#player{
  color:white;
  background-color:black;
  font-size:24px;
  border: 1px solid white;
  text-align:center;
}
```

If you start the game now, you'd have a "ship" with no way to move it. You can fix that with the bold code in Listing 7.10. This handles input, so it should be fast. Add it to the bottom of the callback that uses REFRESH_RATE so that it will be executed frequently.

**Listing 7.10** Moving Your Ship Around

```
$.playground().registerCallback(function(){
...
  if(jQuery.gameQuery.keyTracker[37]){
    var nextpos = $("#player").x()-5;
    if(nextpos > 0){
      $("#player").x(nextpos);
    }
  }
  if(jQuery.gameQuery.keyTracker[39]){
    var nextpos = $("#player").x()+5;
    if(nextpos < PLAYGROUND_WIDTH - playerWidth){
      $("#player").x(nextpos);
    }
  }
  if(jQuery.gameQuery.keyTracker[38]){
    var nextpos = $("#player").y()-5;
    if(nextpos > 0){
      $("#player").y(nextpos);
    }
  }
  if(jQuery.gameQuery.keyTracker[40]){
    var nextpos = $("#player").y()+5;
    if(nextpos < PLAYGROUND_HEIGHT - playerHeight){
```

```
        $("#player").y(nextpos);
      }
    }
  }, REFRESH_RATE);
```

This code is added just above the bottom of your main game loop. gameQuery doesn't come with any fancy key mapping abstractions like some of the other game engines, so we have to figure out these numbers ourselves. 37–40 correspond to the arrow keys, and in order, these key checking statements correspond (in order) to pressing left, right, up and down. Within these blocks, there is code to keep the ship on the screen. For a full list of the numbers that correspond to keys on the keyboard, search for "JavaScript keycodes." As of this writing, the best reference to read more about these keycodes is at https://developer.mozilla.org/en-US/docs/DOM/KeyboardEvent#Key_location_constants.

With all this code in place, you should have a ship that you can drive around for a game that looks something like Figure 7.3.

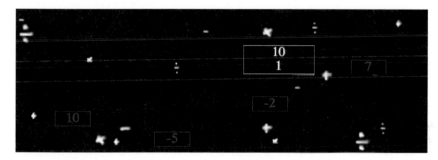

**Figure 7.3** A drivable ship

# Recipe: Enemy Collisions

Now that you have a ship and enemies, you should handle the first aspect of their interaction, which is some result when they touch. You could consider the enemies as collectable objects and add to a score when they are encountered. Casting them as enemies, as you have done, could suggest that the player ship be hurt or destroyed when they are touched. It's a fairly philosophical point, though. We'll be shooting things at them later, so we shouldn't get too friendly. Replace the enemy update loop (inside of the main loop) with the code in Listing 7.11 to handle collisions.

**Listing 7.11** Dealing with Collisions

```
$(".enemy").each(function(){
  this.enemy.update();
  if(($(this).x() + enemyWidth) < 0){
    $(this).remove();
  } else {
    var collided = $(this).collision("#playerBody,.
➥"+$.gQ.groupCssClass);
    if(collided.length > 0){
      $("#player")[0].player.value += $(this)[0].enemy.value;
      $("#player")[0].player.number = $(this)[0].enemy.value;
      $("#player .value").html($("#player")[0].player.value);
      $("#player .number").html($("#player")[0].player.number);
      $(this).remove();
    }
  }
});
```

Now when you run into an enemy ship, three things happen. First, the player `value` attribute has the enemy `value` added to it and updates the corresponding html. You could think of this as the player's score. Second, the enemy `number` attribute is assigned to the player `number` attribute, and the html is updated. This ends up being a player's ammunition. Last, the enemy ship is removed.

# Recipe: Shooting

You have your ships; you have your ammo. All that's left to make this a shooter is the ability to shoot. First, you need another global variable for the speed of the missile, as in the bold line of Listing 7.12.

**Listing 7.12** missile speed

```
function Player(){
  this.speed = 5;
  this.value = 10;
  this.number = 1;
};

var missileSpeed = 10;
```

Then you need to add a new layer to your layer initialization code, as shown in Listing 7.13.

**Listing 7.13** Missile Layer

```
.addSprite("playerBody",{animation: '', posx: 0, posy: 0, width:
➡playerWidth, height: playerHeight})
.end()
.addGroup("playerMissileLayer",{width: PLAYGROUND_WIDTH, height:
➡PLAYGROUND_HEIGHT}).end()
```

We'll get to the code for actually adding the missiles in Listing 7.15. For now, add the code in Listing 7.14 to handle collisions with enemy ships. This code goes right after the logic for handling collisions on enemies, and right before your key tracking code in the fast callback function (that ends with REFRESH_RATE).

**Listing 7.14** Missile Collision Detection

```
$(".enemy").each(function(){
  ...
});
$(".playerMissiles").each(function(){
  var posx = $(this).x();
  if(posx > PLAYGROUND_WIDTH){
    $(this).remove();
  }else{
    $(this).x(missileSpeed, true);
    var collided = $(this).collision(".enemy,."+$.gQ.groupCssClass);
    if(collided.length > 0){
      collided.each(function(){
        var possible_value = $(this)[0].enemy.value +
➡$('#player')[0].player.number;
        if(possible_value < 10000 && possible_value > -10000){
          var thisEnemy = $(this)[0].enemy;
          thisEnemy.value = possible_value;
          $(thisEnemy.node[0]).text(thisEnemy.value)
        };
      })
      $(this).remove();
    };
  };
});
```

First, we determine if the missile was able to fly past all the enemy ships and end up past the right side of the playground. If it did, you can remove it. If it still is on the screen, it moves a bit to the right. Then we check to see if any missiles collided with an enemy. We loop through those that did, adding the value of the missile to the value of the enemy ship, but with one caveat. We don't change the ship value if it would end up less than –10000 or greater than 10000. Finally, we remove the missile that collided.

Next, you need the code to actually generate the missiles (triggered by pressing the spacebar). You could put this inside of the main update loop, but you need faster reactions to the fire button than that. In addition, you don't want anything in that loop that isn't completely necessary, or it can slow down the game. Listing 7.15 shows the code you need, which you can put just above the `startGame` function at the bottom of the file.

**Listing 7.15**  Missile Creation

```
$(document).keydown(function(e){
  if(e.keyCode === 32){
      var playerposx = $("#player").x();
      var playerposy = $("#player").y();
      var name = "playerMissile_"+(new Date()).getTime();
      $("#playerMissileLayer").addSprite(name, {posx: playerposx
➥+ playerWidth, posy: playerposy, width: playerWidth/2,height:
➥playerHeight/2});
        $("#"+name).addClass("playerMissiles, player");
        $("#"+name).html("<div>"+$("#player")[0].player.number+"</div>");
  }
});

$.playground().startGame();
```

We start by using jQuery's (not gameQuery's) `keydown` function to check for spacebar presses (keycode 32). We store the position of the ship to be used later, and then we generate a `name` (through the `(new Date()).getTime()` function you previously used), which becomes the `id` of the sprite. We set the width and height as one-half of the player ship values and the position to be just to the right of the ship. We add the `playerMissiles` class that you need for the code in Listing 7.14 to have something to loop through to test collisions. The last line adds the html. As you might expect, you now need to add some styling for your missiles. You can add the code in Listing 7.16 to the bottom of game.css. Let's style the `number` class similarly because the numbers are actually missiles loaded up and ready to fire.

**Listing 7.16**  Styling Your Missiles

```
.playerMissiles{
  text-align:center;
  border: solid 1px green;
```

```
  font-size:24px;
  color:green;
  background-color:black;
}
.number{
  color:green;
}
```

# Recipe: Powerups

You might not be that excited by addition or the bit of subtraction that we snuck in there. That's okay. This recipe adds a wealth of complexity to what happens when you shoot an enemy ship.

Again, we'll start by adding a couple variables just under `missileSpeed` with Listing 7.17.

**Listing 7.17**  Variables for Symbol Array

```
var missileSpeed = 10;
var symbols = ["+", "-", "*", "/", "%", "|", "&", "<<", ">>"];
var symbolIndex = 0;
```

You may recognize these symbols as what JavaScript (and many other programming languages) recognize as the following: "addition," "subtraction," "multiplication," "division," "modulo" (getting the remainder of division), "binary or," "binary and," "bitwise left shift," and "bitwise right shift." The plan is to "attack" with all these functions, not just addition. Next you need to replace the original html of the `playerBody` element with the slightly longer code in Listing 7.18. The bolded portions indicate the new code.

**Listing 7.18**  Adding a Symbol Indicator to playerBody

```
$("#player")[0].player = new Player();
$("#playerBody").html("<span class='value'>"+$("#player")[0].player.
➡ value+"</span><br />(<span class='symbol'>"+symbols[symbolIndex]+
➡"</span>) <span class='number'>"+$("#player")[0].player.number+
➡"</span>");
```

Here, you're mostly just slipping in the symbol between a pair of parentheses. Next, you need to make a change to the logic in your missile collision detection code so that it can update based on any mathematical function conveyed by the symbols, rather than just addition. You can accomplish this with the code in Listing 7.19.

**Listing 7.19** Smarter Missile Collisions

```
$(".playerMissiles").each(function(){
  var posx = $(this).x();
...
      collided.each(function(){
        var possible_value = Math.round(eval($(this)[0].enemy.value +
➥" " + symbols[symbolIndex] + " " + $('#player')[0].player.number));
        if(possible_value < 10000 && possible_value > -10000){
...
    };
});
```

Only one line has actually changed here. Now, the possible value is wrapped with a
`Math.round` function so that the player doesn't get confused when division causes things
to get extremely small and fractional. In addition, you now are "evaling" the entire line, which
amounts to one string. What `eval` does is attempt to interpret the string passed in as a parameter, as if it is valid JavaScript code. You could have gone through the trouble of creating functions for each symbol, and passing in each operand, but for your purposes here, `eval`
does the trick.

## warning

**NEVER EVER USE EVAL!**   …or so the saying goes. There are a few good reasons
for this. Architecturally, it encourages sticking a bunch of variables and strings
together, which is hard to debug and maintain. From a performance standpoint, it
is also not good because it requires invoking the JavaScript interpreter in ways that
performance can't benefit as well from browser optimizations.

The scariest bit is the oft-cited security issues that `eval` opens you up to. What
are we worried about? Mostly it's cross-site scripting (XSS), which is a much easier
attack when generating the different pieces of the eval'd statement based on the
URL, form input, or through any other user submitted free-form text.

Okay, fine. I can't bear the guilt. If you're worried about `eval`, use the code in Listing 7.20
instead, placing the `functionEval` function near the top of the file (just below declaring the
`symbolIndex` variable) and calling it from the line altering the assignment of the `possible_`
`value` variable that had the evil `eval` call in Listing 7.19.

**Listing 7.20**   No More eval

```
var symbols - ["+", "-", "*", "/", "%", "|", "&", "<<", ">>"];
var symbolIndex = 0;

function functionEval(enemyValue, symbol, missileValue){
  switch(symbol){
    case "+":
      return enemyValue + missileValue;
    case "-":
      return enemyValue - missileValue;
    case "*":
      return enemyValue * missileValue;
    case "/":
      return enemyValue / missileValue;
    case "%":
      return enemyValue % missileValue;
    case "|":
      return enemyValue | missileValue;
    case "&":
      return enemyValue & missileValue;
    case "<<":
      return enemyValue << missileValue;
    case ">>":
      return enemyValue >> missileValue;
  };
};
...
var possible_value = Math.round(functionEval($(this)[0].enemy.value,
➥symbols[symbolIndex], $('#player')[0].player.number));
```

You have just one last piece of code to add, which enables you to cycle through your possible functions. It is in Listing 7.21.

**Listing 7.21**   Cycling Through Your Functions

```
$(document).keydown(function(e){
  if(e.keyCode === 32){
      var playerposx = $("#player").x();
      var playerposy = $("#player").y();
      var name = "playerMissile_"+(new Date()).getTime();
      $("#playerMissileLayer").addSprite(name, {posx: playerposx
➥+ playerWidth, posy: playerposy, width: playerWidth/2,height:
➥playerHeight/2});
      $("#"+name).addClass("playerMissiles");
      $("#"+name).html("<div>"+$("#player")[0].player.number+"</div>");
```

```
  } else if(e.keyCode === 70){
    symbolIndex = (symbolIndex+1)%symbols.length;
    $("#player .symbol").text(symbols[symbolIndex]);
  };
});
```

This code will be executed when you press the "f" key. It adds 1 to the `symbolIndex`, and when it gets to the maximum value, it goes back down to 0 by virtue of the modulo operator. (You can play the game a little with this function if you're not sure how it works.) Then the html of the player symbol is updated to reflect the currently selected symbol.

After all this, you should end up with something like Figure 7.4.

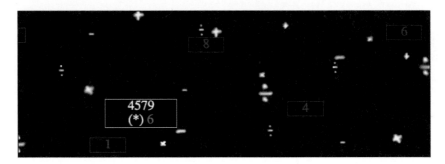

**Figure 7.4**   The finished game

# Summary

This chapter used the DOM-rendering-based game engine gameQuery to build a mathematical shooter. While we were at it, we had a chance to cover different types of browser rendering technologies (3-D canvas, 2-D canvas, SVG, DOM, and CSS3) at a high level and talk a bit about why everyone hates `eval` so much (security, performance, and architecture).

Most shooting games just deal with subtraction. You shoot the enemy, and their hit points drop until they hit 0 or below, and they disappear or explode. Or they shoot you to similar effect. What you created is quite a bit more flexible and could even be helpful for drilling on binary operators if you are less familiar with them.

As far as where to head next with gameQuery, it has a few features that were not discussed, such as the Sound Wrapper API, animations, tilemaps, and sprite manipulations such as scaling and rotating.

With this game specifically, there are a few obvious places for you to take it next. You could have a top scrolling game within an hour just by flipping the x and y properties and rotating some images by 90 degrees. You could establish goals, winning/losing states, and levels. With that, you could demand more attention and aspiration, with increasing skill being required as progress is made. The score could represent some kind of intermittent goal. You could make some of the weapons (functions) unlockable, rather than all of them being immediately available. The weapons could follow multiple trajectories with different speeds. The enemies could as well. There could be a big, bad boss. Overall, it is very abstract in its current form, somewhat like a pinball game in an undecorated cabinet.

# CHAPTER 8

# FPS

Before polygons and multiple camera angles informed how modern 3-D games could work, games with raycaster-based rendering such as *Doom* and the game you build in this chapter provided a convincing pseudo-3D experience. With this first-person perspective, you can invite players to view the world you create through the eyes of a soldier, a secret agent, or someone mostly running away from the undead. With an over-the-shoulder camera, the techniques in this chapter also lend themselves to creating the type of perspective you would need for a racing game or first person RPG.

# Recipe: Getting Started with Jaws

In the last chapter, we managed to sneak in a 3-D technique with parallax scrolling background images, which is frequently used in 2-D games, especially platformers, to give a sense of broader world motion. This chapter tackles another fake 3-D effect known as *raycasting*. Don't confuse this with the vastly more complicated 3-D rendering technique known as *raytracing*. We will get into the details of this game shortly, but in brief, using a raycaster means you first lay out a map in a two-dimensional way and then "cast" rays out from your perspective to the walls to find their distances, and render them as appropriate sizes.

> ## note
>
> There is one more popular fake 3-D effect known as *isometric projection*. Thinking back (or ahead if you're that young and awesome) to 8th-grade art class, do you remember when you had to draw a cube in three dimensions, so you tilted it to the side and moved the view angle more to the top? This is what an *isometric perspective* looks like. We use this technique in Chapter 10, "RTS."
>
> There are many games that render in this style. Some early examples are *Q*bert* for the Atari, or *Marble Madness*, *Snake Rattle 'n Roll*, and *Solstice* for the NES. Games such as *Final Fantasy Tactics* for the PlayStation and the MMO Sim *Habbo Hotel* demonstrate its versatility as a more modern technique as well.
>
> If you can't recognize the art in these games as isometric projection, you could also identify use of this technique by your potential confusion of having to remember things such as how pressing "up" actually means "up and right" (or is it "up and left?"), "right" moves you "right and down," and so on. Take care if you decide to employ this technique with directional input controls rather than a point-and-click interface.

In many of the chapters to this point, you could rely on your game engines to do much of the work. Because most game engines don't come with a raycaster on board, you need to build it yourself.

Because of this, you might wonder if you should use a game engine at all. Despite the complexity of the things you have to build from scratch, in this chapter the author has taken the liberty of answering, "Yes, you want a game engine." Organizing code, managing the game loop, preloading sprites, and accepting input may seem like trivial tasks, but generally speaking, aiming for simplicity is an architectural choice worth considering. On the other hand, you might have goals to reduce dependencies on external libraries, choose single-purpose tools, or optimize the code.

So what can Jaws do for you? Well, to kick things off, get a basic html file going with the code in Listing 8.1.

**Listing 8.1**   A Basic html File

```
<html>
  <head>
    <title>FPS</title>
    <link rel="stylesheet" type="text/css" href="game.css" />
</head>
  <body>
    <canvas id="canvas"></canvas>
    <script type="text/javascript" src="jaws.js"></script>
    <script type="text/javascript" src="game.js"></script>
    <script>
      jaws.start(Game);
    </script>
  </body>
</html>
```

Nothing too exotic here. You load a style sheet, add a `canvas` element with an `id` of `canvas`, load the game engine, load your JavaScript file for the game, and run an inline script to start the jaws engine, passing in a value of `Game`. To see what `jaws.start(Game);` does, set up your game.js file, as shown in Listing 8.2.

**Listing 8.2**   game.js

```
var Game = function(){
  this.setup = function() {
    alert("running setup");
  };
}
```

You make use of the other Jaws-defined methods of `draw` and `update` in a little while, but for now, just notice how simply you can initialize the game in Jaws. Before moving on, let's get the css file in place with the code in Listing 8.3.

**Listing 8.3**   game.css

```
#canvas{
  position:absolute;
  width:600px;
  height:300px;
  z-index:-1;
}
```

With that all in place, you should see the Jaws loading screen and an alert box like in Figure 8.1. There are two things to notice here. First, Jaws has grabbed onto the first canvas element that it saw. You didn't have to explicitly call a method or pass an id. Second, it runs the `setup` function automatically (and only once) by virtue of the `start` function.

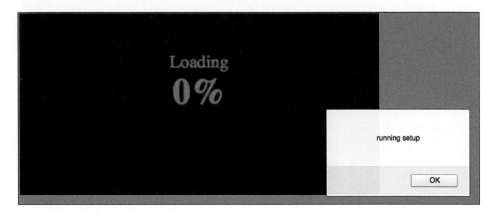

**Figure 8.1**   Loading with Jaws

## Recipe: Creating a 2-D Map

To get your raycaster going, you need to start with a 2-D map of the area. First, update the code in game.js to reflect Listing 8.4.

**Listing 8.4**   Adding the Map

```
var Game = function(){
  var map = [ [1,1,1,1,1,1,1,1,1,1,1,1,1,1,1,1],
      [1,-1,-1,-1,-1,-1,-1,-1,-1,-1,-1,-1,-1,-1,1],
      [1,-1,-1,-1,-1,-1,-1,0,-1,2,3,1,-1,-1,-1,1],
      [1,1,-1,-1,-1,-1,-1,-1,-1,-1,-1,-1,-1,-1,1],
      [1,-1,-1,-1,-1,-1,-1,-1,-1,-1,-1,-1,-1,-1,1],
      [1,-1,-1,-1,-1,-1,-1,-1,-1,-1,-1,-1,-1,-1,1],
      [1,-1,-1,-1,-1,-1,-1,-1,-1,-1,-1,-1,-1,-1,1],
      [1,-1,3,-1,-1,-1,-1,-1,-1,-1,-1,-1,-1,-1,1],
      [1,-1,-1,-1,-1,-1,-1,-1,-1,-1,-1,2,-1,-1,-1,1],
      [1,-1,-1,1,-1,-1,-1,-1,-1,3,-1,-1,-1,-1,-1,1],
      [1,-1,-1,-1,-1,-1,-1,-1,-1,-1,-1,-1,-1,-1,1],
      [1,-1,-1,-1,-1,-1,-1,-1,-1,-1,-1,-1,-1,-1,1],
      [1,-1,-1,-1,-1,-1,1,-1,-1,2,-1,-1,-1,-1,-1,1],
```

```
           [1,-1,-1,-1,-1,-1,-1,-1,-1,-1,-1,-1,-1,-1,1],
           [1,-1,-1,-1,-1,-1,-1,-1,-1,-1,-1,-1,-1,-1,1],
           [1,1,1,1,1,1,1,1,1,1,1,1,1,1,1]];
    var minimap = {
      init: function(){
        this.element = document.getElementById('minimap');
        this.context = this.element.getContext("2d");
        this.element.width = 300;
        this.element.height = 300;
        this.width = this.element.width;
        this.height = this.element.height;
        this.cellsAcross = map[0].length;
        this.cellsDown = map.length;
        this.cellWidth = this.width/this.cellsAcross;
        this.cellHeight = this.height/this.cellsDown;
        this.colors = ["#ffff00", "#ff00ff", "#00ffff", "#0000ff"];
        this.draw = function(){
          for(var y = 0; y < this.cellsDown; y++){
            for(var x = 0; x < this.cellsAcross; x++){
              var cell = map[y][x];
              if (cell===-1){
                this.context.fillStyle = "#ffffff"
              }else{
                this.context.fillStyle = this.colors[map[y][x]];
              };
              this.context.fillRect(this.cellWidth*x, this.cellHeight*y,
➥this.cellWidth, this.cellHeight);
            };
          };
        };
      }
    };
    this.draw = function(){
      minimap.draw();
    };
    this.setup = function() {
      minimap.init();
    };
}
```

Here, you added the two-dimensional array `map`. –1 is empty space, and 0-3 are different types
of walls. In your setup function, you have deleted the `alert` statement and are now initializing
the `minimap` object with the `init` function. The `draw` function, which Jaws is kind enough to
run in a loop for us, calls the `minimap`'s `draw` function.

Now let's discuss the `minimap` object. This separate canvas element stores your 2-D overview of the map. The `init` function is called, which makes the attributes declared as `this.myAttributeNameHere` available outside of the context. First, let's get the canvas element and its context. Next we explicitly set the height and width of the canvas object. You may think that height and width of the canvas context would be inherited from the style attributes of the canvas element that you will be declaring in the CSS. This is NOT true, so you have to set it explicitly. We then set these properties to shorter names for convenience. Next we find the number of cells in the x-axis and the y-axis, and use these to determine the size of the cells. In the last line before the draw function, we establish an array of colors to distinguish walls of different types.

In our draw method, we loop through each outer element of the `map` array (the y-axis), looping through every subarray (the x-axis), drawing a white cell for empty space or a color that is mapped to the index of the color array referenced by the cell position in the map. The parameters passed to `fillRect` are x position (from left), y position (from top), width, and height.

Let's catch our html and css up to speed with the JavaScript we added starting with a new canvas element as in the bold line of Listing 8.5.

**Listing 8.5**  Adding the minimap to index.html

```html
<canvas id="canvas"></canvas>
<canvas id="minimap"></canvas>
<script type="text/javascript" src="jaws.js"></script>
```

Lastly, we'll add the following styles to this element by adding the code in Listing 8.6 to our game.css file.

**Listing 8.6**  Styling the minimap Element

```
...
#minimap{
  border:1px solid black;
  position:absolute;
  top:350px;
  width:300px;
  height:300px;
}
```

Because we position the element absolutely, the `top` attribute indicates where we want it to appear on the page. `width` and `height` behave as expected for the element, but remember, as pointed out earlier, these values do not transfer to the deceptively homonymous `width` and `height` JavaScript attributes of the context object derived from this canvas element.

With all that in place, you should be able to load index.html in your browser and see your minimap appear, as shown in Figure 8.2.

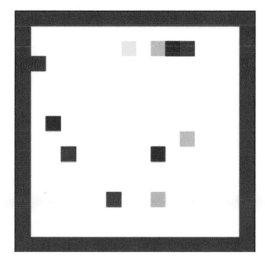

**Figure 8.2**  The minimap

# Recipe: Adding a Player

You have your 2-D map. Next we'll need something to explore it with. To put a player object on the screen, use the updated version of game.js found in Listing 8.7.

**Listing 8.7** Putting the player on the minimap

```
var Game = function(){
  var player = {
    init: function(){
      this.x = 10;
      this.y = 6;
      this.draw = function(){
        var playerXOnMinimap = this.x * minimap.cellWidth;
        var playerYOnMinimap = this.y * minimap.cellHeight;
        minimap.context.fillStyle = "#000000";
        minimap.context.beginPath();
        minimap.context.arc(minimap.cellWidth*this.x,
➥minimap.cellHeight*this.y, minimap.cellWidth/2, 0, 2*Math.PI, true);
        minimap.context.fill();
      };
    }
  }
  var map = [[1,1,1,1,1,1,1,1,1,1,1,1,1,1,1,1],
  ...
  var minimap = {
  ...
  };
  this.draw = function(){
    minimap.draw();
    player.draw();
  };
  this.setup = function() {
    minimap.init();
    player.init();
  };
}
```

You can ignore the unbolded lines here. We added three important sections. Starting from the bottom, we now initialize the `player` object in the same way as the `minimap`, and register the `player.draw` function to be run inside of the `draw` function, which loops indefinitely. As for the `player` object at the top, we define the coordinates where the player starts, and then rely on some of the minimap attributes to draw a black circle at the player position.

Next, we will be introduce the movement of the player. You might expect up and down to correspond with movement along the y-axis, and right and left to correspond with movement along the x-axis. Perspective is going to be important later, so we have to take a different approach to movement, with some keys to turn the player and others to go forward and backward.

Now we can use the code in Listing 8.8 to add an `update` function. As with `draw`, this will be looped indefinitely by Jaws. The `update` function can appear directly following the `draw` function.

**Listing 8.8**  Registering Input

```
this.update = function(){
  if(jaws.pressed("left")) { player.direction = -1 };
  if(jaws.pressed("right")) { player.direction = 1 };
  if(jaws.pressed("up")) { player.speed = 1 };
  if(jaws.pressed("down")) { player.speed = -1 };

  if(jaws.on_keyup(["left", "right"], function(){
    player.direction = 0;
  }));
  if(jaws.on_keyup(["up", "down"], function(){
    player.speed = 0;
  }));
  player.move();
};
} //this is the end of the file
```

With these lines of code, we register whether or not a player is attempting to turn or move. Then we call the `move` function to register the results. Besides adding a move method, we have some other changes to the beginning of this file. These are in the bold lines of Listing 8.9.

**Listing 8.9**  Moving the player

```
var Game = function(){
  var player = {
    init: function(){
      this.x = 10;
      this.y = 6;
      this.direction = 0;
      this.angle = 0;
      this.speed = 0;
      this.movementSpeed = 0.1;
      this.turnSpeed = 4 * Math.PI / 180;
      this.move = function(){
        var moveStep = this.speed * this.movementSpeed;
        this.angle += this.direction * this.turnSpeed;
        var newX = this.x + Math.cos(this.angle) * moveStep;
        var newY = this.y + Math.sin(this.angle) * moveStep;
        if (!containsBlock(newX, newY)){
          this.x = newX;
```

```
        this.y = newY;
      };
    };
    this.draw = function(){
      var playerXOnMinimap = this.x * minimap.cellWidth;
      var playerYOnMinimap = this.y * minimap.cellHeight;
      minimap.context.fillStyle = "#000000";
      minimap.context.beginPath();
      minimap.context.arc(minimap.cellWidth*this.x,
➡minimap.cellHeight*this.y, minimap.cellWidth/2, 0, 2*Math.PI, true);
      minimap.context.fill();
      var projectedX = this.x + Math.cos(this.angle);
      var projectedY = this.y + Math.sin(this.angle);
      minimap.context.fillRect(minimap.cellWidth*projectedX
➡- minimap.cellWidth/4, minimap.cellHeight*projectedY -
➡minimap.cellHeight/4, minimap.cellWidth/2, minimap.cellHeight/2);
      };
    }
  };
  function containsBlock(x,y) {
    return (map[Math.floor(y)][Math.floor(x)] !== -1);
  };
```

We start by setting `direction` to 0, which indicates we are not attempting to turn the player. Setting `angle` to 0 means that we start out facing to the right. The `speed` at 0 describes that we are not attempting to move forward or backward. The `movementSpeed` describes how fast we will travel while moving, and the `turnSpeed` describes how fast we can rotate. The fancy-looking arithmetic involving `Math.PI` there is a conversion from 4 degrees (out of 360 in a full circle) to .0698 radians (in which 2 times Pi would be the equivalent of 360 degrees). Just as we reference Pi to convert degrees to radians to draw circles, we will need to convert degree measurements to radians to apply trig functions like sine or cosine.

> ## warning
>
> **TRIGONOMETRY AHEAD** If you don't know much about trigonometry, don't worry. All we are doing in this chapter is figuring out how angles and sides of triangles fit together. There will be explanations along the way, but if all you can do today is copy the functions, you will still be able to make the game. There will always be more to learn, so don't feel too bad if you get a bit lost for a moment or need more practice in one area or another.

The `move` method has our first uses of trigonometric functions in this game. The goal here is to update the x and y coordinates of the player. We start by getting the `moveStep` variable, which you can think of as the distance forward that your player wants to travel. But this alone is not enough information to determine x and y coordinates. Next, we update the angle that the player is facing if we are in the process of turning. So now you know how far the player would like to travel and in what direction. By using the trig functions (sine, cosine, and tangent), you can determine the ratios of the sides of a triangle. In this triangle, the direction the player faces is the hypotenuse (the longest side of a triangle), the x-axis is the adjacent side, and the y-axis is the opposite side. For x, use the cosine function to get the ratio of the adjacent side over the hypotenuse (`moveStep`). When you multiply by the length of the hypotenuse, you get a distance along the x-axis. By adding this to the current x position, you can find the `newX` where the player would like to be.

To determine a new y position, we can take a similar approach but apply the sine function to the angle to determine the ratio of the opposite side (y-axis) over hypotenuse (`moveStep`). As before, we multiply this ratio by the length of the hypotenuse to find a distance that the player is attempting to move to. Then we add this distance to the current position to get a `newY` value.

To prevent the player from walking into walls, we pass these values into the `containsBlock` function, which checks to see if the player is attempting to move within the space that a block is occupying. Use of the `floor` function is one method of stopping updates to any position from values inside of each cell (that is, x-position 5 through 5.999 and y-position 4 through 4.999). If the block is empty, allow the player to be updated.

In the `draw` function, add an indicator of which direction the player is facing. Use the trigonometric functions similarly to the `move` function, but don't worry about whether a player can actually move to the location. Just plot it. For `fillRect`, we are indicating a fairly small rectangle, which is why we divide the `cellWidth` and `cellHeight` by 2 In the third and fourth parameters. As for the division by 4 in the first two parameters, we do this to ensure that our direction indicator rotates evenly around the player circle.

# Recipe: Raycasting Top View

Now that you have a basic map, let's do some raycasting. We won't achieve our ideal of fake 3-D just yet, but you can create a `raycaster` object that contains the bulk of complexity in the game.

First, let's replace our main `setup` and `draw` functions with the code in Listing 8.10. Don't confuse this `draw` function with the one for `player` or `minimap`. This one is the main `draw` function that delegates to those two more-specific functions.

**Listing 8.10**   Setting Up Your raycaster

```
this.draw = function(){
  minimap.draw();
  player.draw();
  raycaster.castRays();
};
this.setup = function() {
  minimap.init();
  player.init();
  raycaster.init();
};
```

Nothing much new here. We're setting up the `raycaster` object in `setup` and calling the `castRays` function in the `draw` loop. Let's create your `raycaster` object, along with these two methods, with the bold code in Listing 8.11. This can appear just below where the `Game` function is started (on line 1).

**Listing 8.11**   The raycaster Object

```
var Game = function(){
  var raycaster = {
    init: function(){
      var numberOfRays = 300;
      var angleBetweenRays = .2 * Math.PI /180;
      this.castRays = function() {
        for (var i=0;i<numberOfRays;i++) {
          var rayNumber = -numberOfRays/2 + i;
          var rayAngle = angleBetweenRays * rayNumber + player.angle;
          this.castRay(rayAngle);
        }
      }
    }
  }
  var player = {
```

Let's pretend for a second that the last line calling another `raycaster` function isn't there. We'll add that in the next listing. As with the other objects in this game, we are putting all of our methods inside of the `init` function. We will want 300 rays to shoot out from our player at consistent angle intervals. To get a view field of view that is acceptably broad, we set our `angleBetweenRays` variable to .2 degrees, but convert it inline into radians by multiplying times pi and dividing by 180.

In the `castRays` function, we execute the loop 300 times, to the end of determining an angle and using that in our `castRay` function. Because we want the rays to be cast on either side of the player, we subtract one-half of the rays from the loop index and store this as `rayNumber`. Then, we can multiply the `rayNumber` times the `angleBetweenRays` to get the angle (positive or negative) from the center. We add that product to `player.angle` to get each `rayAngle` that we pass as an argument to `castRay`. Let's implement this function with the bold code in Listing 8.12.

**Listing 8.12**   Casting Rays

```
var raycaster = {
  init: function(){
    this.castRays = function() {
  ...
    }
    this.castRay = function(rayAngle){
      var twoPi = Math.PI * 2;
      rayAngle %= twoPi;
      if (rayAngle < 0) rayAngle += twoPi;
      var right = (rayAngle > twoPi * 0.75 || rayAngle < twoPi * 0.25);
      var up = rayAngle > Math.PI;
      var slope = Math.tan(rayAngle);
      var distance = 0;
      var xHit = 0;
      var yHit = 0;
      var wallX;
      var wallY;
      var dX = right ? 1 : -1;
      var dY = dX * slope;
      var x = right ? Math.ceil(player.x) : Math.floor(player.x);
      var y = player.y + (x - player.x) * slope;
      while (x >= 0 && x < minimap.cellsAcross && y >= 0 && y <
➥minimap.cellsDown) {
        wallX = Math.floor(x + (right ? 0 : -1));
        wallY = Math.floor(y);
        if (map[wallY][wallX] > -1) {
          var distanceX = x - player.x;
          var distanceY = y - player.y;
          distance = Math.sqrt(distanceX*distanceX +
➥distanceY*distanceY);
          xHit = x;
          yHit = y;
          break;
        }
        x += dX;
        y += dY;
```

```
        }
        slope = 1/slope;
        dY = up ? -1 : 1;
        dX = dY * slope;
        y = up ? Math.floor(player.y) : Math.ceil(player.y);
        x = player.x + (y - player.y) * slope;
        while (x >= 0 && x < minimap.cellsAcross && y >= 0 && y <
➥minimap.cellsDown) {
            wallY = Math.floor(y + (up ? -1 : 0));
            wallX = Math.floor(x);
            if (map[wallY][wallX] > -1) {
              var distanceX = x - player.x;
              var distanceY = y - player.y;
              var blockDistance = Math.sqrt(distanceX*distanceX +
➥distanceY*distanceY);
                if (!distance || blockDistance < distance) {
                  distance = blockDistance;
                  xHit = x;
                  yHit = y;
                }
                break;
            }
            x += dX;
            y += dY;
        }
        this.draw(xHit, yHit);
    };
    this.draw = function(rayX, rayY){
      minimap.context.beginPath();
      minimap.context.moveTo(minimap.cellWidth*player.x, minimap.
➥cellHeight*player.y);
      minimap.context.lineTo(rayX * minimap.cellWidth, rayY *
➥minimap.cellHeight);
      minimap.context.closePath();
      minimap.context.stroke();
    }
  }
};
```

When you're presented with a function this large, it helps to glance down at what it returns, what it calls, or any side effects (variables) that the function sets. If you look just above the `draw` function declaration, you may notice that the most important thing that this does is find the `xHit` and `yHit` variables, which are the x and y map coordinates of the block that the ray hits. Then these coordinates are passed to the draw function. Keep that goal in mind as you step through the function.

We'll be working with the radian equivalent of 360 degrees (Math.PI * 2) a good bit, so you can set that to a variable called `twoPi`. Next, we mod (`%`) the value of the angle by `twoPi` so that it does not get larger than (the radian equivalent of) 360 degrees. Then we add `twoPi` to it if it is small, so that we won't have to work with negatives. After that, we determine which quadrant it is in. This simply means if the ray is pointing, say, up and to the right, versus down and to the left.

Next, we get the `slope` of the angle. When we use the tangent function, we discover the ratio of length of the "opposite" side (y) over the length of the "adjacent" side (x). When we multiply this by `dX` (change in x) in a few lines, we will find the change in y, or `dY`. We need these values because we want to know where to check for a new block if the immediate space is empty, which we will see in just a second.

After setting `slope`, we initialize a few more variables on speculation. We set the `distance`, which is the length from the player to a terminating block, to zero. `xHit` and `yHit` will store the specific location where a collision between ray and block occurs. `wallX` and `wallY` will store the more general map coordinates of the block that was hit. `dX` is either one unit to the right (+1), or one unit to the left (–1), depending on which direction the ray is headed. `dY` is the change in y, proportional to the change in x (`dX`) as determined by the `slope`. x and y together form the current cell position on the map that the ray is going through.

Inside of the `while` loop, we are looking for a hit, and when we get it, we'll leave with the `break` keyword. The loop conditions indicate that we will also stop if we reach the edge of the map. Inside of the loop, we set `wallX` and `wallY` to be the cell that we're currently investigating. The `if` statement checks to see if there is a block in the cell. If there is, we have a hit, so we set `distanceX` and `distanceY` to the distances from the player. Then we discover the straight-line distance from the player by applying the Pythagorean theorem to those distances. Then we update the most important variables (because they are what we need for the `draw` function), the `xHit` and `yHit`, to store the exact locations of the collision. The last thing we do if we have a hit is break out of the while statement.

In the event that we do not have a hit, we add increment x and y to cast a bit further and try again. Note that if you wanted to have a very large map, it would be a good idea to limit the viewing distance. A ray without a hit until the edge of the map could be expensive and slow down the other rays.

On the following lines, we do essentially the same thing, but this time, we try for a vertical hit. One notable difference is that there is an additional conditional check to see if the horizontal distance was larger, and only replacing that distance if it was. Everything else is essentially the same but shifted slightly. It may seem like a good candidate for refactoring by compressing everything into one function, but those efforts will be complicated by how many variables these sections share, as well as the fairly large number of tiny variations between the two. You may end up with something smaller yet harder to read and maintain.

Finally, the `draw` function is called. Here we draw a line from the player to the point where the ray collided with a block. Don't forget that `lineTo` is the function that draws, and `moveTo` is more like picking up the pencil and setting it down at the position you indicate (in this case, the player).

Then, you cast 299 more rays for each execution of the draw loop, producing a new and improved minimap that looks something like Figure 8.3.

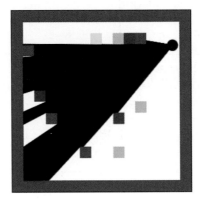

**Figure 8.3**  Casting rays in 2-D

You could stop here, add some shooting (and more geometry), and end up with a pool game or a game resembling the Atari tank shooter *Combat*, but with the next recipe, we'll aim a little higher and shoot for something closer to *Golden Eye* for the Nintendo 64.

# Recipe: Fake 3D with Raycasting

The last recipe set up most of what we need to make faking 3-D happen, but we still haven't rendered anything to the main canvas. Let's start by updating the draw and setup functions with the code in Listing 8.13.

**Listing 8.13**  Updating the draw and setup Functions

```
this.draw = function(){
  minimap.draw();
  player.draw();
  canvas.blank();
  raycaster.castRays();
};
```

```
this.setup = function() {
  minimap.init();
  player.init();
  raycaster.init();
  canvas.init();
};
```

There are two new function calls here. You have a canvas object, which will be initialized in the same way as your objects have been so far, which is why you call `canvas.init()` in the setup function. Remember that this function runs only once when the game begins. In your draw function, which loops many times per second, you call the `blank` function that will draw the ground and sky. We will be adding the canvas object in a minute, but first, we have a few updates to make to the raycaster. We will need to add the bolded lines in Listing 8.14.

**Listing 8.14** Updates to raycaster

```
var raycaster = {
  init: function(){
    this.castRays = function() {
...
      for (var i=0;i<numberOfRays;i++) {
...
        this.castRay(rayAngle, i); //replaces this.castRay(rayAngle);
      }
    }
    this.castRay = function(rayAngle, i){ //replaces this.castRay =
➥function(rayAngle);
...
      this.draw(xHit, yHit, distance, i, rayAngle); //replaces
➥this.draw(xHit, yHit);
    };
    // next line replaces this.draw = function(rayX, rayY){
    this.draw = function(rayX, rayY, distance, i, rayAngle){
...
      var adjustedDistance = Math.cos(rayAngle - player.angle) *
➥distance;
      var wallHalfHeight = canvas.height / adjustedDistance / 2;
      var wallTop = Math.max(0, canvas.halfHeight - wallHalfHeight);
      var wallBottom = Math.min(canvas.height, canvas.halfHeight +
➥wallHalfHeight);
      canvas.drawSliver(i, wallTop, wallBottom, "#000")
    }
  }
};
```

Because of our rendering needs, we have more data to pass around. In the first four bolded lines of this listing, we indicate that we will need the ray number, `i`, as well as the distance to the collision and the angle of the ray.

Next, in our `draw` function, we end up with a call to `canvas.drawSliver`. We will get to this in a minute, but for now, notice that the parameters we pass in are an x-axis position, `i`, the y-axis positions of the top and bottom of the wall, and a color, hardcoded to black. The preceding four bolded lines are how we determine these values.

We start by getting the `adjustedDistance` by multiplying the distance of the player to the collision by the cosine of the player's angle minus the direction of the ray. Remember that the `rayAngle` is taking the player angle into account already. By subtracting it, you can treat the angle independently, essentially the same as when the player angle is 0. The cosine of the resulting angle is the ratio of the distance of where the middle ray would collide with the wall divided by the distance along the ray where the collision actually occurs. By multiplying the cosine of the angle times `distance`, you get that somewhat hypothetical distance of where a collision would occur if the ray in question was in the middle of the player's field of vision.

The reason why you do this is so that you don't get a "fish-eye" effect as a result of wall sections to the side technically being farther away. The effect looks like the wall being taller in the center and shorter on the sides. How about a real-life example? If you look straight at a wall that is 20 feet away, do you get the feeling that the sections of the wall to the left and right are further away? Not really, right? That's what you achieve with this extra bit of trigonometry.

After we determine the adjusted distance, we use this to find what one-half of the height of the wall would be. With that value, we can figure out the position of the top and bottom of the wall. The min and max functions here ensure that we don't attempt to go beyond the dimensions of the canvas. The last thing to do with our raycaster is call the canvas's `drawSliver` function.

> ## tip
>
> After adding the canvas object, if you want to check out the fish-eye effect in action, just substitute this line
>
> ```
> var wallHalfHeight = canvas.height / adjustedDistance / 2;
> ```
>
> for this line
>
> ```
> var wallHalfHeight = canvas.height / distance / 2;
> ```

So far we have three calls to a canvas object that we have not actually created yet. To do so, let's add the code from Listing 8.15 above the main `draw` function, just below the end of the `minimap` object.

**Listing 8.15** Adding the canvas Object

```
var canvas = {
  init: function(){
    this.element = document.getElementById('canvas');
    this.context = this.element.getContext("2d");
    this.width = this.element.width;
    this.height = this.element.height;
    this.halfHeight = this.height/2;
    this.ground = '#DFD3C3';
    this.sky = '#418DFB';
    this.blank = function(){
      this.context.clearRect(0, 0, this.width, this.height);
      this.context.fillStyle = this.sky;
      this.context.fillRect(0, 0, this.width, this.halfHeight);
      this.context.fillStyle = this.ground;
      this.context.fillRect(0, this.halfHeight, this.width,
➡this.height);
    }
    this.drawSliver = function(sliver, wallTop, wallBottom, color){
      this.context.beginPath();
      this.context.strokeStyle = color;
      this.context.moveTo(sliver + .5, wallTop);
      this.context.lineTo(sliver + .5, wallBottom);
      this.context.closePath();
      this.context.stroke();
    }
  }
};
```

As with the other objects, we wrap the code inside with the `init` function. We get the canvas element, return the context, set a few variables related to its dimensions, and set color values to represent the sky (blue) and the ground (sand color).

Our `blank` function starts by clearing the canvas and then draws the sky and the ground. We call this in the draw loop before each execution of `castRays`, which calls `drawSliver` for each ray. We use typical canvas drawing functions in the `drawSliver` function. The only thing that might seem a bit out of place here is the .5 offset that we add to the x position of the line to draw. If you're wondering what this does, try deleting the "+ .5" and you will see the colors of the sky and ground bleeding through the walls.

With all that in place, you should finally be able to see from the player's point of view with something like Figure 8.4.

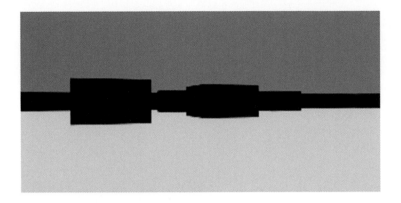

**Figure 8.4**  Raycasting!

# Recipe: Adding a Camera

Now that we have a raycaster, we have more options for what types of games we could make, most of those amounting to standard shooters. In this recipe, we'll dodge a bullet implementation and instead expose some features of canvas you might not know about yet. We'll be doing this by equipping the player with a camera, instead of a gun. This is not completely without precedent. For example, *Pokemon Snap* and *Pilot Wings* for Nintendo 64 both involve taking pictures.

First, let's address some changes that we need to make to our html file with Listing 8.16.

**Listing 8.16**  Camera Added to html File

```
...
<img id="camera" src="camera.png">
<div id="screenshot-wrapper"><canvas id="screenshot"></canvas></div>
```

```
<script type="text/javascript" src="jquery.js"></script>
<script type="text/javascript" src="filtrr2.js"></script>
<script type="text/javascript" src="jaws.js"></script>
<script type="text/javascript" src="game.js"></script>
<script>
  jaws.start(Game);
</script>
...
```

First, we add the image of the camera. Next, we add a new canvas tag that will show the pictures that we take with the camera, along with its wrapper. After that, we add the JavaScript library filtrr, as well as jQuery, which it depends on.

Next, you need to style your new elements by adding the styling in Listing 8.17 to game.css.

**Listing 8.17**   Styling the Camera Elements

```
#screenshot-wrapper{
  position:absolute;
  left:700px;
  border:1px solid black;
}
#camera{
  width:100px;
  position:absolute;
  left:505px;
  top:180px;
}
```

Nothing too surprising here. Next we'll update our game.js file, starting with the bold line changes to update and setup found in Listing 8.18.

**Listing 8.18**   Starting the Camera in game.js

```
this.setup = function() {
  camera.init();
...
};
this.update = function(){
...
  if(jaws.on_keyup(["up", "down"], function(){
      player.speed = 0;
  }));
  if(jaws.pressed("space")) {
    camera.takePicture();
```

```
  };
  player.move();
};
```

Just as with other objects, we run its `init` function in the `setup` function. In the `update` function, after the other key bindings, we add a call to run `camera.takePicture` when the spacebar is pressed.

The only thing left now is to add our `camera` object with the code in Listing 8.19. It can be placed just above the main `draw` function for the game.

**Listing 8.19**   The camera Object

```
var camera = {
  init: function(){
    this.context = document.getElementById('screenshot').
➥getContext('2d');
    var filtered = false;
    var f;
    $("#screenshot").on("click", function() {
      if(filtered){
        filtered = false;
        f.reset().render();
      } else{
        filtered = true;
        f = Filtrr2("#screenshot", function() {
          this.expose(50)
          .render();
        }, {store: false});
      };
    });
    this.takePicture = function(){
      var image = new Image();
      image.src = canvas.element.toDataURL('image/png');
      image.onload = function() {
        camera.context.drawImage(image,0,0);
      }
      filtered = false;
    }
  }
};
this.draw = function(){
```

Inside the `init` function, we start by setting the context of the canvas of the screenshot element. Next, we set variable `f` to hold the object we will use in the filtrr code to come, and set `filtered` to false because we haven't filtered anything yet. Next, we bind a click function to the screenshot element so that when it is clicked, it applies or removes a filter. In both branches of the if/else statement, you must call the render function on the object. The reset function before the render will remove the filter. The other branch applies an expose filter to the object, which makes it lighter.

> ## tip
>
> filtrr can be a bit tricky to set up and interface with, but after you do, you can apply a wide variety of filters to your images. Here are some examples of filters you could use instead of `this.expose(50)`:
>
> ```
> this.adjust(10, 25, 50)
> this.brighten(50)
> this.alpha(50)
> this.saturate(50)
> this.invert()
> this.posterize(10)
> this.gamma(50)
> this.contrast(50)
> this.sepia()
> this.subtract(10, 25, 50)
> this.fill(100, 25, 50)
> this.blur('simple')
> this.blur('gaussian')
> this.sharpen()
> ```

Lastly, we have a `takePicture` function that is called whenever the spacebar is pressed. In this function, we create a new image, set the source of the image to be a URI encoding of the main canvas element, and draw the image in the screenshot box after it loads. The details about encoding images and canvas elements as data URIs are beyond the scope of this recipe, but this is a handy technique to keep in mind. Some would suggest Googling for data uri to learn more. If you're enjoying the approach we've been taking with lightweight and scrappy tools so far, try http://duckduckgo.com instead. It's a hacker-friendly search engine with privacy in mind.

In addition to adding a HUD or a "heads-up display" camera, what we have done in this recipe is add the ability to take a picture of our canvas, save it to a data URI, display it in a canvas, and manipulate the image. See the results in Figure 8.5.

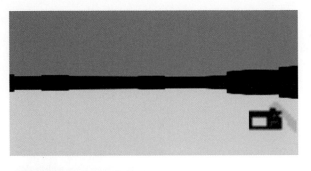
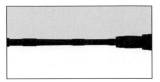
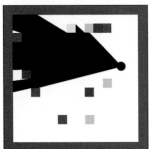

**Figure 8.5** A picture with the filter applied

Before leaving this recipe, you should make note of a couple of things. First, notice that you accidentally add a video camera feature if you hold down the spacebar while you move around. Second, you can use the `toDataURL` function in other ways than you have here. You could put snapshots in local storage or on a server to create a photo album. You could also call `window.open(canvas.element.toDataURL('image/png'));` to bring up the image in a new window. If you do this, the entire image will be encoded visibly in the URL bar, which means you can simply copy the URL and send it to someone to show a particular state of the canvas element. The last thing to notice is that your camera doesn't show up in the pictures. This is because the camera is a DOM element sitting on top of the canvas. It is not part of the canvas that is copied.

# Recipe: Making the World a More Photogenic Place

Your raycaster is shaping up nicely, and you even have a way to take pictures when you see things that you like in your virtual world. It could be a little more likeable though. You added different types of blocks with the intention of creating some difference between them. Right now they are all black.

To address that, we will introduce a new object (the `palette`) into the game. Let's start by initializing it in the setup function with the code in Listing 8.20.

**Listing 8.20**   setup Function with palette

```
this.setup = function() {
...
  palette.init();
};
```

Next, let's create our `palette` object with the code in Listing 8.21. This code can live under the `camera` object and above the `draw` function.

**Listing 8.21**   The palette Object

```
var palette = {
  init: function(){
    this.ground = '#DFD3C3';
    this.sky = '#418DFB';
    this.shades = 300;
    var initialWallColors = [[85, 68, 102],
                             [255, 53, 91],
                             [255, 201, 52],
                             [118, 204, 159]];
    this.walls = [];
    for(var i = 0; i < initialWallColors.length; i++){
      this.walls[i] = [];
      for(var j = 0; j < this.shades; j++){
        var red = Math.round(initialWallColors[i][0] * j /
➥this.shades);
        var green = Math.round(initialWallColors[i][1] * j /
➥this.shades);
        var blue =  Math.round(initialWallColors[i][2] * j /
➥this.shades);
        var color = "rgb("+red+","+green+","+blue+")";
        this.walls[i].push(color);
      };
    };
  }
}
```

We start by declaring the sky and ground colors that were previously in the `canvas` object. Now that we have an object specifically concerned with storing colors, it makes sense for them to be here. Look at Listing 8.22 to see what changes we need to make in the `canvas` object.

Back to Listing 8.21, the `shades` property refers to how many shades of color each of the walls will have. The `initialWallColors` describes what the lightest version of the color is. This is the color that we will show when we are the closest to the wall. Next, we set about populating the `walls` array with an array of shades for each wall type. The first in the array will be black, and the last will be the color prescribed by `initialWallColors`.

> **note**
>
> There are various ways to describe colors within JavaScript and CSS. Here, we opted for the rgb format because we can more easily manipulate the rgb values individually. It is also helpful that they are encoded in base 10 (decimal) rather than base 16 (hexadecimal) like the #ff23e9 type format is. There are ways to convert between them, but we saved a good bit of code by using this format.

**Listing 8.22**  Updates to the canvas Object

```
var canvas = {
  init: function(){
...
    //this.ground = '#DFD3C3'; // we can delete this line
    //this.sky = '#418DFB'; // this one too
    this.blank = function(){
      this.context.clearRect(0, 0, this.width, this.height);
      this.context.fillStyle = palette.sky;
       this.context.fillRect(0, 0, this.width, this.halfHeight);
      this.context.fillStyle = palette.ground;
      this.context.fillRect(0, this.halfHeight, this.width, this.
height);
    }
...
  }
};
```

Next, we need to make some adjustments to the `castRay` function of our `raycaster` object by adding the bolded code in Listing 8.23.

**Listing 8.23**  Adjustments to raycaster's castRay Function for Colored Walls

```
this.castRay = function(rayAngle, i){
...
  var wallType;
  while (x >= 0 && x < minimap.cellsAcross && y >= 0 && y <
➥minimap.cellsDown) {
```

```
...
    if (map[wallY][wallX] > -1) {
...
        wallType = map[wallY][wallX];
        break;
    }
...
  }
...
  while (x >= 0 && x < minimap.cellsAcross && y >= 0 && y <
➥minimap.cellsDown){
...
    if (map[wallY][wallX] > -1) {
...
        if (!distance || blockDistance < distance) {
...
            wallType = map[wallY][wallX];
        }
        break;
    }
...
  }
  this.draw(xHit, yHit, distance, i, rayAngle, wallType); // also
➥passing the wallType
};
```

The changes here are in order to pass the `raycaster.draw` function the `wallType` variable that describes which type of block the ray collided with. As the final piece of this recipe, let's look at how we use this in the draw function with the code in Listing 8.24.

**Listing 8.24** Drawing Colors and Shades

```
this.draw = function(rayX, rayY, distance, i, rayAngle, wallType){
  minimap.context.beginPath();
  minimap.context.moveTo(minimap.cellWidth*player.x,
➥minimap.cellHeight*player.y);
  minimap.context.lineTo(rayX * minimap.cellWidth, rayY *
➥minimap.cellHeight);
  minimap.context.closePath();
  minimap.context.stroke();
  var adjustedDistance = Math.cos(rayAngle - player.angle) * distance;
  var wallHalfHeight = canvas.height / adjustedDistance / 2;
  var wallTop = Math.max(0, canvas.halfHeight - wallHalfHeight);
  var wallBottom = Math.min(canvas.height, canvas.halfHeight +
➥wallHalfHeight);
```

```
    var percentageDistance = adjustedDistance /
➥Math.sqrt(minimap.cellsAcross * minimap.cellsAcross +
➥minimap.cellsDown * minimap.cellsDown);
    var brightness = 1 - percentageDistance;
    var shade = Math.floor(palette.shades * brightness);
    var color = palette.walls[wallType][shade];
    canvas.drawSliver(i, wallTop, wallBottom, color)
  }
```

On the first line, notice that we now need the extra `wallType` parameter to be passed into the function. Use this as our first index of the multidimensional `palette.walls` array. To get the shade, we do something a bit more complicated. We use the Pythagorean theorem to determine the maximum distance a ray can travel (from one corner of the screen to the corner diagonal). We divide the `adjustedDistance` by this in order to determine the proportion of how much of the screen the ray is going through before hitting a wall, compared to how much distance it could cover.

## note

The Pythagorean theorem says that for a right triangle (one with a 90-degree angle), the length of the hypotenuse is equal to the square root of the sum of the square of each remaining side. The equation looks like this:

h = Math.sqrt(sideOne * sideOne + sideTwo * sideTwo);

This percentage has an inverse relationship with `brightness`, so when the distance of the ray shortens, the `brightness` approaches 1 (100%). We get the `shade` by multiplying this `brightness` by the number of shades that are possible, and rounding down. We then look up the color in the `palette.walls` table that we created earlier. Lastly, we pass this color into our canvas object, and it behaves completely as expected. If everything went according to plan, you should see something like Figure 8.6.

## tip

Creating the lookup table ahead of time is the type of optimization that you should consider if you're worried about doing too many calculations and slowing down your draw loop. If there are things that can be known ahead of time, it can be good to figure it out once rather than doing so in a recurring loop.

Also keep in mind that what might be an optimization in one browser, could be a detriment in another. Test your target browsers.

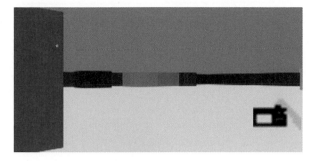

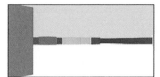

**Figure 8.6** Shading and color!

# Recipe: Adding a Friend or Foe

Right now your character is all alone, just moving around a big square and taking pictures. Add the dinosaur from Chapter 3, "Party," to keep her company.

We'll start off with a slight change to the inline script of our html file found in Listing 8.25 to preload the dino asset.

**Listing 8.25** Preloading the Dino Asset

```
...
<script>
  jaws.assets.add(["dino.png"])
  jaws.start(Game);
</script>
...
```

As you may have expected, next, we'll have to initialize our `dino` object in the `setup` function with the code in Listing 8.26.

**Listing 8.26**  Initializing the Dino

```
this.setup = function() {
...
  dino.init();
};
```

Before we get to our dino object, there are a few updates to make elsewhere. First, let's prepare the `raycaster` object to support the dino with the code in Listing 8.27.

**Listing 8.27**  Updates to raycaster

```
var twoPi = Math.PI * 2;
var raycaster = {
  init: function(){
    this.maxDistance = Math.sqrt(minimap.cellsAcross *
➥minimap.cellsAcross + minimap.cellsDown * minimap.cellsDown);
    var numberOfRays = 300;
    var angleBetweenRays = .2 * Math.PI /180;
    this.castRays = function() {
      foregroundSlivers = [];
      backgroundSlivers = [];
      minimap.rays = [];
      dino.show = false;
      for (var i=0;i<numberOfRays;i++) {
        var rayNumber = -numberOfRays/2 + i;
        var rayAngle = angleBetweenRays * rayNumber + player.angle;
        this.castRay(rayAngle, i);
      }
    }
    this.castRay = function(rayAngle, i){
    rayAngle %= twoPi;
    if (rayAngle < 0) rayAngle += twoPi;
      var right = (rayAngle > twoPi * 0.75 || rayAngle < twoPi * 0.25);
      var up = rayAngle > Math.PI;
      var slope = Math.tan(rayAngle);
      var distance = 0;
      var xHit = 0;
      var yHit = 0;
      var wallX;
      var wallY;
      var dX = right ? 1 : -1;
      var dY = dX * slope;
      var x = right ? Math.ceil(player.x) : Math.floor(player.x);
      var y = player.y + (x - player.x) * slope;
      var wallType;
```

```
        while (x >= 0 && x < minimap.cellsAcross && y >= 0 && y <
➥minimap.cellsDown) {
        wallX = Math.floor(x + (right ? 0 : -1));
        wallY = Math.floor(y);
        if (map[wallY][wallX] > -1) {
          var distanceX = x - player.x;
          var distanceY = y - player.y;
          distance = Math.sqrt(distanceX*distanceX +
➥distanceY*distanceY);
          xHit = x;
          yHit = y;
          wallType = map[wallY][wallX];
          break;
        } else{
          if(dino.x === wallX && dino.y === wallY){
            dino.show = true;
          };
        };
        x += dX;
        y += dY;
      }
      slope = 1/slope;
      dY = up ? -1 : 1;
      dX = dY * slope;
      y = up ? Math.floor(player.y) : Math.ceil(player.y);
      x = player.x + (y - player.y) * slope;
      while (x >= 0 && x < minimap.cellsAcross && y >= 0 && y <
➥minimap.cellsDown) {
        wallY = Math.floor(y + (up ? -1 : 0));
        wallX - Math.floor(x);
        if (map[wallY][wallX] > -1) {
          var distanceX = x - player.x;
          var distanceY = y - player.y;
          var blockDistance = Math.sqrt(distanceX*distanceX +
➥distanceY*distanceY);
          if (!distance || blockDistance < distance) {
            distance = blockDistance;
            xHit = x;
            yHit = y;
            wallType = map[wallY][wallX];
          }
          break;
        }else{
          if(dino.x === wallX && dino.y === wallY){
            dino.show = true;
          };
        };
```

```
        x += dX;
        y += dY;
      }
      if(dino.show === true){
        var dinoDistanceX = dino.x + .5 - player.x;
        var dinoDistanceY = dino.y + .5 - player.y;
        dino.angle = Math.atan(dinoDistanceY/dinoDistanceX) -
➥player.angle;
        dino.distance = Math.sqrt(dinoDistanceX*dinoDistanceX +
➥dinoDistanceY * dinoDistanceY);
      };
      minimap.rays.push([xHit, yHit]);
      var adjustedDistance = Math.cos(rayAngle - player.angle) *
➥distance;
      var wallHalfHeight = canvas.height / adjustedDistance / 2;
      var wallTop = Math.max(0, canvas.halfHeight - wallHalfHeight);
      var wallBottom = Math.min(canvas.height, canvas.halfHeight +
wallHalfHeight);
      var percentageDistance = adjustedDistance / this.maxDistance;
      var brightness = 1 - percentageDistance;
      var shade = Math.floor(palette.shades * brightness);
      var color = palette.walls[wallType][shade];
      if(adjustedDistance < dino.distance){
        foregroundSlivers.push([i, wallTop, wallBottom, color]);
      }else{
        backgroundSlivers.push([i, wallTop, wallBottom, color]);
      };
    }
  }
};
```

Because we will be making use of it later, we can move the twoPi variable out of the raycaster.

As for the raycaster, enough has changed here that the entire object has been listed. Let's go through each bold section to note the additions. First, we have introduced a maxDistance variable to describe the maximum distance that a player could view the map (corner-to-corner diagonally).

On each call to castRays, we initialize three new arrays to keep track what we will render. As you will see later, we now rely on our raycaster only to describe what will be rendered, rather than calling draw functions directly. We also set the dino.show property to false so that the dino won't render unless we want it to.

We have a new check for the dino in each of the casts along the x-axis and y-axis. If we find the dino there, we set the show property to true.

In the next bolded section, for each ray that is cast, check to see if we intend to show the dino. If we do, we first calculate the x and y distances by adding .5 to each (in order to set the dino in the middle of the block), and subtracting the x and y values of the player object. Then we use the `Math.atan` (arctan) function to get the angle from the ratio of the opposite over the adjacent sides of the triangle. The arctan function is the inverse of the tan function, whereas with the tan function, you get the proportion of the sides by applying the function to the angle; here you do the opposite. Similarly to the player distances, subtract the player angle to gain context of the relationship between dino and player, rather than an absolute angle. To get the straight-line distance from the player to the dino, rely on the Pythagorean theorem (hypotenuse squared equals sideA squared + sideB squared) again.

Next, we push an array of the x and y coordinates describing the ray collision points onto `minimap`'s `ray` array. It is here that we would have called the `draw` function before. The call and the function declaration have both been removed. Since we are now populating arrays rather than drawing, it makes sense just to eliminate the barrier here.

Notice that we have removed calls to render rays on the `minimap`. We will handle those with the array we created to store the rays. Also, our `percentageDistance` variable is now updated to make use of the `maxDistance` property that we set earlier.

The last change in this function is that instead of calling `canvas.drawSliver` directly, we have added a check to see if the wall found in the sliver to be rendered is closer or further away from the player than the dino. If it is close, we add it to the `foregroundSlivers` array. If it is further, we add it to the `backgroundSlivers` array. Remember that these are cleared out with each new call to `castRays`.

Now, our `raycaster` is only responsible for generating what to render. This frees us from the obligation of running it in the draw loop. Alter the `update` function with the code in Listing 8.28 to call `castRays` there.

Listing 8.28   Call castRays from the update Function

```
this.update = function(){
  raycaster.castRays();
  ...
};
```

Our `draw` function has lost the responsibility of running `castRays`, but now we must loop through the arrays we created to actually render the blocks and the dino. Add the bolded code in Listing 8.29 to the main draw function.

**Listing 8.29**  Updates to the main draw Function

```
this.draw = function(){
  minimap.draw();
  player.draw();
  canvas.blank();
  for(var i = 0; i < backgroundSlivers.length; i++){
    canvas.drawSliver.apply(canvas, backgroundSlivers[i]);
  };
  if (dino.show){
    dino.draw();
  };
  for(var i = 0; i < foregroundSlivers.length; i++){
    canvas.drawSliver.apply(canvas, foregroundSlivers[i]);
  };
};
```

Here, we are doing three new things, and the order is important. First, we render each background sliver. Next, we render the dino on top of the background. Lastly, we render the blocks that are in front of the dino. Note the use of the `apply` function that calls the function `drawSliver` with the context of `this` (here it is `canvas`) as the first parameter, and an array of arguments as the second parameter.

We will get to the `dino` object soon. First, let's address the changes we need to make to the `draw` function of `minimap` with the code in Listing 8.30.

**Listing 8.30**  Updates to the minimap draw Function

```
var minimap = {
  init: function(){
...
    this.draw = function(){
...
      for(var i = 0; i < this.rays.length; i++){
        this.drawRay(this.rays[i][0], this.rays[i][1])
      }
    };
    this.drawRay = function(xHit, yHit){
      this.context.beginPath();
      this.context.moveTo(this.cellWidth*player.x,
➥this.cellHeight*player.y);
      this.context.lineTo(xHit * this.cellWidth, yHit *
➥this.cellHeight);
```

```
      this.context.closePath();
      this.context.stroke();
    };
  }
};
```

Most of the code in `minimap` has remained the same. The difference is that now we loop through our `rays` array, passing alone the `xHit` and `yHit` variables to the `drawRay` function, which behaves as it did before. Everything in the `drawRay` function is a direct copy from what previously lived inside of the `raycaster`'s `draw` function with some new variable names.

Finally, let's add the `dino` object above the draw function and below the `palette` object with the code in Listing 8.31.

### Listing 8.31   The dino Object

```
var dino = {
  init: function(){
    this.sprite = new jaws.Sprite({image: "dino.png", x: 0, y:
➥canvas.height/2, anchor: "center"});
    this.x = 12;
    this.y = 4;
    this.show = false;
    this.distance - 10000;
    this.draw = function(){
      this.scale = raycaster.maxDistance / dino.distance / 2;
      this.sprite.scaleTo(this.scale);
      this.angle %= twoPi;
      if (this.angle < 0) this.angle += twoPi;
      this.angleInDegrees = this.angle * 180 / Math.PI;
      var potentialWidth = 300*.2;
      var halfAngularWidth = potentialWidth/2;
      this.adjustedAngle = this.angleInDegrees + halfAngularWidth;
      if(this.adjustedAngle > 180 || this.adjustedAngle < -180){
        this.adjustedAngle %= 180;
      };
      this.sprite.x = this.adjustedAngle/potentialWidth*canvas.width;
      this.sprite.draw();
    };
  }
};
```

We start by creating the jaws sprite as a property of `dino`. When we show the dino, the sprite's x property is our main concern. Anchoring the sprite in the center, and setting the y property to be one-half of the canvas height, will ensure that the dino will be centered along the y-axis.

Next, we set an x and a y property to describe where the dino will appear, considered from a block level. So for our map, that means ranges from 0-15. Don't confuse these with the sprite's x and y attributes, which instead describe where on the canvas to show the sprite. Next we set the show property to false so that the dino is not immediately visible. The distance property is set to a high value initially so that the walls will render from the foregroundSlivers until the dino shows up.

The dino.draw function starts by setting the scale of the sprite to be the maximum distance possible (corner-to-corner of the map) divided by the distance between the player and the dino. It is important to divide by dino.distance so that the dino gets larger as the player gets closer. The 2 is fairly arbitrary but seems to work out well for making the dino look like he is in the cell he is assigned to. Next, we take advantage of the jaws scaleTo function to change the size of the dino. Next, we ensure that the angle is within a positive range and not too large.

Then, we convert the angle to degrees, and assign it to angleInDegrees. We do this because the width of the sliver that we have been using is .2 degrees. We multiply this by 300, our number of rays, to get 60, the "field of vision" of the player. We set this as the potentialWidth, and divide it by 2 to get the degree measurement of one-half of the canvas (halfAngularWidth). This is added to angleInDegrees to make up the adjustedAngle. This describes, along a range from 0 to 60, where our sprite should appear. We make sure that the adjustedAngle is in an appropriate range, and then divide by potentialWidth (60), and multiply by canvas.width (300). The sprite is set to this value between 0 and 300 as the point along the x axis.

Finally, we use Jaws's sprite.draw function to render the sprite. You should now be able to take pictures of the dino as well as the colorful walls. Just for fun, let's change the filter on our camera to the sepia with the code in Listing 8.32.

**Listing 8.32**  Sepia Filter

```
var camera = {
...
//replace this
//this.expose(50)
//with this
  this.sepia()
  .render();
...
}
```

Now, as in Figure 8.7, you can finally take an old-timey photograph of a dinosaur!

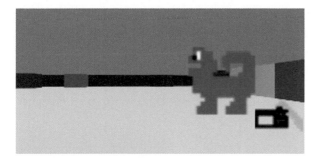

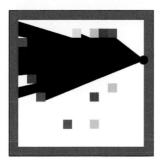

**Figure 8.7** Old-timey dino photo

# Summary

You may have started this chapter without a working knowledge of raycasters or geometry in general, or perhaps the canvas manipulations and dataUri saving and loading were unfamiliar. In the worst case that you were familiar with all these techniques, you now have a basic engine to build games in various genres, including first-person shooters, rail shooters (where you travel along a specified path), survival/horror, racing games, and exploration games such as *Myst*.

Mainly, we used the game looping, input handling, and sprite management capabilities of Jaws, but if you were interested in using it in other contexts, it has other strong features as well. It has support for parallax scrolling, tile maps, and viewports (viewing a portion of a canvas/following a player around) that could come in handy.

As for where to go next with this game, you have many options. If you're focused on missing features, implementing crouching, jumping, and lateral movement could be interesting to attempt. Adding textured, rather than colored, walls could fun, too. If you like taking pictures of prehistoric things, you could add a few wooly mammoths and create a zoo. In a sufficiently large map, playing *Hide and Seek* with virtual critters could be fairly entertaining. You could add a timer, along with a randomly generated map, and critter spawn points if you wanted to create a challenge. Or you could build specific levels. You could also redirect the browser from the interactive fiction game in Chapter 2 to come to this game when you flip the time machine switch.

Naturally, you could take the FPS concept to its logical conclusion, add health, powerups, weapons, and have enemies chase you and throw stuff at you. You could throw stuff at them, too. That said, *Minecraft* and *Myst* both could have ended up as *Doom* clones. Don't be afraid to explore other possibilities.

# CHAPTER 9

# RPG

Engagement in playing a game comes from two possible places: content exploration and challenge. Consider *World of Warcraft* versus *Pong*. In *WoW*, new content is continuously created behind the scenes. *Pong* is all about competing against the computer or a friend. Even challenging modern games tend to have more content exploration mixed into gameplay, and for managing this exploration, no genre is more influential than RPGs. The content density of the NES's *Dragon Warrior* demanded content management interfaces for dialog, shopping, inventory, and battling. The time required to explore these worlds pushed for the convenience of battery-backed saving rather than a clunky password system. Every content-heavy game is borrowing from the tradition of RPGs.

# Recipe: Getting Started with enchant.js

The distinction between subclassifications of action RPGs and turn-based RPGs has faded over time, but in the early days of video game RPGs, there was a pronounced difference between the two. In action RPGs, the combat takes place on the same screen as the exploration of the world. This distinguishes a game such as *The Legend of Zelda* from a turn-based (aka menu-based) RPG such as *Final Fantasy* or *Dragon Warrior*. We explored what would be necessary for an action RPG (collision detection) in other chapters, so in this chapter, we'll be building a system for menu-based combat as well as an inventory, a shopping interface, a leveling system, and a way to save the game.

To get started, let's add the index.html file with the code in Listing 9.1.

**Listing 9.1**   The index.html File

```html
<!DOCTYPE html>
<html>
  <head>
    <meta charset="utf-8">
    <title>RPG</title>
    <script type="text/javascript" src="enchant.js"></script>
    <script type="text/javascript" src="game.js"></script>
    <link rel="stylesheet" type="text/css" href="game.css">
  </head>
  <body>
  </body>
</html>
```

Most of this should look familiar. We load the JavaScript files and the style sheet, as well as setting the title. The fourth line may stand out to you as new. Here, we are setting the encoding of the page. Most of the time, leaving this out (as we have in other recipes) won't cause any problems other than giving you a warning.

Next, let's start a game.css file with the code in Listing 9.2.

**Listing 9.2**   game.css

```css
body {
  margin: 0;
}
```

The last thing that you need to do for this recipe is get your JavaScript stub file for game.js with the code in Listing 9.3.

**Listing 9.3**  game.js Stub

```
enchant();
window.onload = function(){
  var game = new Game(300, 300);
  game.fps = 15;
  game.onload = function(){
    alert("hello");
  };
  game.start();
};
```

The first line makes your core enchant.js classes such as `Game` available. The `window.onload` block executes after the window is loaded. This is so that the `body` element has a chance to load, which is important because creating a new `Game` object amounts to generating two nested `div` tags under `body`. We pass the height and width of the games as parameters to the `Game` constructor. Next, we set the frames per second (fps) of the game. The body of the `game.onload` function is run when we execute the `game.start` function. If you load index.html into a browser, you see the "hello" pop-up in an alert box.

> ## note
>
> There are a couple of features to note about enchant.js. First, if you forgot to wrap the game creation in `window.onload`, in the browser console, enchant.js will give you an error message letting you know what you did wrong. This reflects a robustness with this engine that is not as common as it should be.
>
> The second thing about enchant, although it is as of yet not completely perceivable, is that the engine relies on creating multiple `canvas` objects and other DOM elements to make up a game. We have yet to see an approach that is mixed to this degree.

With that out of the way, let's look into creating the map with the next recipe.

# Recipe: Creating a Map

The map (a big two-dimensional array) amounts to quite a few lines of code, so let's get it live in its own JavaScript file. We need to add the bold line in Listing 9.4 to index.html.

### Listing 9.4  Loading the Map File

```
<script type="text/javascript" src="enchant.js"></script>
<script type="text/javascript" src="map.js"></script>
<script type="text/javascript" src="game.js"></script>
<link rel="stylesheet" type="text/css" href="game.css">
```

Next, we need to make a map.js file to hold the two-dimensional arrays of the background and foreground maps. You can use the code in Listing 9.5 for this.

### Listing 9.5  map.js

```
var mapData = [[1, 1, 1, 1, 1, 1, 1, 1, 1, 1, 1, 1, 1, 1, 1, 1, 1,
1, 1, 1, 1, 1, 1, 1, 1],
    [1, 1, 1, 1, 1, 1, 1, 1, 1, 1, 1, 1, 1, 1, 1, 1, 1, 1, 1, 1, 1,
1, 1, 1, 1],
    [1, 1, 1, 1, 1, 1, 1, 1, 1, 1, 1, 1, 1, 1, 1, 1, 1, 1, 1, 1, 1,
1, 1, 1, 1],
    [1, 1, 1, 1, 1, 1, 1, 1, 1, 1, 1, 1, 1, 1, 1, 1, 1, 1, 1, 1, 1,
1, 1, 1, 1],
    [1, 1, 1, 1, 1, 1, 1, 1, 1, 1, 1, 1, 1, 1, 1, 1, 1, 1, 1, 1, 1,
1, 1, 1, 1],
    [1, 1, 1, 1, 1, 1, 1, 1, 1, 1, 1, 1, 1, 1, 1, 1, 1, 1, 1, 1, 1,
1, 1, 1, 1],
    [1, 1, 1, 1, 1, 1, 1, 1, 1, 1, 1, 1, 1, 1, 1, 1, 1, 1, 1, 1, 1,
1, 1, 1, 1],
    [1, 1, 1, 1, 1, 1, 1, 1, 1, 1, 1, 1, 1, 1, 1, 1, 1, 1, 1, 1, 1,
1, 1, 1, 1],
    [1, 1, 1, 1, 1, 1, 1, 1, 1, 1, 1, 1, 1, 1, 1, 1, 1, 1, 1, 1, 1,
1, 1, 1, 1],
    [1, 1, 1, 1, 1, 1, 1, 1, 1, 1, 1, 1, 1, 1, 1, 1, 1, 1, 1, 1, 1,
1, 1, 1, 1],
    [1, 1, 1, 1, 1, 1, 1, 1, 1, 1, 1, 1, 1, 1, 1, 1, 1, 1, 1, 1, 1,
1, 1, 1, 1],
    [1, 1, 1, 1, 1, 1, 1, 1, 1, 1, 1, 1, 1, 1, 1, 1, 1, 1, 1, 1, 1,
1, 1, 1, 1],
    [1, 1, 1, 1, 1, 1, 1, 1, 1, 1, 1, 1, 1, 1, 1, 1, 1, 1, 1, 1, 1,
1, 1, 1, 1],
    [1, 1, 1, 1, 1, 1, 1, 1, 1, 1, 1, 1, 1, 1, 1, 1, 1, 1, 1, 1, 1,
1, 1, 1, 1],
    [1, 1, 1, 1, 1, 1, 1, 1, 1, 1, 1, 1, 1, 1, 1, 1, 1, 1, 1, 1, 1,
1, 1, 1, 1],
    [1, 1, 1, 1, 1, 1, 1, 1, 1, 1, 1, 1, 1, 1, 1, 1, 1, 1, 1, 1, 1,
1, 1, 1, 1],
    [1, 1, 1, 1, 1, 1, 1, 1, 1, 1, 1, 1, 1, 1, 1, 1, 1, 1, 1, 1, 1,
1, 1, 1, 1],
```

```
    [1, 1, 1, 1, 1, 1, 1, 1, 1, 1, 1, 1, 1, 1, 1, 1, 1, 1, 1, 1, 1, 1,
1, 1, 1, 1],
    [0, 0, 0, 0, 0, 0, 0, 0, 0, 0, 0, 0, 0, 0, 0, 0, 0, 0, 0, 0, 0,
0, 0, 0, 0]];

var foregroundData = [[-1,-1, -1, -1, -1, -1, -1, -1, -1, -1, -1, -1,
3, 3, 3, 3, -1, -1, -1, -1, -1, -1, -1, -1, -1, -1],
    [3,   3, -1, -1, -1, -1, -1, -1, -1, -1, -1, -1,  3, 3, 3, 3, -1, -1,
-1, -1, -1, -1, -1, -1,  -1, -1],
    [-1, 3, -1, -1, -1, -1, -1, -1, -1, -1, -1, -1,  3, 3, 3, 3, -1, -1,
-1, -1, -1, -1, -1, -1, -1, -1],
    [3, -1, -1,  3,  3,   3, -1, -1, -1, -1, -1, -1,  3,  3,  3,  3,  3,
3,  3,  3,  3,  3,  3,  3, 13],
    [-1,-1, -1,  3,  -1,  3, -1, -1, -1,  3, -1, -1, 3, 3, 3, 3, -1, -1,
-1, -1, -1, -1, -1, -1,  3, 13],
    [-1,-1, -1, -1, -1, -1, -1, -1, -1, -1, -1, -1, 3, 3, 3, 3, -1, -1,
-1, -1, -1, -1, -1, -1,  3, 13],
    [-1,-1, -1, -1, -1, -1, -1, -1, -1, -1, -1, -1, 3, 3, 3, 3, -1, -1,
-1, -1, -1, -1, -1, -1,  3, 13],
    [-1,-1, -1, -1, -1, -1, -1, -1, -1, -1, -1, -1, 3, 3, 3, 3, -1, -1,
-1, -1, -1, -1, -1, -1,  3, 13],
    [-1,-1, -1, -1, -1, -1, -1, -1, -1, -1, -1, -1, 3, 3, 3, 3, -1, -1,
-1, -1, -1, -1, -1, -1,  3, 13],
    [-1,-1, -1, -1, -1, -1, -1, -1, -1, -1, -1, -1, 3, 3, 3, 3, -1, -1,
-1, -1, -1, -1, -1, -1,  3, 13],
    [-1,-1, -1, -1, -1, -1, -1, -1, -1, -1, -1, -1, 3, 3, 3, 3, -1, -1,
-1, -1, -1, -1, -1, -1,  3, 13],
    [-1,-1, -1,  3, -1, -1, -1, -1, -1, -1, -1, -1, 3, 3, 3, 3, -1, -1,
-1, -1, -1, -1, -1, -1,  3, 13],
    [-1,-1, -1, -1, -1, -1, -1, -1, -1, -1, -1, -1, 3, 3, 3, 3, -1, -1,
-1, -1, -1, -1, -1, -1,  3, 13],
    [-1,-1, -1, -1, -1,  -1,  1,  1,  1,  1, -1, -1, 3, 3, 3, 3, -1, -1,
-1, -1, -1, -1, -1, -1,  3, 13],
    [-1,-1, -1, -1, -1, -1, -1, -1, -1, -1, -1, -1, 3, 3, 3, 3, -1, -1,
-1, -1, -1, -1, -1, -1,  3, 13],
    [-1,-1, -1, -1, -1, -1, -1, -1, -1, -1, -1, -1, 3, 3, 3, 3, -1, -1,
-1, -1, -1, -1, -1, -1,  3, 13],
    [-1,-1, -1, -1, -1, -1, -1, -1, -1, -1, -1, -1, 3, 3, 3, 3, -1, -1,
-1, -1, -1, -1, -1, -1,  3, 13],
    [-1,-1, -1, -1, -1, -1, -1, -1, -1, -1, -1, -1, 3, 3, 3, 3, -1, -1,
-1, -1, -1, -1, -1, -1,  3, 13],
    [14,14, 14, 14, 14, 14, 14, 14, 14, 14, 14, 14, 14, 14, 14, 14, 14,
14, 14, 14, 14, 14, 14, 14, 14, 14]];
```

Here, we have created the variables mapData and foregroundData. To load the maps with this data, let's head back to our game.js file and add the bolded lines in Listing 9.6.

**Listing 9.6**  Loading the Map

```
enchant();
window.onload = function(){
  var game = new Game(300, 300);
  game.fps = 15;
  game.spriteWidth = 16;
  game.spriteHeight = 16;
  game.preload('sprites.png');
  var map = new Map(game.spriteWidth, game.spriteHeight);
  var foregroundMap = new Map(game.spriteWidth, game.spriteHeight);
  var setMaps = function(){
    map.image = game.assets['sprites.png'];
    map.loadData(mapData);
    foregroundMap.image = game.assets['sprites.png'];
    foregroundMap.loadData(foregroundData);
  };
  var setStage = function(){
    var stage = new Group();
    stage.addChild(map);
    stage.addChild(foregroundMap);
    game.rootScene.addChild(stage);
  };
  game.onload = function(){
    setMaps();
    setStage();
  };
  game.start();
};
```

First, we define new attributes on `game` for the sprite dimensions. Next, we preload the sprites image file. Then we create a map and a foreground map object with the given sprite width and height. We declare two functions, which are called in the `game.onload` function. The first, `setMaps`, assigns the image file used for each map to be sprites.png and loads the corresponding data from map.js. The `setStage` function creates a new enchant.js object, `stage`, of type `Group` that contains everything for this "scene." We use the `addChild` function to add the maps to the stage. Finally, we add the `stage` to the `rootScene` of the game, which for our purposes will be the aerial view of the map. If we had a title screen, this could be the `rootScene` instead. Later, we will create the scenes for battling and shopping as well.

You may wonder what these objects represent in terms of DOM and canvas elements. If you inspect the DOM now, you will see two new divs, each with a nested canvas element. Each of these corresponds with one of our map objects, but the `stage` object merely represents an in-memory collection of elements that are not reflected by the DOM.

With the code from Listing 9.6 in place, after opening index.html in the browser, you should see something like Figure 9.1.

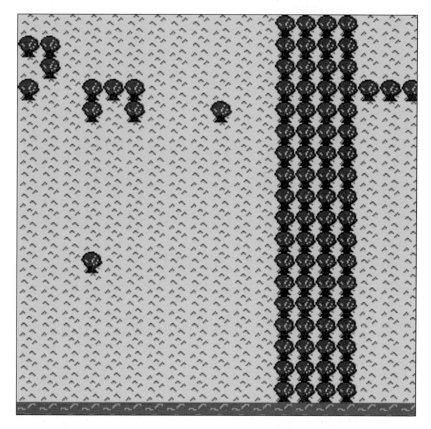

**Figure 9.1** Foreground and background maps loaded

Notice that the transparent portions of the trees allow the grass to show through underneath.

# Recipe: Adding the Player

Now that we have the map laid out, we can add a player object to move around in it. The result of this is a new div absolutely positioned on the screen. Let's look at an updated version of game.js in Listing 9.7 to see what we need.

**Listing 9.7** game.js Updated with Player Movement

```
enchant();
window.onload = function(){
  var game = new Game(300, 300);
  game.spriteSheetWidth = 256;
  game.spriteSheetHeight = 16;
...
  var setStage = function(){
    var stage = new Group();
    stage.addChild(map);
    stage.addChild(player);
    stage.addChild(foregroundMap);
    game.rootScene.addChild(stage);
  };
  var player = new Sprite(game.spriteWidth, game.spriteHeight);
  var setPlayer = function(){
    player.spriteOffset = 5;
    player.startingX = 6;
    player.startingY = 14;
    player.x = player.startingX * game.spriteWidth;
    player.y = player.startingY * game.spriteHeight;
    player.direction = 0;
    player.walk = 0;
    player.frame = player.spriteOffset + player.direction;
    player.image = new Surface(game.spriteSheetWidth,
➥game.spriteSheetHeight);
    player.image.draw(game.assets['sprites.png']);
  };
  player.move = function(){
    this.frame = this.spriteOffset + this.direction * 2 + this.walk;
    if (this.isMoving) {
      this.moveBy(this.xMovement, this.yMovement);
      if (!(game.frame % 2)) {
        this.walk++;
        this.walk %= 2;
      }
      if ((this.xMovement && this.x % 16 === 0) || (this.yMovement &&
➥this.y % 16 === 0)) {
        this.isMoving = false;
        this.walk = 1;
      }
    } else {
      this.xMovement = 0;
      this.yMovement = 0;
      if (game.input.up) {
        this.direction = 1;
        this.yMovement = -4;
```

```
            } else if (game.input.right) {
                this.direction = 2;
                this.xMovement = 4;
            } else if (game.input.left) {
                this.direction = 3;
                this.xMovement = -4;
            } else if (game.input.down) {
                this.direction = 0;
                this.yMovement = 4;
            }
            if (this.xMovement || this.yMovement) {
                var x = this.x + (this.xMovement ? this.xMovement /
➡Math.abs(this.xMovement) * 16 : 0);
                var y = this.y + (this.yMovement ? this.yMovement /
➡Math.abs(this.yMovement) * 16 : 0);
                if (0 <= x && x < map.width && 0 <= y && y < map.height) {
                    this.isMoving = true;
                    this.move();
                }
            }
        }
    };
    game.focusViewport = function(){
        var x = Math.min((game.width - 16) / 2 - player.x, 0);
        var y = Math.min((game.height - 16) / 2 - player.y, 0);
        x = Math.max(game.width,  x + map.width)  - map.width;
        y = Math.max(game.height, y + map.height) - map.height;
        game.rootScene.firstChild.x = x;
        game.rootScene.firstChild.y = y;
    };
    game.onload = function(){
        setMaps();
        setPlayer();
        setStage();
        player.on('enterframe', function() {
            player.move();
        });
        game.rootScene.on('enterframe', function(e) {
            game.focusViewport();
        });
    };
    game.start();
};
```

Going through the bold lines, first, we set the dimensions of the spritesheet because we need these later when we declare the surface of the player. Then, in the setStage function, we now need to add the `player` (remember that this ends up as a div) to the `stage`. We declare `player` as a new sprite with 16-by-16 pixels.

Next we have three player-related functions. Let's jump down to the bottom of the listing (inside of the `game.onload` function) to see how they are called. First, `setPlayer` assigns properties to `player`. `spriteOffset` stores the position where the player sprites start occurring in the spritesheet. (If you open the png file by itself, you can notice that they are not all the way to the left.) `startingX` and `startingY` describe the map cell where the player should start. These are multiplied by 16 (the sprite width). `direction` is a numerical representation of where the player is facing. `walk` is either a 0 or 1 depending on where the `player` is in the process of moving from square to square. The frame is the individual sprite that we want to render, which starts as the `spriteOffset` plus the `direction`. The last thing to do in the `setPlayer` function is to create a new Surface, assign it to `player.image`, and then draw it in the context of the sprites described in the draw function. The `frame` property determines which sprite is drawn.

> ## tip
>
> We've declared some new properties for our player, so it may be hard to keep track of which properties and functions belong to enchant.js (frame and image), which belong to us (everything else), and which belong to native JavaScript (for example, length).
>
> To help keep track, you should keep the documentation for enchant.js handy (http://wise9.github.com/enchant.js/doc/core/en/index.html). The Mozilla Developer Network documentation is a great resource for seeing what is native JavaScript. As for keeping track of your own properties, leaving comments in the code or creating new objects to encapsulate custom properties is your best bet.

Next, we see the `player.move` function called from `player.on("enterframe")`. This is called every time a new frame of player is processed. You can think of it as an update loop just for this object. The `player.move` function makes use of a few attributes, but conceptually, the most important things it does is determine the frame and position of the player.

Let's start from the top of the declaration of `player.move`. In determining the frame, the reason why `direction` is multiplied by 2 is that there are two frames per direction. `walk` is just a 0 or 1 to flip from sprite to sprite. We check to see if the player `isMoving`. Let's follow the else case because it will occur first (`isMoving` is `undefined`).

First, `xMovement` and `yMovement` are initialized to 0. Then, we check to see if we have any input, and set the direction and intended x or y movement. These are more like velocities, so if you change the values, you see the player move more quickly or slowly. Next, if there is some intended motion, the variable x or y will be set to the current player position plus the width of the sprite (16 for positive values, 0 for 0, and –16 for negative values). The last conditional here determines whether the intended motion is within the bounds of the map. If it is, `isMoving` is set to `true`, and we recursively call this function `move` again.

Now, we once again update the frame of the sprite. `ifMoving` is true, so we call the enchant.js function `moveBy` to move the sprite by `xMovement` and `yMovement`. If the frame is even, then we set `walk` to be 0. The next conditional statement checks to see if we are in the exact center of a square and there is some intended motion. If this is the case, then we set `walk` to 1, but more important, we set `isMoving` to false. The next time this function executes, which will be a result of a sprite refresh, it will follow the else path, looking for user input and starting the cycle again.

We have seen simpler methods of updating the x and y position of sprites on the screen in other chapters of this book, but this one achieves the classical RPG walking pattern of moving square by square.

The `focusViewport` function, which runs every time the scene is updated, sets the x and y position of the screen so that the player always appears in the middle of the screen if possible.

## note

While we're discussing viewports, we should try to keep a couple of concepts separate. The "viewport" that we are referencing here refers to the camera that follows the player around. Sometimes, a game engine provides high-level functionality to allow you to pin a viewport (or camera) to a specific object as you have done here.

There is a related concept of the viewport meta-tag extension, which is useful controlling rendering on mobile devices. For games, disabling zooming can make sense, but for the love of all that is not 20/20 vision, don't disable zooming when people need to read, click links, and see detail on pictures. This meta extension is used like this:

```
<meta name="viewport" content="width=device-width, user-scalable=no">
```

Mobile Safari (the iPhone browser) has two more meta-tag extensions: apple-mobile-web-app-status-bar-style and apple-mobile-web-app-capable. The first enables you to control the style of the status bar. The second enables you to set mobile Safari in full-screen mode.

On the nonmobile side of things, HTML5's full-screen API enables you to take up the full screen with the inside of your browser window alone. Everything from operating system toolbars to the URL bar of the browser window disappears. This currently has support on all nonmobile browsers (except Internet Explorer), but lacks support on all mobile browsers (except Firefox mobile). The trick with this one is that it must be triggered by a user action, and it asks users if they want to be in full-screen mode. In a typical web app, this would be a bad user experience, but gamers would likely respond more positively to the question "Allow Full Screen?".

With all that code in place, you should be set to open index.html in a browser and see the character on the screen, as shown in Figure 9.2. Use the arrow keys to let him walk around.

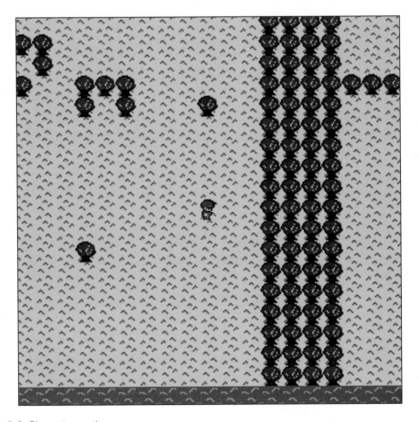

**Figure 9.2** Character on the screen

# Recipe: Adding a Collision Layer

Our character can walk through trees right now. Let's fix that with a couple quick changes to game.js. In Listing 9.8, we'll change the `setMaps` function to create a collision layer based on the sprite types that appear in `foregroundMap`.

**Listing 9.8** Adding Collision Data to the Map

```
var setMaps = function(){
  map.image = game.assets['sprites.png'];
  map.loadData(mapData);
  foregroundMap.image = game.assets['sprites.png'];
  foregroundMap.loadData(foregroundData);
  var collisionData = [];
  for(var i = 0; i< foregroundData.length; i++){
    collisionData.push([]);
    for(var j = 0; j< foregroundData[0].length; j++){
      var collision = foregroundData[i][j] %13 > 1 ? 1 : 0;
      collisionData[i][j] = collision;
    }
  }
  map.collisionData = collisionData;
};
```

Here, we create a two-dimensional array that every sprite type in the foreground map except for –1 (blank), 0 (grass), 1 (water), and 13 (trees you can walk through, good for secret paths) as 0. Everything else is set as 1, which means you cannot walk through them.

Now that we have the collision data set as an attribute of map, we need to implement the actual detection. We do this inside our `player.move` function with the bolded line in Listing 9.9.

**Listing 9.9** Testing for Collisions

```
player.move = function(){
  this.frame = this.spriteOffset + this.direction * 2 + this.walk;
  if (this.isMoving) {
...
  } else {
...
    if (this.xMovement || this.yMovement) {
      var x = this.x + (this.xMovement ? this.xMovement /
➡ Math.abs(this.xMovement) * 16 : 0);
      var y = this.y + (this.yMovement ? this.yMovement /
➡ Math.abs(this.yMovement) * 16 : 0);
      if (0 <= x && x < map.width && 0 <= y && y < map.height &&
➡ !map.hitTest(x, y)) {
        this.isMoving = true;
        this.move();
      }
    }
  }
};
```

`hitTest` and `collisionData` are both provided by enchant.js. Now you can only walk through the special trees (all the way on the right side of the screen). You can still walk through the water. In case you didn't notice yet, the water has two layers. The background layer is the full sprite, but the foreground layer is transparent on the top half. This makes it look like the player is wading in.

# Recipe: Status Screen

Let's start treating our player as more than just a thing that can walk around trees. Let's give him some attributes to brag about. For starters, we'll need to enable a new key to display the current player status. We can accomplish this with a new key binding along with a complementary event listener. We can put the key binding right at the top of game.js with the bolded line in Listing 9.10.

**Listing 9.10** Binding the Spacebar to the "a" Key

```
enchant();
window.onload = function(){
  var game = new Game(300, 300);
  game.keybind(32, 'a');
```

At first glance, this may look like we are binding the "a" key. We are actually binding the spacebar, the keycode of which is 32. enchant.js has its own idea of what keys should be bound to what it calls "buttons" internally. The arrow keys are bound by default to corresponding "buttons," and an "a button" and "b button" are left unassigned. It may seem opinionated to not give everything a constant as in the jaws or (the small) atom engines. This likely comes from enchant's focus on mobile, where generally, the keyboard does not apply. It has an implementation of both a virtual directional and analog pad in its ui extension. If you go the mobile route, putting virtual directional pads and buttons on the screen that are clickable/touchable makes a bit more sense than going through the keyboard.

> ## note
>
> If you're looking for yet another input option, you should check out the gamepad API. It lets you bind events to button presses on a controller connected to your computer. For the console gaming fans out there, this may be a nice change of pace from the mouse/touch/keyboard options.

Next, let's create the event listener for our "a button," so that when it is pressed, we display the status. We'll add this near the bottom of game.js in `game.onload` with the bolded code in Listing 9.11.

**Listing 9.11**   Listener for the "a Button"

```
game.onload = function(){
  setMaps();
  setPlayer();
  setStage();
  player.on('enterframe', function() {
    player.move();
    if (game.input.a) {
      player.displayStatus();
    };
  });
  ...
```

It should be clear that our next goal will be to implement the `displayStatus` function, but what we're displaying are attributes of player. Then there's the issue of physically drawing the object. Let's take on all these changes in Listing 9.12.

**Listing 9.12**  Creating How to and What to Display

```
var setStage = function(){
...
  stage.addChild(foregroundMap);
  stage.addChild(player.statusLabel);
  game.rootScene.addChild(stage);
};
var player = new Sprite(game.spriteWidth, game.spriteHeight);
var setPlayer = function(){
...
  player.name = "Roger";
  player.characterClass = "Rogue";
  player.exp = 0;
  player.level = 1;
  player.gp = 100;
  player.hp = 10;
  player.maxHp = 10;
  player.mp = 0;
  player.maxMp = 0;
  player.statusLabel = new Label("");
  player.statusLabel.width = game.width;
  player.statusLabel.y = undefined;
  player.statusLabel.x = undefined;
  player.statusLabel.color = '#fff';
  player.statusLabel.backgroundColor = '#000';
};
player.displayStatus = function(){
  player.statusLabel.text =
    "--" + player.name + " the " + player.characterClass +
    "<br />--HP: "+player.hp + "/" + player.maxHp +
    "<br />--MP: "+player.mp + "/" + player.maxMp +
    "<br />--Exp: "+player.exp +
    "<br />--Level: " + player.level +
    "<br />--GP: " + player.gp;
};
```

Now, in our `setStage` function, we add the label that we fill with text when we call `player.displayStatus`. When there is no text there, it hides itself. We will use that rather than explicit removal and addition to toggle between showing and hiding the label.

Next, in our `setPlayer` function, we initialize values for typical RPG-centric attributes such as gp to stand for gold pieces, hp to stand for hit points, and so on. One that may stand out is characterClass. We might want to say "class" instead, but "class" is a reserved word in JavaScript, so it's not great to use that here.

Then, we get into the attributes of the status label. First, we initialize it as an empty string. Remember that this means that it will be hidden until it is filled with text. We set the `width` as the `width` of the `game`. Assigning `x` and `y` to `undefined` may seem a little odd. The reason for doing so is that the default value of these attributes is 0, which places the label at the top-left corner of the map, no matter where "Roger the Rogue" goes. Specifying them as `undefined` does exactly what we want by always putting them at the top of the screen we are looking at. It makes the code simpler, and for this game at least, we can trust it.

After setting the colors, let's move on to the `displayStatus` function. This simply sets the text of the label to be a concatenated string made up of player attributes. HTML is interpreted inside of labels, so for easy formatting, we add a few `<br />` tags.

You're almost done with this recipe, but you don't have any way to remove the label (set text to an empty string) right now. To that end, let's make the status disappear if you press any of the walking keys. This requires just a few updates with the bold lines in Listing 9.13 to the input handling code inside of the `player.move` function.

**Listing 9.13** Updated Input Handling to Remove Status Message

```
if (game.input.up) {
  this.direction = 1;
  this.yMovement = -4;
  player.statusLabel.text = "";
} else if (game.input.right) {
  this.direction = 2;
  this.xMovement = 4;
  player.statusLabel.text = "";
} else if (game.input.left) {
  this.direction = 3;
  this.xMovement = -4;
  player.statusLabel.text = "";
} else if (game.input.down) {
  this.direction = 0;
  this.yMovement = 4;
  player.statusLabel.text = "";
}
```

And with that, you can have a status message appear like in Figure 9.3 that disappears when you start walking.

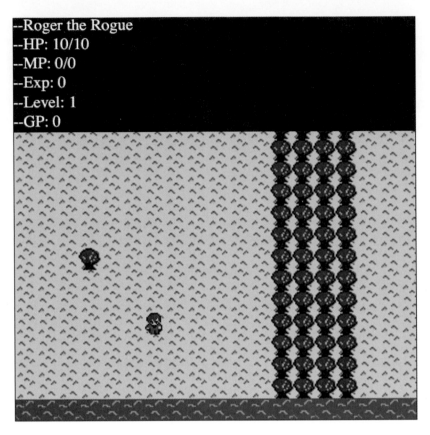

**Figure 9.3** Status message

# Recipe: Talking to NPCs

Nonplayable characters (NPCs) are game characters that exist in the game world that you cannot play as. Some of them are shopkeepers; some of them give helpful advice. Some of them just announce the name of the town and what its defining characteristic is. They give a sense of a living world with their concerns, humor, inanity, and distraction. Let's just make one that says "hello."

If we're going to have a player talk to something, the first thing we'll need to know is what is directly in front of the player. We can accomplish this with three new functions of player in Listing 9.14 added after the `player.move` function.

**Listing 9.14**    Functions for Determining What Sprite Is in Front of the Player

```
player.square = function(){
  return {x: Math.floor(this.x /game.spriteWidth), y:
➥Math.floor(this.y/game.spriteHeight)}
}
player.facingSquare = function(){
  var playerSquare = player.square();
  var facingSquare;
  if(player.direction === 0){
    facingSquare = {x: playerSquare.x, y: playerSquare.y + 1}
  }else if (player.direction === 1) {
    facingSquare = {x: playerSquare.x, y: playerSquare.y - 1}
  }else if (player.direction === 2) {
    facingSquare = {x: playerSquare.x + 1, y: playerSquare.y}
  }else if (player.direction === 3) {
    facingSquare = {x: playerSquare.x - 1, y: playerSquare.y}
  }
  if ((facingSquare.x < 0 || facingSquare.x >= map.width/16) ||
➥(facingSquare.y < 0 || facingSquare.y >= map.height/16)) {
    return null;
  } else {
    return facingSquare;
  }
}
player.facing = function(){
  var facingSquare = player.facingSquare();
  if (!facingSquare){
    return null;
  }else{
    return foregroundData[facingSquare.y][facingSquare.x];
  }
}
```

The first function returns an object that describes the square that the player is in. The `facing-Square` function returns a similar object one square in front of the player, but if the player is looking beyond the edge of the map, it returns `null`. The third function, `facing`, also returns `null` if the player is looking beyond the edge of the map. If not, it returns the sprite number from `foregroundData`.

Directly after the code from Listing 9.14, let's add the objects we need to make an NPC talk. We can do this with the code in Listing 9.15.

**Listing 9.15**  Objects to Let the NPC Talk

```
var npc = {
  say: function(message){
    player.statusLabel.height = 12;
    player.statusLabel.text = message;
  }
}
var greeter = {
  action: function(){
    npc.say("hello");
  }
};
var spriteRoles = [,,greeter,,,,,,,,,,,,,]
```

First, the npc object itself just contains one method, say, which updates the status with what-ever message is passed in. Next, the greeter object is responsible for saying "hello" via the npc's say function. Last, we have a spriteRoles array that tracks an object type for every sprite in sprites.png. Here, you can see that the greeter is in index 2, so spriteRoles[2] returns the greeter object. We could say 0 or undefined or null between each comma, but the implicit undefined return value of calling an index with nothing there will work fine for our purpose.

The last major change we need to make is inside of your game.onload function. Instead of simply calling displayStatus when the A button is pressed, we now have to check whether the player will talk to someone instead. The updated game.onload function is in Listing 9.16, with the bold lines showing the additional code that is necessary.

**Listing 9.16**  Checking Whether to Display Status or Execute a Sprite's Action

```
game.onload = function(){
  setMaps();
  setPlayer();
  setStage();
  player.on('enterframe', function() {
    player.move();
    if (game.input.a) {
      var playerFacing = player.facing();
      if(!playerFacing || !spriteRoles[playerFacing]){
        player.displayStatus();
      }else{
        spriteRoles[playerFacing].action();
      };
    };
  });
};
```

```
  game.rootScene.on('enterframe', function(e) {
    game.focusViewport();
  });
};
```

Here, we wait for the A button (spacebar) to be pressed. If the player faces a square with a sprite, then we check the number of the sprite against the index of that `spriteRoles` array. If we find one (such as `greeter` in index 2), then we execute the action of the sprite object. In this case, the eventual effect is that the `statusLabel` will be updated to say "hello."

The only change left now is that you need a sprite in your `foregroundData` array inside of map.js to have a 2 in it somewhere. Then you can talk to that sprite, and it will say "hello." This technique could be adapted for the trees as well. You would just need to add a tree object in the same way as greeter, and then add it at index 3 of the `spriteRoles` array instead of 2.

# Recipe: Creating an Inventory

Let's give the rogue a few items to help him out. First, we'll be introducing a new spritesheet with the bolded lines in Listing 9.17.

**Listing 9.17**   New Spritesheet for Items

```
window.onload = function(){
...
  game.spriteSheetHeight = 16;
  game.itemSpriteSheetWidth = 64;
  game.preload(['sprites.png', 'items.png']);
```

Because this spritesheet only has four items, it will be 64 pixels wide (4 times 16). In the next line, we preload this spritesheet along with your main spritesheet.

Next, let's take a new approach to showing and hiding our status label. Before, we could just hide by deleting text and show it by inserting text. We need something a bit more comprehensive now. In Listing 9.18, we'll alter the `displayStatus` function and add a `clearStatus` function directly underneath it.

**Listing 9.18**   Toggling Visibility of Status

```
player.displayStatus = function(){
  player.statusLabel.text =
  "--" + player.name + " the " + player.characterClass +
  "<br />--HP: "+player.hp + "/" + player.maxHp +
```

```
    "<br />--MP: "+player.mp + "/" + player.maxMp +
    "<br />--Exp: "+player.exp +
    "<br />--Level: " + player.level +
    "<br />--GP: " + player.gp +
    "<br /><br />--Inventory:";
    player.statusLabel.height = 170;
    player.showInventory();
  };
player.clearStatus = function(){
    player.statusLabel.text = "";
    player.statusLabel.height = 0;
    player.hideInventory();
  };
```

Much of the displayStatus function has remained the same. The difference is now we introduce a showInventory function and set an explicit height for the statusLabel. In the clearStatus function, in addition to setting the text to an empty string, we set the height as 0 and call hideInventory.

We will get to hideInventory and showInventory momentarily, but first, let's replace the old way of clearing the label with our new clearStatus function. You may recall that this happens when an arrow key is pressed. The bold lines in Listing 9.19 show how our input handling has changed.

**Listing 9.19**  Calling clearStatus When Arrow Keys Are Pressed

```
if (game.input.up) {
  this.direction = 1;
  this.yMovement = -4;
  player.clearStatus();
} else if (game.input.right) {
  this.direction = 2;
  this.xMovement = 4;
  player.clearStatus();
} else if (game.input.left) {
  this.direction = 3;
  this.xMovement = -4;
  player.clearStatus();
} else if (game.input.down) {
  this.direction = 0;
  this.yMovement = 4;
  player.clearStatus();
}
```

After this simple replacement, there is one more block of code to visualize the inventory in the status screen. Just below the player.facing function, add the bold lines from Listing 9.20.

**Listing 9.20**   Showing and Hiding the Inventory

```
player.facing = function(){
...
}
player.visibleItems = [];
player.itemSurface = new Surface(game.itemSpriteSheetWidth,
➥game.spriteSheetHeight);
player.inventory = [0, 1, 2, 3];
player.hideInventory = function(){
  for(var i = 0; i < player.visibleItems.length; i++){
    player.visibleItems[i].remove();
  }
   player.visibleItems = [];

};
player.showInventory = function(){
  if(player.visibleItems.length === 0){

    player.itemSurface.draw(game.assets['items.png']);
    for (var i = 0; i < player.inventory.length; i++){
      var item = new Sprite(game.spriteWidth, game.spriteHeight);
      item.y = 130;
      item.x = 30 + 70*i;
      item.frame = player.inventory[i];
      item.scaleX = 2;
      item.scaleY = 2;
      item.image = player.itemSurface;
      player.visibleItems.push(item);
      game.rootScene.addChild(item);
    }
  }
};
```

First, we initialize a new array for visible items. We keep this reference simply so that we can delete them later. Next, we initialize a new `Surface` that our sprites will rely on to know what asset is acting as the spritesheet. Notice that we are referring to our smaller width for this spritesheet rather than the larger one we use for the sprites.png file.

Next, we set an array of objects that the player has. By default, we give him everything for now. Then we fill out the `hideInventory` function. In this, which is triggered as part of the `clearStatus` function based on directional input, we loop through all the items that are visible and remove them (from the DOM). Then, we empty the `visibleItems` array.

`showInventory` starts by seeing if `visibleItems` is empty. We perform this check so that, at most, four items display, even if the spacebar is held down. We draw the surface, which functions less like "drawing" and more like selecting what image file your spritesheet is using. Then, for each item in the player's inventory, we create a new sprite and set the placement, frame, and scale. We ensure it uses the correct spritesheet (surface). Because we need to be able to delete it later, we add it to the `visibleItems` array. Lastly, we add it to the `rootScene`, finally allowing it to appear on the screen.

See the results of opening the index file in a browser and pressing the spacebar, as shown in Figure 9.4.

# Recipe: Creating a Shop

Is that a sword? And a dragon's paw? Woah woah. That's way too much power for a rogue to have without having to work for it a bit first. In this recipe, we'll create a shop so that he'll have to earn that dragon paw.

The first thing you'll have to do is change a "-1" to a "4" somewhere in your `foregroundData` array in map.js. This puts the lucky cat sprite somewhere on the screen. If you "talk" to the cat now, you can see your inventory. You need to adjust your `spriteRoles` array and add a new object to get her to do something else. For now, let's just have her say "ahoy." Seems like something a talking merchant cat would say. You can achieve this with the bolded portions of Listing 9.21.

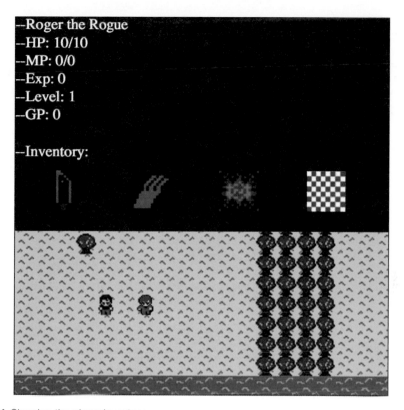

**Figure 9.4** Showing the player inventory

**Listing 9.21** Making Your Cat Talk

```
var greeter = {
  action: function(){
    npc.say("hello");
  }
};
var cat = {
  action: function(){
    npc.say("ahoy");
  }
};
var spriteRoles = [,,greeter,,cat,,,,,,,,,,,]
```

Before going further in turning your cat into a proper merchant, let's clear out the player's inventory. See Listing 9.22 for how to accomplish this.

**Listing 9.22**  Clearing the Player's Inventory

```
//Find this line:
//player.inventory = [0, 1, 2, 3];
//and change it to this:
player.inventory = [];
```

You can give a little more detail on the game's items with the bold code in Listing 9.23.

**Listing 9.23**  game.items with More Detail

```
enchant();
window.onload = function(){
...
  game.preload(['sprites.png', 'items.png']);
  game.items = [{price: 1000, description: "Hurter", id: 0},
              {price: 5000, description: "Drg. Paw", id: 1},
              {price: 5000, description: "Ice Magic", id: 2},
              {price: 60, description: "Chess Set", id: 3}]
```

Next, we'll be reusing our `showInventory` function inside of the shop, so we'll need to make the vertical position adaptable. First, we need to change the `displayStatus` function with the bolded line in Listing 9.24.

**Listing 9.24**  Update Call to displayStatus

```
player.displayStatus = function(){
...
  player.showInventory(0);
};
```

We now pass a value to the function so that we can set it lower. For this particular call, it is fine where it is, so we just pass 0. Next, with the bolded lines in Listing 9.25, we'll make the corresponding update to the function, with one additional change.

**Listing 9.25**  showInventory Updated

```
player.showInventory = function(yOffset){
  if(player.visibleItems.length === 0){
    player.itemSurface.draw(game.assets['items.png']);
    for (var i = 0; i < player.inventory.length; i++){
      var item = new Sprite(game.spriteWidth, game.spriteHeight);
      item.y = 130 + yOffset;
      item.x = 30 + 70*i;
```

```
...
      game.currentScene.addChild(item);
    }
  }
};
```

We also had to change `rootScene` to `currentScene` to accommodate for our ability to call this from more than one scene. To do this, we use the `pushScene` function of game. With the bold code in Listing 9.26, let's make the cat open up shop instead of just saying hi.

**Listing 9.26**   pushScene to Open Up Shop

```
var greeter = {
  action: function(){
    npc.say("hello");
  }
};
var shopScene = new Scene();
var cat = {
  action: function(){
    game.pushScene(shopScene);
  }
};
```

If you want to talk to the cat now, your game would look like it was frozen because there is nothing in the scene. Your controls would stop working because input is tied to the `enter-frame` event of the `player` sprite. That sprite may look like it is there, but it is tied to the `root-Scene`, which we are no longer in the context of. The player sprite will not update, so none of the code inside of the `player.on('enterframe', function() {}` block will run, which includes input handling.

To define what we need for the shop, let's make a small change to `game.onload` by adding the bold line in Listing 9.27.

**Listing 9.27**   Starting the Shop

```
game.onload = function(){
  setMaps();
  setPlayer();
  setStage();
  setShopping();
  player.on('enterframe', function() {
...
  });
```

```
    game.rootScene.on('enterframe', function(e) {
      game.focusViewport();
    });
};
```

Next, let's define this function. This encompasses the rest of the recipe, so we will break it up into Listing 9.28 through Listing 9.33. They all follow each other in sequence in the code.

Listing 9.28 shows the first part of our `setShopping` function, occurring after our cat's new identity (included here for context).

**Listing 9.28**  setShopping Started

```
    var shopScene = new Scene();
    var cat = {
      action: function(){
        game.pushScene(shopScene);
      }
    };
    var spriteRoles = [,,greeter,,cat,,,,,,,,,,];
    var setShopping = function(){
      var shop = new Group();
      shop.itemSelected = 0;
      shop.shoppingFunds = function(){
        return "Gold: " + player.gp;
      };
  ...
```

To start, we declare a new `Group` called `shop`. This contains the text and sprites that we render, and we also liberally overload it with extra properties and functions. Speaking of properties and functions, we add those to `shop`. `itemSelected` keeps track of the index of the item that is being considered for purchase among the array of available items we will later expose. `shoppingFunds` gives a textual representation of how much the player has to spend.

In Listing 9.29, we draw maneki.

**Listing 9.29**  Drawing Maneki

```
 ... //listing 9.28
shop.drawManeki = function(){
  var image = new Surface(game.spriteSheetWidth,
➥game.spriteSheetHeight);
  var maneki = new Sprite(game.spriteWidth, game.spriteHeight);
  maneki.image = image;
```

```
    image.draw(game.assets['sprites.png']);
    maneki.frame = 4;
    maneki.y = 10;
    maneki.x = 10;
    maneki.scaleX = 2;
    maneki.scaleY = 2;
    this.addChild(maneki);
    this.message.x = 40;
    this.message.y = 10;
    this.message.color = '#fff';
    this.addChild(this.message);
};
... //listing 9.30
```

All this code should look fairly familiar given the sprites and labels that we have previously drawn. Notice that this has both and adds them both to `shop`. However, you may wonder what `this.message` is. This is a `shop.message`, which we have yet to set but will function as what the cat is saying to you.

In Listing 9.30, we draw the items for sale.

**Listing 9.30** Drawing the Items for Sale

```
... //listing 9.29
shop.drawItemsForSale = function(){
  for(var i = 0; i < game.items.length; i++){
    var image = new Surface(game.itemSpriteSheetWidth,
➥game.spriteSheetHeight);
    var item = new Sprite(game.spriteWidth, game.spriteHeight);
    image.draw(game.assets['items.png']);
    itemLocationX = 30 + 70*i;
    itemLocationY = 70;
    item.y = itemLocationY;
    item.x = itemLocationX;
    item.frame = i;
    item.scaleX = 2;
    item.scaleY = 2;
    item.image = image;
    this.addChild(item);
    var itemDescription = new Label(game.items[i].price + "<br />" +
➥game.items[i].description);
    itemDescription.x = itemLocationX - 8;
    itemDescription.y = itemLocationY + 40;
    itemDescription.color = '#fff';
    this.addChild(itemDescription);
    if(i === this.itemSelected){
```

```
        var image = new Surface(game.spriteSheetWidth,
➥game.spriteSheetHeight);
        this.itemSelector = new Sprite(game.spriteWidth,
➥game.spriteHeight);
        image.draw(game.assets['sprites.png']);
        itemLocationX = 30 + 70*i;
        itemLocationY = 160;
        this.itemSelector.scaleX = 2;
        this.itemSelector.scaleY = 2;
        this.itemSelector.y = itemLocationY;
        this.itemSelector.x = itemLocationX;
        this.itemSelector.frame = 7;
        this.itemSelector.image = image;
        this.addChild(this.itemSelector);
      };
    };
  };
... //listing 9.31
```

This entire function is a `for` loop that executes once for each of the items in the game's items array. It has three primary duties per item. First, it draws the sprite of the sprite image that corresponds with the item. Second, it writes out the price and description of the item. (This is why we beefed up our item descriptions earlier.) The last thing that it does is draw the player sprite faced in the up direction toward the item. Notice that we are not overwriting the `player` variable used in the overworld, but rather describing the player sprite as `shop.itemSelector`.

In Listing 9.31, we create a couple of new event handlers.

**Listing 9.31**   shop's Event Handlers

```
... //listing 9.30
shop.on('enter', function(){
  shoppingFunds.text = shop.shoppingFunds();
});
shop.on('enterframe', function() {
  setTimeout(function(){
    if (game.input.a){
      shop.attemptToBuy();
    } else if (game.input.down) {
      shop.message.text = shop.farewell;
      setTimeout(function(){
        game.popScene();
        shop.message.text = shop.greeting;
      }, 1000);
    } else if (game.input.left) {
      shop.itemSelected = shop.itemSelected + game.items.length - 1;
```

```
            shop.itemSelected = shop.itemSelected % game.items.length;
            shop.itemSelector.x = 30 + 70*shop.itemSelected;
            shop.message.text = shop.greeting;
        } else if (game.input.right) {
            shop.itemSelected = (shop.itemSelected + 1) % game.items.length;
            shop.itemSelector.x = 30 + 70*shop.itemSelected;
            shop.message.text = shop.greeting;
        }
    }, 500);
    player.showInventory(100);
    shoppingFunds.text = shop.shoppingFunds();
});
... //listing 9.32
```

In the `enter` event handler (executed once when the sprite first appears), we set the text for the player's funds. This will be updated on purchase, so it may not seem important here, but if a player gains or loses cash elsewhere, we need this value to be correct upon entry to the shop.

Next, in the `enterframe` handler (executes in a loop), we start with a `setTimeout` function in order to wait one-half a second before accepting input so that the player doesn't accidentally buy something upon entering the shop. We bind the A button (spacebar) to an `attemptToBuy` function. Down will set a farewell message from the cat and wait one second before going back to the over world map. It also resets the message so that the cat doesn't say goodbye when you go back in. Left and right change the item that you may attempt to buy, along with updating the selection sprite (player facing up) and resetting the cat's message to the greeting. `show-Inventory` makes use of the change we made earlier to accept the y offset of 100, placing the player's inventory lower than on the over world map. We also update the `shoppingFunds` text here. The reason for calling both of these here is that they can change when something is purchased.

In Listing 9.32, we create the consequences of trying to buy something.

**Listing 9.32**   Attempting to Buy an Item

```
... //listing 9.31
shop.attemptToBuy = function(){
    var itemPrice = game.items[this.itemSelected].price;
    if (player.gp < itemPrice){
        this.message.text = this.apology;
    }else{
        player.visibleItems = [];
        player.gp = player.gp - itemPrice;
        player.inventory.push(game.items[this.itemSelected].id);
        this.message.text = this.sale;
```

```
    }
  };
  ... //listing 9.33
```

First, we set `visibleItems` to an empty array so that the inventory can render properly for multiple items. If the player doesn't have enough gp, the cat apologizes for your poverty. If the item can be purchased, the player's gp is reduced by the cost of the item, the numerical representation of the object is added to the player's inventory array, and the cat congratulates you on your purchase. The display of your new gp total and inventory are handled in Listing 9.31.

To finish this recipe, we have a smattering of property assignments and function calls in Listing 9.33.

**Listing 9.33**  Function Calls and Property Assignments for the Shop

```
  ... //listing 9.32
    shop.greeting = "Hi!  I'm Maneki. Meow. I sell things.";
    shop.apology = "Meow... sorry, you don't have the money for this.";
    shop.sale = "Here ya go!";
    shop.farewell = "Come again! Meow!";
    shop.message = new Label(shop.greeting);
    shop.drawManeki();
    var shoppingFunds = new Label(shop.shoppingFunds());
    shoppingFunds.color = '#fff';
    shoppingFunds.y = 200;
    shoppingFunds.x = 10;
    shop.addChild(shoppingFunds);
    shop.drawItemsForSale();
    shopScene.backgroundColor = '#000';
    shopScene.addChild(shop);
  };
```

The first four lines are the different things that the cat might say. The next is the label that contains it. After that, we call the function to draw the cat along with its message. Then, to the `shop` group, we add the label for `shoppingFunds`, which can be updated upon purchase. Following that, in `drawItemsForSale`, we draw the sprites for the items, their prices, their descriptions, and the player sprite acting as a selector. We set the background for the whole scene as black, and finally, add the `shop` to the `shopScene`. Figure 9.5 shows what happens when we get into the shopping screen and buy the chess set.

You will also be able to see an updated inventory on the over world interface as part of the status screen.

**Figure 9.5** Chess set acquired!

# Recipe: Creating a Battle Interface

In a standard RPG, a player directly or indirectly makes progress through battles. Sometimes when a battle is won, it means you saved some part of the world and all the NPCs start thanking you. Other times, it's just for the gold and experience. Battles can be triggered randomly by walking around, being in a particular location, or being in a location and chatting with some object, monster, or person. For our purposes, we'll just introduce another character that fights you when you talk to him.

As with the cat merchant, we'll need to add the character's sprite to the map. We'll use sprite number 15 for this. Somewhere in the `foregroundData` array in map.js, change a -1 to a 15.

Next, let's add this brawler character near where we added the cat. See the bolded lines in Listing 9.34.

**Listing 9.34**  Adding the Brawler Character

```
var shopScene = new Scene();
var cat = {
  action: function(){
    game.pushScene(shopScene);
  }
};
var battleScene = new Scene();
var brawler = {
  maxHp: 20,
  hp: 20,
  sprite: 15,
  attack: 3,
  exp: 3,
  gp: 5,
  action: function(){
    player.currentEnemy = this;
    game.pushScene(battleScene);
  }
};
var spriteRoles = [,,greeter,,cat,,,,,,,,,,,brawler]
```

As with the cat and the shopScene, we first add the scene where the brawler appears, the `battleScene`. Next, we add a few attributes to the brawler that are relevant to the battle (as well as what happens when you win a battle), and set the action to start the new scene. We also give the player a reference to which enemy he is fighting. Lastly, we modify the sprite roles so that in the 16th position of the array, this variable is stored for reference. Remember that because arrays are 0 indexed (they start at 0), this will be [15], not [16]. Also remember that the reason for it being in that position is the index corresponds with the sprite number.

Next, we have some changes to make to the player. See the bold lines in Listing 9.35.

**Listing 9.35**  Changes to player to Enable Leveling and Attacking

```
var player = new Sprite(game.spriteWidth, game.spriteHeight);
var setPlayer = function(){
...
  // player.hp = 10; // delete this
  ///player.maxHp = 10; // delete this
  // player.mp = 0; // delete this
  // player.maxMp = 0; // delete this
  player.gp = 100;
  player.levelStats = [{},{attack: 4, maxHp: 10, maxMp: 0, expMax: 10},
                       {attack: 6, maxHp: 14, maxMp: 0, expMax: 30},
```

```
                        {attack: 7, maxHp: 20, maxMp: 5, expMax: 50}
  ];
  player.attack = function(){
    return player.levelStats[player.level].attack;
  };
  player.hp = player.levelStats[player.level].maxHp;
  player.mp = player.levelStats[player.level].maxMp;
```

In our player object, we can no longer get by with the simple assignments for hp, maxHp, mp, and maxMp. Delete the old attributes that are bolded and commented out with //. Now, they will be referenced through the player's level according to the levelStats array. The attack function will be used during combat. This is where we might add the power of a weapon should your character equip one. The expMax stores the maximum number of experience points needed before leveling up. If you wonder why the array starts with an empty object, this lets us keep consistency between the player's level, which typically is not 0-indexed, and the array data structure that is 0-indexed.

Next, update the HP and MP portions of your displayStatus function according to the bold lines in Listing 9.36.

**Listing 9.36**  Updated Way of Displaying the Player's Status

```
player.displayStatus = function(){
  player.statusLabel.text =
    "--" + player.name + " the " + player.characterClass +
    "<br />--HP: "+player.hp + "/" +
➥player.levelStats[player.level].maxHp +
    "<br />--MP: "+player.mp + "/" +
➥player.levelStats[player.level].maxMp +
  ...
};
```

Here we reference the attributes of the player through the context of the current level.

We have one small change to game.onload to initiate our battling code. Add the bold line in Listing 9.37.

**Listing 9.37**  Set Up the Battle When the Game Starts

```
game.onload = function(){
  setMaps();
  setPlayer();
  setStage();
```

```
    setShopping();
    setBattle();
...
```

We will address what `setBattle` momentarily, but first we have one last change. In the game.css file, add the code from Listing 9.38.

**Listing 9.38**  Highlighting the Selected Battle Option

```
.active-option{
 color:red;
}
```

With this in place, we will color the option we select (Fight, Magic, or Run) red so that we know which option we are choosing.

Now, let's begin the code for `setBattle`. This will be broken into many listings, and like the code for `setShopping`, they will all appear sequentially, beginning with Listing 9.39.

**Listing 9.39**  A Few Objects to Set Right Away

```
var spriteRoles = [,,greeter,,cat,,,,,,,,,,,brawler]
var setBattle = function(){
  battleScene.backgroundColor = '#000';
  var battle = new Group();
  battle.menu = new Label();
  battle.menu.x = 20;
  battle.menu.y = 170;
  battle.menu.color = '#fff';
  battle.activeAction = 0;

... //listing 9.40
```

To start, directly under `spriteRoles`, we start the `setBattle` function declaration and set a black background for the scene. Then, we add `battle` to act as a container for our sprites, labels, and properties. The `battle.menu` is the (white) text showing our battle options.

Next, in Listing 9.40, we introduce another label, `playerStatus`, to describe the current hp and mp of the `player`.

**Listing 9.40** A Label for the Status of the Player

```
... //listing 9.39
    battle.getPlayerStatus = function(){
      return "HP: " + player.hp + "<br />MP: " + player.mp;
    };
    battle.playerStatus = new Label(battle.getPlayerStatus());
    battle.playerStatus.color = '#fff';
    battle.playerStatus.x = 200;
    battle.playerStatus.y = 120;
... //listing 9.41
```

This should be fairly clear at this point, so let's move on to the `hitStrength` function in
Listing 9.41.

**Listing 9.41** Determining How Many hp a Hit Will Deduct

```
... //listing 9.40
battle.hitStrength = function(hit){
  return Math.round((Math.random() + .5) * hit);
};
... //listing 9.42
```

We could rely strictly on the attack (and potentially defense) values to determine how many hit
points to deduct from a player or enemy. This function adds a bit of randomness so that battles
are less predictable.

In Listing 9.42, we take care of what happens when a player wins.

**Listing 9.42** Winning a Battle

```
... //listing 9.41
battle.won = function(){
  battle.over = true;
  player.exp += player.currentEnemy.exp;
  player.gp += player.currentEnemy.gp;
  player.currentEnemy.hp = player.currentEnemy.maxHp;
  player.statusLabel.text = "You won!<br />" +
    "You gained "+ player.currentEnemy.exp + " exp<br />"+
    "and " + player.currentEnemy.gp + " gold pieces!";
  player.statusLabel.height = 45;
  if(player.exp > player.levelStats[player.level].expMax){
    player.level += 1;
    player.statusLabel.text = player.statusLabel.text +
      "<br />And you gained a level!"+
```

```
        "<br />You are now at level " + player.level +"!";
      player.statusLabel.height = 75;
    }
  };
  ... //listing 9.43
```

When a player wins a battle, with the code in Listing 9.42, we set `battle.over` to true so that our higher-level functions can pop out of the scene. Then, the player is awarded with the experience points and gold of the enemy. If the player exceeds the experience threshold for the current level, he levels up. The enemy's hit points are reset for the next battle. We set the `statusLabel` (the one on the over world scene) to describe the victory. If you were so inclined, you could instead use one of the `battleScene`'s labels for this purpose.

In Listing 9.43, we take care of what happens when a player loses.

**Listing 9.43**  Losing a Battle

```
  ... //listing 9.42
battle.lost = function(){
    battle.over = true;
    player.hp = player.levelStats[player.level].maxHp;
    player.mp = player.levelStats[player.level].maxMp;
    player.gp = Math.round(player.gp/2);
    player.statusLabel.text = "You lost!";
    player.statusLabel.height = 12;
  };
  ... //listing 9.44
```

In Listing 9.43, we show what happens when you lose. Similar to winning, we set `battle.over` to true in preparation to pop the scene. We reset the player's hit points and magic points so that he can fight again, and take away one-half of his gold. Again, we rely on the over world scene message to describe what happened.

In Listing 9.44, we add code necessary for the player to attack and be attacked.

**Listing 9.44**  When Attacks Happen

```
  ... //listing 9.43
battle.playerAttack = function(){
    var currentEnemy = player.currentEnemy;
    var playerHit = battle.hitStrength(player.attack());
    currentEnemy.hp = currentEnemy.hp - playerHit;
    battle.menu.text = "You did " + playerHit + " damage!";
    if(currentEnemy.hp <= 0){
```

```
      battle.won();
    };
  };
battle.enemyAttack = function(){
  var currentEnemy = player.currentEnemy;
  var enemyHit = battle.hitStrength(currentEnemy.attack);
  player.hp = player.hp - enemyHit;
  battle.menu.text = "You took " + enemyHit + " damage!";
  if(player.hp <= 0){
    battle.lost();
  };
};
... //listing 9.45
```

In Listing 9.44, we have the functions for player and enemy attacks. In both cases, we calculate the strength of the hit based on the attacker's strength and the randomness we get from the `hitStrength` function. Then we subtract the hit from the hit points, set a message, and when there is a victor, call the `won` or `lost` function.

In Listing 9.45, we outline what happens with each battle action that the player can take.

**Listing 9.45**  Possible Actions to Take in Battle

```
... //listing 9.44
battle.actions = [{name: "Fight", action: function(){
    battle.wait = true;
    battle.playerAttack();
    setTimeout(function(){
      if(!battle.over){
        battle.enemyAttack();
      };
      if(!battle.over){
        setTimeout(function(){
          battle.menu.text = battle.listActions();
          battle.wait = false;
        }, 1000)
      } else {
        setTimeout(function(){
          battle.menu.text = "";
          game.popScene();
        }, 1000)
      };
    }, 1000);
  }},
  {name: "Magic", action: function(){
    battle.menu.text = "You don't know any magic yet!";
```

```
    battle.wait = true;
    battle.activeAction = 0;
    setTimeout(function(){
      battle.menu.text = battle.listActions();
      battle.wait = false;
    }, 1000);
  }},
  {name: "Run", action: function(){
    game.pause();
    player.statusLabel.text = "You ran away!";
    player.statusLabel.height = 12;
    battle.menu.text = "";
    game.popScene();
  }}
];
... //listing 9.46
```

Listing 9.45 covers what can happen when we select a given option. Starting from the bottom, Run pauses the game input with the enchant.js pause function and sets the statusLabel describing your cowardice when you exit the scene. Then, it prepares the battle menu so that when you battle again, you will not see a flash of the old menu. Lastly, it pops out of the scene, back to the over world.

The Magic option does not currently do anything very interesting. It just sets a delay while telling you that you don't have any magic yet. You might wonder why it explicitly waits with setTimeout rather than relying on game.pause. The reason for this and for setting battle. wait is that outside of this code we may have collected input multiple times, so it will try to run this code multiple times. Even if we pause input at the very top of the function, we are too late.

The Fight action is the most complex. Again, we get explicit about waiting so that we can block input. We call playerAttack that we defined previously, and we set a timeout to ensure that our playerAttack messages have a chance to display. If the enemy is still alive, then we give him a chance to attack. If the player is still alive, then we wait again. After we wait, we show the menu and enable input for another round of combat. If the battle is over, then we reset the menu for the next fight, and pop out of the scene.

In Listing 9.46, we handle the display for the battle actions.

### Listing 9.46 Displaying Our Options for Combat

```
... //listing 9.45
battle.listActions = function(){
  battle.optionText = [];
  for(var i = 0; i < battle.actions.length; i++){
```

```
      if(i === battle.activeAction){
        battle.optionText[i] = "<span class='active-option'>"+ battle.
    actions[i].name + "</span>";
      } else {
        battle.optionText[i] = battle.actions[i].name;
      }
    }
    return battle.optionText.join("<br />");
  };
  ... //listing 9.47
```

Listing 9.46 shows what we use to display our options. We loop through the array of actions that we just declared, building a new array. We store the name, and if it is selected as the current option that would be executed by pressing the A Button (spacebar), we add our css class so that it will appear red instead of white. At the end of the loop, we join our array elements into a string with a break tag separating them.

In Listing 9.47, we set up the attributes for the player and enemy sprites.

**Listing 9.47**   Adding the Player and the Enemy

```
  ... //listing 9.46
 battle.addCombatants = function(){
    var image = new Surface(game.spriteSheetWidth, game.
 spriteSheetHeight);
    image.draw(game.assets['sprites.png']),
    battle.player = new Sprite(game.spriteWidth, game.spriteHeight);
    battle.player.image = image;
    battle.player.frame = 7;
    battle.player.x = 150;
    battle.player.y = 120;
    battle.player.scaleX = 2;
    battle.player.scaleY = 2;
    battle.enemy = new Sprite(game.spriteWidth, game.spriteHeight);
    battle.enemy.image = image;
    battle.enemy.x = 150;
    battle.enemy.y = 70;
    battle.enemy.scaleX = 2;
    battle.enemy.scaleY = 2;
    battle.addChild(battle.enemy);
  };
 battle.addCombatants();
  ... //listing 9.48
```

In Listing 9.47, we create the addCombatants function and then immediately call it. The reason for declaring a function instead of just running it sequentially is just for clarity. This code should all look familiar to you.

In Listing 9.48, we add the handler for when the battle starts.

**Listing 9.48**   The Handler for When the Battle Starts

```
... //listing 9.47
battleScene.on('enter', function() {
  battle.over = false;
  battle.wait = true;
  battle.menu.text = "";
  battle.enemy.frame = player.currentEnemy.sprite;
  setTimeout(function() {
    battle.menu.text = battle.listActions();
    battle.wait = false;
  }, 500);
});
... //listing 9.49
```

The handler for battleScene in Listing 9.48 is run once when the battle starts. The battle has just begun, so it sets over to false. Then it sets wait to true so that input is halted. It sets the menu text to an empty string so that players don't see undefined as a battle option. The reason for setting the enemy frame here is so that it would be possible to fight more than one type of enemy and have their sprite show up. After we have waited one-half second, we show the menu to the player to indicate that action can be taken, and with battle.wait set to false, we are ready for input.

In Listing 9.49, we add the handler for the loop that executes during the battle.

**Listing 9.49**   The Handler to Loop During Battle

```
... //listing 9.48
battleScene.on('enterframe', function() {
  if(!battle.wait){
    if (game.input.a){
      battle.actions[battle.activeAction].action();
    } else if (game.input.down){
      battle.activeAction = (battle.activeAction + 1) %
➥battle.actions.length;
      battle.menu.text = battle.listActions();
    } else if (game.input.up){
      battle.activeAction = (battle.activeAction - 1 +
➥battle.actions.length) % battle.actions.length;
```

```
      battle.menu.text = battle.listActions();
    }
    battle.playerStatus.text = battle.getPlayerStatus();
  };
})
... //listing 9.50
```

In Listing 9.49, which loops during the battle, we see what all the waiting was about. If `battle.wait` is set to true, we don't accept any input. Otherwise, the up and down arrow keys select the active action and update the text to reflect which action is selected. The A Button (spacebar) takes whatever action is highlighted. Also in this loop, we make updates to the player's hit point display with the `getPlayerStatus` function.

In Listing 9.50, we add a handler for leaving the battle mode.

**Listing 9.50**  What Happens When We Leave the Scene

```
... //listing 9.49
battleScene.on('exit', function() {
  setTimeout(function(){
    battle.menu.text = "";
    battle.activeAction = 0;
    battle.playerStatus.text = battle.getPlayerStatus();
    game.resume();
  }, 1000);
});
... //listing 9.51
```

In Listing 9.50, we are introduced to a new kind of event handler. This runs when we pop the scene and head back to the over world. We reset the menu and which battle option is selected. Then we update the player's hit point display so that when another fight breaks out, we don't see old information. If the game is paused, we resume here after waiting for 1 second. The reason to pause when we leave like this is so that the player doesn't accidentally reenter the battle by holding down the spacebar too long.

In Listing 9.51, we add the large pieces of functionality we created to the battle scene.

> **tip**
>
> If managing the scenes, inner logic, and transitions between everything is confusing, especially if this becomes a larger game for you, you might want to implement a "state machine" to help keep things organized. This lets you define what to do

when entering and leaving a state, as well as what states can go to other states, and by what function call they may transition. We approach some of this with our event handlers, but when we jump from the level of a scene to a state within that scene, our interface to transition and work with variables can be inconsistent.

You can find a well-tested and popular state machine at https://github.com/jakesgordon/javascript-state-machine.

**Listing 9.51**   Building the Scene

```
... //listing 9.50
  battle.addChild(battle.playerStatus);
  battle.addChild(battle.menu);
  battle.addChild(battle.player);
  battleScene.addChild(battle);
}; //closing the setBattle function
```

Recall that the code since Listing 9.39 has been running inside of the context of the `setBattle` function. This code is executed only once on `game.onload` for the setup, and then all your functions and properties of `battle` are called from within the scene event handlers, one of which behaves as an update/draw loop. With that context in mind, we can now do our final bit of setting up the `battleScene`. Here, we add the remaining child objects to our `battle`, which is an instance of `Group`, add `battle` to the `battleScene`, and write our final closing brace for this recipe.

If you pick a fight with the guy with the hat, you will see something like Figure 9.6.

# Recipe: Saving Your Game with HTML5's Local Storage API

With all that leveling up and buying items, you might want to hang onto the progress you make. To do this, we'll use HTML5's local storage capabilities. You could base this on events, but for simplicity's sake, let's just set a timer for saving variables to local storage. Add the bold lines in Listing 9.52.

**Listing 9.52**   Saving Variables to Local Storage at a 5-Second Interval

```
game.onload = function(){
  game.storable = ['exp', 'level', 'gp', 'inventory'];
  game.saveToLocalStorage = function(){
    for(var i = 0; i < game.storable.length; i++){
```

```
      if(game.storable[i] === 'inventory'){
        window.localStorage.setItem(game.storable[i],
➥JSON.stringify(player[game.storable[i]]));
      } else {
        window.localStorage.setItem(game.storable[i],
➥player[game.storable[i]]);
      }
    }
  };
  setInterval(game.saveToLocalStorage, 5000);
...
```

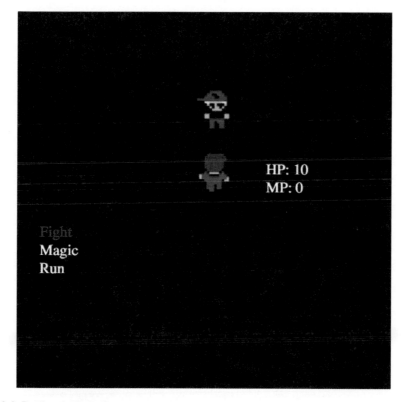

**Figure 9.6** Battling the hatted guy

First, we set an array with the names of the properties of `player` that we want to store. Then, we run through the array and call `window.localStorage.setItem(keyName, value);` to store a value. Local storage only saves strings, which means that `inventory` is a special case because it is an array. Therefore, we need to call `JSON.stringify` on it before we can save it. You might think that integers will be a problem, too. In their case, the issue is with the reading, rather than the writing. Let's take a look at reading from local storage with the bold code in Listing 9.53.

**Listing 9.53** Reading from Local Storage

```
player = new Sprite(game.spriteWidth, game.spriteHeight);
var setPlayer = function(){
  player.spriteOffset = 5;
...
  player.characterClass = "Rogue";
  if (window.localStorage.getItem('exp')) {
    player.exp = parseInt(window.localStorage.getItem('exp'));
  } else {
    player.exp = 0;
  }
  if (window.localStorage.getItem('level')) {
    player.level = parseInt(window.localStorage.getItem('level'));
  } else {
    player.level = 1;
  }
  if (window.localStorage.getItem('gp')) {
    player.gp = parseInt(window.localStorage.getItem('gp'));
  } else {
    player.gp = 100;
  }
  if (window.localStorage.getItem('inventory')) {
    player.inventory = JSON.parse(window.localStorage.
getItem('inventory'));
  } else {
    player.inventory = []; //This is originally further down in the
➥file.
  }
  player.levelStats = [{},{attack: 4, maxHp: 10, maxMp: 0, expMax: 10},
                  {attack: 6, maxHp: 14, maxMp: 0, expMax: 30},
                  {attack: 7, maxHp: 20, maxMp: 5, expMax: 50}
  ];
```

Here, we attempt to read each value from local storage. If it is there, we call `parseInt` to convert the strings to integers. `inventory` is a special case again, and we call `JSON.parse` to convert the `stringified` array back into a normal JavaScript array that we can use. If we don't find the object in local storage, we set each with the defaults that we used before. Make sure to remove the code that set these values in the last recipe. Most are near this area, but in the last recipe, `player.inventory = [];` is further down in the file, just above the declaration for `player.hideInventory`.

The result of this is that your experience, level, inventory, and gp will be saved to and reloaded from local storage, even if you close the browser.

> **note**
>
> It is out of scope for this book to cover every aspect of HTML5, but there are two more client-side storage options to be aware of. The first is called sessionStorage. This will allow you to throw away the data when the browser tab is closed.
>
> If you want to store more complex (relational) data, there are also relational data storage options such as the IndexedDB (Chrome, Firefox, and IE) or Web SQL Database (Chrome, Safari, Opera, iOS, Android, and Opera Mobile).

# Summary

In this chapter, we created a basic RPG from scratch in enchant.js, implementing a world map, a dialogue system, a store, a battle interface, an inventory, a leveling system, and a way to pick up where you left off by storing your data with HTML5's local storage.

If you want to add more features to this game, an obvious place to start would be with more content such as characters, weapons, armor, magic, dialogue, enemies, and so on. Creating a larger narrative around the game could also make it more interesting. The player's battle abilities could be more fleshed out. Currently, even if we had the ice magic, it wouldn't be functional, and none of the other items would do anything tangible either. It would not be difficult to add something to his attack power. In addition, the player always goes first, player and enemy attacks never miss, and the player can always run away. Introducing attributes such as speed, accuracy, and agility could give the game a more dynamic feel. The visuals during battle are also a little light. It might be nice to have a backdrop of some sort with visible effects for hits. Maybe you decide that turn-based combat is too complicated or not as exciting as collision-based combat like in an action RPG. If you made it through this chapter, pulling in some collision detection concepts from earlier chapters shouldn't be a problem for you.

If you want to explore enchant.js more, you are in luck. It has perhaps the fullest API of any of the engines covered so far. Some of the unique features that were not talked about include the CanvasGroup alternative to Group, the Sound API, the ParallelAction object, and Timelines and Tweens for animations. What's more, enchant.js features plug-ins for, among other things, connecting to Twitter or the wise9 distribution platform. (They make enchant.js.) They even have an avatar animation server where you can swap out aspects of the character such as hair or clothes, just like with Mr. Potato Head. If you're thinking of writing your own engine, definitely spend some time looking through enchant's clever and unexpected feature set.

# CHAPTER 10

# RTS

What's better than playing an RPG and being a hero? Commanding an entire army of heroes. Some of this genre's canonical games include *Starcraft* and *Warcraft* (not to be confused with the MMORPG *World of Warcraft*), but it's influence can be seen in other sim games such as *Sim City* or *Roller Coaster Tycoon* as well. In addition, turn-based tactical battle systems, with similar interfaces, appear in turn-based contexts as well. Examples would be the *Tactics Ogre* and *Final Fantasy Tactics* franchises, as well as classical abstract, turn-based strategy board games like chess. Many team sports games contain RTS elements as well, but with familiar (sports) theming, and more specific objectives ways of "attacking" your opponent, like kicking a field goal.

# We Need a Server

In this chapter, we'll be building out an RTS in crafty.js, with a little help from node and socket. io. For our RTS, we'll be making a game that is similar to the board game *Stratego*, but real-time rather than turn-based.

*Stratego* is a two-player game, with a red army on one side and a blue army on the other. Each player controls units of varying strengths, with the ultimate goal of capturing the other player's flag. This is a game of hidden ("imperfect") information, as opposed to a game with "perfect information" like chess, where both players have access to the same information about the game state, such as where the enemy's rooks and pawns are. In this game, you only know what unit the other player has advanced once a skirmish breaks out with one of your units. Over time, you guess more and more of what they have and form your strategy as you learn more.

In Chapter 6, "Fighting," we created a two-player fighting game, but we did not have the constraint of needing to hide information. To accomplish that in real time, and without the absurdity of taping a cardboard dividing wall down the center of the monitor to prevent "screen-peeking," our only option is to give each player a screen. Before implementing the game, let's figure out how to solve this problem.

So far, we have only dealt with *client-side code*. This means code that runs on your browser. You open an html file on your browser, and it loads the JavaScript on the interpreter of your browser. Unplug your Ethernet cable and turn your Wi-Fi off, and this code will still work.

Now, we are pushing ourselves into the territory of *server-side code*. This is code that runs on a (sometimes specially built) computer and is available over a network through some protocol to be accessed by other computers. When you visit a website, you are visiting a physical "server" somewhere—that is, a computer that is running a program to interpret your request and give you a response (often through the HTTP protocol). What may be confusing is that these pieces of metal, plastic, and silicon (what we normally call "computers") are called "servers," and they gain this title of "server" by running these special programs which are called…I'm sorry…they are called "servers" also.

You can distinguish between them by referring to the special computer type as machines, boxes, boxen, cages, physical servers, things in the data center, or by their marketing term, the cloud, which hints at a more complex and abstract (virtualized) configuration of boxen where you wouldn't be able to easily point to one and say, "My data is on this computer."

As for the special programs running on a server, we describe them by getting specific about what protocol they communicate in. So we have HTTP servers, web servers, database servers, as well as app servers that often focus on a specific language or framework. As a side note, much of the web revolves around a related concept called *web services or APIs* where you can retrieve, edit, and push data. These are related enough that if people referred to the programmatic interface of Twitter (the API) as a "Tweet Server," they wouldn't be too far off.

> ## note
>
> You will be using your computer as the server, running a node "server" with a socket.io running alongside it. There are ways to expose your computer on a local network or across the web, but it is often simpler to upload and run your program somewhere else. This is called *hosting*.
>
> Physical, managed, and dedicated (not shared) servers, can cost a good bit of money. There are some general options for configuring your own "virtual" server such as Linode, Amazon.com's EC2, and Rackspace, but if you're just looking to get something online easily, something preconfigured with your "application stack" (node.js, Ruby on Rails, and so on) such as heroku or nodejitsu is a good option. If you are just getting started with node, nodejitsu.com would be a good place to start your hunt for a hosting option. It is cheap ($3/month). Unlike open-source software, with hosting, it's hard not to give up some cash to get something that works. If you are looking to set up your own hosting environment, nodejitsu and nodester both have open source tools that would enable these possibilities on one of the virtual options such as Linode, EC2, or Rackspace.
>
> As for setting up a domain name such as jsarcade.com, the steps can vary significantly depending on who you choose for a hosting company. This process forces you to deal with another company, called a Domain Registrar, and pay them something around $10 per year to own the domain. I would recommend namecheap.com, iwantmyname.com, or gandi.net. Avoid godaddy.com.

With that terminology out of the way, let's get back to our goal of presenting related but different information to two players. In short, we need a server (hardware and software) to accomplish this. This approach has other advantages as well. First, in addition to information hiding, having a server gives you the ability to run code in the background without holding up rendering. In addition to slow code, bad performance might indicate a need to increase your server's capabilities, giving us an option to buy rather than build a better user experience. Conversely, in many cases, relying on the client-side interpreter in the browser can take some of the load off a server because there is not one central choke point where slow code holds everyone up.

Second, rather than players downloading all the code to their browser to interpret, it runs on a server, and you can show them only what you want them to see (commonly, this means html, css, images, and client-side JavaScript). You can keep your server-side code out of their hands altogether if you want, giving you different distribution opportunities (selling your game) than you might have otherwise.

Lastly, anything you show or accept from the client can be changed. If your game is popular enough, and you have some incentives for player performance in the game such as virtual goods or a leaderboard, some players will cheat. To guard against this, compressing your JavaScript so that it is unreasonable can keep out the laziest and dumbest hackers. Following that, you would want a policy for client-side code that you only expose visual functionality such as `drawAThing()` or boring functionality such as `handleInput()`, but not something like `winGame()` or `getRareItemThatIsSupposedToBeAFiveDollarInGamePurchase()`. As a general rule, if it is anything players would brag about accomplishing, don't let them do it by exposing the code, and by this standard, even `handleInput()` is suspect because it could be scripted for gold farming and automated leveling.

On extremely popular games, player-hackers will go as far as cloning your game entirely and creating programs to do totally unexpected things. There are a few problems they can create, such as unbalancing a game's economic system or negatively affecting your average player's experience in any number of ways. Another way to look at it is that you have accidentally designed a second game, where the goal is to understand and control the primary game. In their own way, these player-hackers might be requesting features, benignly exposing security vulnerabilities, designing levels, or creating content (such as new levels, new characters, music remixes, or translation patches) for other player-hackers, as well as normal players. Keep in mind that if your game is open source, you may be primarily building for this type of player.

## Recipe: Getting Node

Now that we know what a server does, let's go get one. Again, we'll be running the "server" on your computer acting as the physical "server," so you won't play against friends outside of your network unless you go through some additional steps to expose your server (self-hosting) or track down a server online. Node, like many software libraries, has many paths to getting the code. There are package managers for specific languages such as Ruby gems or Python eggs. There are source files (binary files) that contain code (often in the C language) that you would compile and install for your specific architecture. There are OS-specific package managers such as Mac's homebrew or Debian Linux's package manager run with apt-get. The web framework we'll be using, node.js, even has its own called npm (node package manager).

For installing node.js though, you have simpler options for Mac and Windows. Go to http://nodejs.org/download and, as of this writing, you will see a page like Figure 10.1. If you click the Windows or Apple logo, you'll download an installer that you can use in a step-by-step wizard to install node. (npm comes with it, but more on that later.) These wizards present the easiest options for the Mac and Windows users. The Linux users might be used to the harder options (using the command line) by now. Anyone taking the command-line options of installing need either the Terminal program in Mac or Linux, or for Windows, putty, or cygwin. If you have one of those terminal programs, Joyent (the driving force behind node) has a wiki page for installing from package managers here:

https://github.com/joyent/node/wiki/Installing-Node.js-via-package-manager

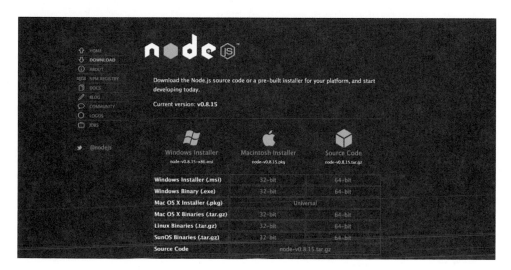

**Figure 10.1** The node.js downloads page

As you share and borrow more code, you'll see git and github referenced frequently. Git is a *version control system* that is, at its core, just a much more sane option than naming your files something like myFileLatest.ext, myFileBest.ext, myFileActuallyLatest.ext, myFileActuallyLatestJune.ext, and so on. Github is a service that hosts source code to backup and share. It is not a package management system like those mentioned earlier, but it is a very popular way to share JavaScript code. You may end up downloading code from it more often than any other option.

After following the directions particular to your operating system and preferred installation method, you should have node all ready to go. If you go to your terminal and type `node`, you will see a ">" prompt. You can treat this just like you would a JavaScript console in your browser. You can say things like `1+3` and get `4` back. You can write JavaScript functions. One major difference is that it will not have access to anything like `window` or `document`. The reason is that those are browser objects, and you're not in the browser anymore! Congratulations. All that confusion around managing different versions of different types of browsers is gone. You are only accountable for 1 (consistent) interpreter now, until you get back to the browser at least. You are using JavaScript as a real language, without all the weird baggage that browsers bring to the party. Press Control-C to exit the interpreter.

You now have a JavaScript interpreter that you can run from the terminal program by typing node. We were trying to write a server as well. Create a file called httpserver.js and put the code from Listing 10.1 in it. Then in your terminal, run this command to start your server: node httpserver.js.

**Listing 10.1**  An HTTP Server in Node

```
console.log("ahoy hoy, check me out at http://localhost:1234");
var http = require('http');
http.createServer(function (request, response) {
  console.log("Request received.");
  response.write('<h1>AHOY HOY!</h1>');
  response.end();
}).listen(1234);
```

You are used to the console.log function from working in the browser. Here, it prints to your terminal. In the second line, node brings in its http package to act as a server for you. Next, run the createServer function, passing in a function that describes what to do when a request comes in. When that happens, we write another message to the terminal, fill in a header tag with an elated message, and close the connection. If you don't close the connection with response.end, you see a spinner on your web page, and it will look like nothing is happening. The listen(1234) function that you are chaining specifies the port number that you are making available to view this server in action.

Speaking of viewing this server in action, visit http://localhost:1234 because the terminal indicates you should and open the console. You would see something like Figure 10.2 if you were using Firefox and opened the Script tab in Firebug. Similarly, on the Sources tab of the Chrome developer tools, you will not see the server.js file listed. The browser has no idea that you used JavaScript. You have liberated it from the browser. All your browser knows is that it visited an HTTP server and got a header tag in response, but it has no idea that you're using JavaScript, rather than Ruby, Python, Perl, Java, or PHP for a server-side language.

## note

JavaScript in some form is the language of the browser, and there is no escaping that fact. Despite having a choice of any number of server-side languages, and even if you prefer them to JavaScript, using the same language on the server-side as the client-side language makes sense for two reasons.

First, during development, it reduces the amount of time to change your brain to think in one language versus the other. The result of using two languages is typically that people spend more time with the server-side language. They end up caring for that code more in every way, and the front end languishes as an auxiliary nice-to-have or poorly implemented guessed-at code. The user experience suffers terribly. Using the same server-side language forces developers to at least know how to care for the front-end code just as much. Secondly, using the same language in both contexts means that code can more easily be shifted between the client side and the server side, or even shared between them. Libraries can even come with complementary code to support both contexts, as you will see with socket.io.

**Figure 10.2** The httpserver.js file is for your eyes only.

# Recipe: Real Time with Socket.io

Before you start the game, there is just one technology left to understand, which is socket.io. So far, you have created an http server that responds to any path and parameters at localhost:1234 in exactly the same way. For asynchronous operations, you could use this server to communicate with hidden information and calculations. Then you could make that information available at different paths such as localhost:1234/playerOne. For complex routing and other higher-level features, you might consider express.js, which sits on top of node. To get real-time updates from this system, you could use Ajax like you did in previous chapters, which means that every time you want new information from the server, you execute a new HTTP request and get back an HTTP response. For this to work, you need a path (and/or parameters) for every type of information, or you could accept a large response and filter through it to get only the information you want.

There are variations on the Ajax solution for two-way communication. The most recent is a new protocol called *web sockets*. This can be faster and consume less bandwidth than Ajax solutions. It is not supported in every browser though, so what socket.io does is create a unified API for all these technologies. If one technology doesn't work, it falls back to the next one.

To use socket.io, you need to download it with the node package manager by running `npm install socket.io@0.9.11 -g` on the command line. This will install socket.io somewhere on your file system. The terminal output will describe where exactly. Then in the same directory where you will end up putting all of the project files (index.html, game.js, and server.js), run the following command at the terminal: `npm link socket.io`.

This adds a local pointer to your global npm package. And with that, you've taken care of the server setup.

> ## note
>
> Many times, you see instructions to download a module with npm using the –g flag, so to install socket.io, you would run `npm install socket.io -g`.
>
> This makes the npm package globally available across your system. One downside with this is that when you have different projects, you may need to guarantee your old projects do not break when you update packages. So in those cases, you would want to install packages locally. On the other hand, for a package such as a testing framework that you use outside of your project on the command line, you would want to install this globally.
>
> For simplicity's sake, take the global option for socket.io, but to future-proof this recipe, we have locked the instructions to download the specific version `@0.9.11`. Otherwise, an update to socket.io could cause a breaking change to the code in this book.

The socket.io module includes the client-side JavaScript file as well, and if you want to dig for it in the file that the terminal said it was in, I won't stop you. However, for your convenience, it is also sitting in the rts/initial/ directory of this book's project files.

Next, create three files, starting with the index.html in Listing 10.2.

**Listing 10.2**  Starter HTML index File

```
<!DOCTYPE html>
<html>
  <head>
    <title>RTS</title>
  </head>
  <body>
    <script src="socket.io.js"></script>
    <script src="crafty.js"></script>
```

```
    <script src="game.js"></script>
  </body>
</html>
```

The index.html file sets the title, loads the socket.io client code that you pulled from the module (the server code is still in the package manager), and adds a new game.js file.

Next, use the code in Listing 10.3 in a newly created game.js file.

**Listing 10.3**   The game.js File with socket.io Client Code

```
window.onload = function() {
  var socket = io.connect('http://localhost:1234');
  socket.on('started', function(data){
    console.log(data);
  });
};
```

This file waits for the window to load and follows that up by attempting to connect with the socket at port 1234. Here, the on function waits to hear the server say "started," and executes the anonymous function to log the data when it does. If you run this code right now (by visiting `http://localhost:1234`), you can see an error message in the console. However, if you left your httpserver.js file running at port 1234, you can see the request attempt to be handled by it, with the message Request Received. Before you make your socket.io server, shut down that HTTP server by either closing that window (or tab) in the terminal that contains it or typing control and C together to "kill" its process.

Now you need a socket.io server that can communicate with the game.js file (that is, making use of the client library that you added earlier). Now add a server.js file with the code in Listing 10.4.

**Listing 10.4**   The socket.io Server File

```
var io = require('socket.io').listen(1234);
io.sockets.on('connection', function (socket) {
  socket.emit('started', {ahoy: "hoy"});
});
```

This code adds a `socket.io` server using node's `require` keyword and sets it up at port 1234. Then, we see our on function (just like in the client code), which listens for a connection event, and responds by sending a message to your client code via `emit` (which can also be used to send data from the client to this server). This message is labeled as started, which is the event that the client code in Listing 10.3 has been waiting for. The client code takes the message object and prints it to the console.

To see this in action, you need to run `node server.js` on the terminal to start the socket.io server. Then open the index.html file in your browser. If you open up the browser console, you can see the message is being passed in. In addition, you can watch the server logging and printing its information in the terminal window similar to Figure 10.3. Everything printed might not make sense to you, but if something is going wrong while building a game with a client/server setup, check here in addition to the browser console for errors. For example, a fairly common mistake is forgetting to turn the server on, which you can tell by looking here. Also, if your server is started, but you visit the wrong URL, your best indication would be if there was no connection code coming from the terminal.

**Figure 10.3**  Example output from the server

With all that out of the way, it is time to finally start building our game.

# Recipe: Creating an Isometric Map with crafty.js

Of all the game engines covered so far, crafty is definitely one of the more mature. It features a robust component-entity system, has an active community, great documentation, and good support for modules (built and supported by said community).

In spite of these good points, it is not yet common practice for HTML5 game engines to follow the lead of node modules like socket.io and create complementary server and client interfaces. Because of that, barring some serious edits, you're stuck using crafty only for the client-side code. Let's start by drawing an isometric board with crafty by adding the bold code in Listing 10.5 to our game.js file.

**Listing 10.5**  Drawing an Isometric Board with Crafty

```javascript
window.onload = function() {
  Crafty.init();
  Crafty.viewport.scale(3.5);
  var iso = Crafty.isometric.size(16);
  var mapWidth = 20;
  var mapHeight = 40;
  Crafty.sprite(16, "sprites.png", {
    grass: [0,0,1,1],
    selected _ grass: [1,0,1,1],
    blue _ box: [2,0,1,1],
    blue _ one: [3,0,1,1],
    blue _ two: [4,0,1,1],
    blue _ three: [5,0,1,1],
    blue _ bomb: [6,0,1,1],
    blue _ flag: [7,0,1,1],
    red _ box: [8,0,1,1],
    red _ one: [9,0,1,1],
    red _ two: [10,0,1,1],
    red _ three: [11,0,1,1],
    red _ bomb: [12,0,1,1],
    red _ flag: [13,0,1,1],
    selected _ box: [14,0,1,1]
  });
  var setMap = function(){
    for(var x = 0; x < mapWidth; x++) {
      for(var y = 0; y < mapHeight; y++) {
        var bias = ((y % 2) ? 1 : 0);
        var z = x+y + bias;
        var tile = Crafty.e("2D, DOM, grass, Mouse")
          .attr('z',z)
          .areaMap([7,0],[8,0],[15,5],[15,6],[8,9],[7,9],[0,6],[0,5])
          .bind("MouseOver", function() {
            this.addComponent("selected _ grass");
            this.removeComponent("grass");
          }).bind("MouseOut", function() {
            this.addComponent("grass");
            this.removeComponent("selected _ grass");
          });
```

```
        iso.place(x,y,0, tile);
      }
    }
  };
  setMap();
  var socket = io.connect('http://localhost:1234');
  socket.on('started', function(data){
    console.log(data);
  });
};
```

When the window loads, we start by initializing crafty. Next, because your sprites are only 16-by-16 pixels, you need to scale up your viewport size. Next, we initialize an isometric crafty object to use for placing our sprites. Then set map dimensions. After that, describe the sprites that appear in the game; then declare their position and dimensions, and give them labels.

In the `setMap` function, loop through each x and y position based on the `mapWidth` and `mapHeight`. The z index (what layer the tile is in) of each tile here is a little tricky. In the top row, the z index is 0 through 19. The pattern for what the z index is in subsequent rows depends on which row it is in. For tiles on even rows, the z index value of the tile immediately down and to the right and the tile immediately down and to the left must have a larger value. If this is not the case, the overlapping of the tiles will not work out correctly. This is what the `bias` value achieves.

The tiles are declared as new entities with the `Crafty.e` function, which contains an array-like string that lists the components. Looking at the list, you can see the type of flexibility the system provides. In addition to allowing for placement of isometric tiles, the 2D component supports the `areaMap` function that determines the pixel boundaries of the tile by tracing a path from each x/y pair passed as a parameter. The DOM component enables drawing the entity and placing it in the DOM structure. Adding the `grass` component sets the sprite for each tile. Also in this block, you can take advantage of the `Mouse` component's capabilities to create a hover state to highlight the tile that the mouse is on top of.

## note

There is a `canvas` component you could use in place of DOM, but it does not support scaling, which you need given the small sprite size. So use the DOM component here.

We have created an isometric map with a hover state showing a tile highlighted blue. Open index.html in a browser, and you should see something like Figure 10.4.

**Figure 10.4**  Isometric map with a highlighted tile

# Recipe: Drawing the Units

Let's get back to our server, which you may have left running, happily pushing less than useful data to the page. That's fine, but we need to change it now. If it is still running and you change it, it won't be automatically updated with new instructions, so you will want to kill the server process by going to the terminal window that it is running in and pressing Control and C together on the keyboard. This goes for any time you change the server file, and not just this time.

> ## tip
>
> If you want your server to be aware of changes to a file, you probably want some technology (possibly an npm package) that contains some of these words: hot reload, live reload, file watcher, or demon, daemon, or forever.
>
> Things change fast in the node world, and at some point, I can see being able to run `server.js -reload` at the command line or specifying auto-reloading in a configuration file. For now, the npm packages nodemon and supervisor are popular options to achieve this functionality.

On the server.js file, let's first change the call on connection to be something a little more useful with the code in Listing 10.6. The bold lines replace your old call emitting `started`.

**Listing 10.6**   Emitting place units to the Client

```
var io = require('socket.io').listen(1234);
io.sockets.on('connection', function (socket) {
  var units = placeUnits();
  socket.emit('place units', units);
  // socket.emit('started', {ahoy: "hoy"}); //This line has to go

});
```

Here, we set `units` to whatever is returned by the yet to be defined `placeUnits`, and then `emit` that to the connecting client. Now, with the code in Listing 10.7, let's define `placeUnits`. It is a rather long listing, but it is mostly repetitive after the first 10 lines. You can place this code at the top of server.js.

**Listing 10.7**   Determining unit Placement in server.js

```
var placeUnits = function(){
  var yLocations = [2, 4, 6, 8, 10, 12, 14, 16, 18, 20, 22, 24, 26, 28,
➥30, 32, 34, 36, 38];
  var pickY = function(alignment){
    var y = Math.floor(Math.random(yLocations.length)*yLocations.length);
    return yLocations.splice(y, 1) - alignment;
  };
  var xPositionRed = 18;
  var xPositionBlue = 1;

  return [
    {color: "red",
    type: "one",
    xPosition: xPositionRed,
    yPosition: pickY(1)},
    {color: "red",
    type: "one",
    xPosition: xPositionRed,
    yPosition: pickY(1)},
    {color: "red",
    type: "one",
    xPosition: xPositionRed,
    yPosition: pickY(1)},
    {color: "red",
    type: "two",
    xPosition: xPositionRed,
    yPosition: pickY(1)},
    {color: "red",
    type: "two",
```

```
    xPosition: xPositionRed,
    yPosition: pickY(1)},
{color: "red",
 type: "three",
    xPosition: xPositionRed,
    yPosition: pickY(1)},
{color: "red",
 type: "three",
    xPosition: xPositionRed,
    yPosition: pickY(1)},
{color: "red",
 type: "bomb",
    xPosition: xPositionRed,
    yPosition: pickY(1)},
{color: "red",
 type: "flag",
    xPosition: xPositionRed,
    yPosition: pickY(1)},
{color: "blue",
 type: "one",
    xPosition: xPositionBlue,
    yPosition: pickY(0)},
{color: "blue",
 type: "one",
    xPosition: xPositionBlue,
    yPosition: pickY(0)},
{color: "blue",
 type: "one",
    xPosition: xPositionBlue,
    yPosition: pickY(0)},
{color: "blue",
 type: "two",
    xPosition: xPositionBlue,
    yPosition: pickY(0)},
{color: "blue",
 type: "two",
    xPosition: xPositionBlue,
    yPosition: pickY(0)},
{color: "blue",
 type: "three",
    xPosition: xPositionBlue,
    yPosition: pickY(0)},
{color: "blue",
 type: "three",
    xPosition: xPositionBlue,
    yPosition: pickY(0)},
{color: "blue",
```

```
    type: "bomb",
    xPosition: xPositionBlue,
    yPosition: pickY(0)},
    {color: "blue",
    type: "flag",
    xPosition: xPositionBlue,
    yPosition: pickY(0)}
  ]
};
```

We set the yLocations array with all the vertical positions possible for units to appear. Then we define a function to pull a random index from this array, remove the element at that index, and return its value. The alignment parameter serves as a way to allow units of both sides to appear the same distance from their respective edges of the map. Without this, the most convenient way to do this would be to have a yLocations array for both red and blue units, allowing only even values in one and only odd values in the other. Next, we set the xPositions for red and blue.

What is ultimately returned from this function is a long array of units. We assign the color and type as string values that you can later use to determine the sprite. The xPosition is based on the xPosition variables of the respective color, and the yPosition is determined randomly by the pickY function. The assignment of these properties is repeated for each unit type, in some cases doing it multiple times per unit.

Remember to restart your server at this point so that these changes will be picked up.

The responsibility of actually drawing the units on the page is on the client. You can ship as much processing and preparation as you want to the server, but at some point, the browser is what actually renders the colors, images, and text. To make this happen, first, we have to adjust the socket.io listener to be ready for the place units message to come with the bold code in Listing 10.8. This can replace your old listener code in game.js.

**Listing 10.8**   Listening to the Server for place units

```
var socket = io.connect('http://localhost:1234');
// replace this line: socket.on('started', function(data){
socket.on('place units', function(units){
// replace this line: console.log(data);
placeUnits(units);

});
```

Here, we listen for the server to tell us about the new units. Then we call a `placeUnits` function to loop through our array of `units` and put them on the map. Let's define that function with the code in Listing 10.9. We can place this code directly above Listing 10.8 in game.js.

**Listing 10.9** The placeUnits Function in game.js

```
var placeUnits = function(units){
  for(var i = 0; i < units.length; i++){
    var componentList = "2D, DOM, Mouse, " + units[i].color + " _ " +
➥units[i].type;
    var unit = Crafty.e(componentList)
          .attr('z',100)
          .areaMap([7,0],[8,0],[14,3],[14,8],[8,12],[7,12],[2,8],[2,3]);
    iso.place(units[i].xPosition,units[i].yPosition,0, unit);
  };
}
```

We loop through the `units` array, adding a new entity for each unit. The unit's sprite is added to the component list by adding the color and type to form the sprite label. The z index is set at 100 because we don't mind if our units overlap one another, but we need them to be in front of the z index of each map tile. The `areaMap` again determines the dimensions of the sprite by connecting the dots specified by the x and y coordinates passed in as parameters. Finally, the unit is placed according to the isometric rules so that it will appear within the bounds of the grass tile it is on top of.

With all that set, and assuming you have restarted your server, you will see a new placement of the units each time you refresh the page. It will look something like Figure 10.5.

# Recipe: Moving Units

Now that we have units on the board, we need a way to move them around. This means adding two new click handlers: one for the units and one for the tiles. The first change we'll make, with the bold code in Listing 10.10, is to add the click handler to each tile inside of the `setMap` function of game.js.

**Listing 10.10** Click Handler for Tiles

```
var unitClicked = null;
var setMap = function(){
...
.bind("MouseOver", function() {
  this.addComponent("selected _ grass");
```

```
    this.removeComponent("grass");
}).bind("MouseOut", function() {
    this.addComponent("grass");
    this.removeComponent("selected _ grass");
}).bind("Click", function() {
    if(unitClicked){
        moveUnit(this);
    }
});
iso.place(x,y,0, tile);
```

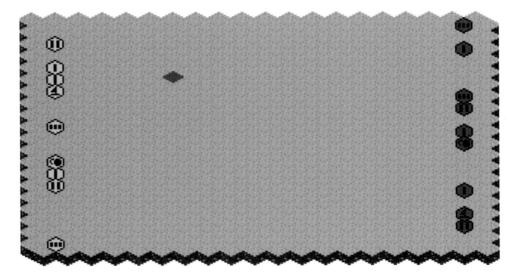

**Figure 10.5** Randomly placed units on the map

Before the setMap function, we declare a new variable that will store a unit that is clicked. Then, inside of the setMap function, in the bolded section, we bind a click handler to each tile that, if a unit has been clicked, executes the moveUnit function. With the bolded lines in Listing 10.11, let's define the moveUnit function. You can do this just under the declaration of unitClicked and before setMap.

**Listing 10.11** Declaring the moveUnit Function

```
var unitClicked = null;

var moveUnit = function(place){
    var xDistance = Math.abs(unitClicked.x - place.x);
    var yDistance = Math.abs(unitClicked.y - place.y);
    var distance = Math.sqrt(Math.pow(xDistance, 2) + Math.pow(yDistance,
2)*4);
```

```
    unitClicked.tween({x: place.x, y: place.y}, Math.round(distance*3))
    unitClicked.addComponent(unitClicked.trueSprite);
    unitClicked = null;
};

var setMap = function(){
```

Here, we calculate the difference in the x positions and y positions of the `unitClicked` and the `place`, where the `place` is the patch of grass we're sending the `unitClicked` to. After we adjust the unit code, `place` will also refer to the location of the second unit clicked. Now that we have the x and y distances between the sections, we use our old friend the Pythagorean theorem to find the straight-line distance between the points. Notice that you multiply the y component by four in this calculation because the map, despite containing twice as many vertical positions, is one-half as high as it is wide. Then, in the tween function, we pass the coordinates as where the unit is headed, and the result of the distance calculation is to give an appropriate number of milliseconds over which to display this movement. Multiply this by 3 to slow this movement down a bit. Next, we flip the `unitClicked` back to its original sprite and set `unitClicked` to null.

---

### note

We intentionally slowed down the movement of these units by multiplying the distance by 3. In a game where you control just one unit, like a fighting game, you would be likely to want faster motion. Partly because slowing down the movement gives players time to think, and partly because there are many more units to keep track of, slowing down the movement is a sensible choice here.

You can experiment with the number of units and how fast they move as you see fit. You might also want to play with unit types all having a different speed.

---

Next, let's introduce a new and improved `placeUnits` function with the bolded code in Listing 10.12.

**Listing 10.12** placeUnits Updated with Clicking and Moving

```
var placeUnits = function(units){
    for(var i = 0; i < units.length; i++){
        var unitSprite = units[i].color + " _ " + units[i].type;
        var componentList = "2D, DOM, Mouse, Tween, " + unitSprite;
        var unit = Crafty.e(componentList)
            .attr('z',100)
            .areaMap([7,0],[8,0],[14,3],[14,8],[8,12],[7,12],[2,8],[2,3]);
        unit.trueSprite = unitSprite;
        unit.bind("Click", function() {
```

```
    if(unitClicked){
      if(unitClicked !== this){
        moveUnit(this);
      };
    }else{
      this.removeComponent(this.trueSprite);
      this.addComponent('selected _ box');
      unitClicked = this;
    };
  });
  iso.place(units[i].xPosition,units[i].yPosition,0, unit);
};
}
```

Because we need to reuse the variable describing the sprite, we now calculate it before we use it in the component list. In the third bold line, we attach it as the `trueSprite` of the `unit`. Next, we have a click handler that, when there is a unit that has been clicked, and it is not the current unit being clicked, moves the unit to the position of the current unit being clicked. If a unit has not already been clicked, we show the unit being clicked as a box by swapping its `trueSprite` with the `selected _ box` sprite, and then we set the unit being clicked to the `unitClicked`.

Now, you can move sprites around, after clicking around a bit, and moving some sprites, you can open index.html in your browser to see something like Figure 10.6. Again, don't forget to start your server.

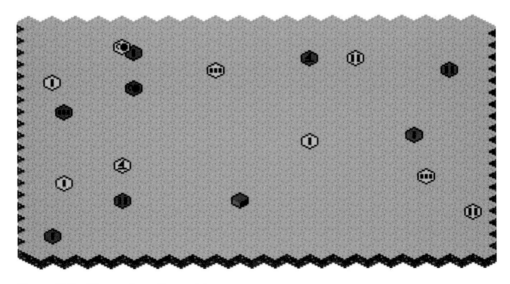

**Figure 10.6**  After moving units around

# Recipe: Player Specific Control and Visibility

Now we have a game where you can move different colored tiles around a map. We're at the "bad art installation" stage of building where our only options are either to make it better or to change the sprites to something topical and claim that it's experimental/pop art so that no one judges us too harshly. Let's take option one by giving each player control over one of the colors, and hide the face values (I, II, III, bomb, flag) of the other colored tokens.

The server.js file is the most basic, so let's start there. Note that up until this point, we have only been using your server to set up the board. We'll go beyond that in this recipe. Insert the bold lines from Listing 10.13 just below the `placeUnits` function and above the connection handler.

**Listing 10.13** room and player Attributes

```
var playerId = 0;
var playerColor = function(){
  return (!(playerId % 2)) ? "red" : "blue";
}
var roomId = function(){
  return "room" + Math.floor(playerId / 2);
}
var units;
var io = require('socket.io').listen(1234);
```

We start by giving `playerId` an initial value of 0. We will increment this with every connection. Next, we declare a function that will set even numbered players to red and odd numbered players to blue. Next, we declare a second function that gives each sequential set of two players their own room. The `Math.floor` function here allows every two players to be in the same room. Lastly, we declare the units variable so that you can preserve the first value of it for the second player to join a room.

Now let's head into the code for the connection handler of server.js with the bolded lines in Listing 10.14.

**Listing 10.14** Updates to the connection Handler

```
var io = require('socket.io').listen(1234);
io.sockets.on('connection', function (socket) {
  socket.playerColor = playerColor();
  socket.roomId = roomId();
  var player = {id: playerId,
             color: socket.playerColor,
             room: socket.roomId }
```

```
    socket.emit('initialize player', player);
    socket.join(socket.roomId);
    if(!(playerId % 2)){
      units = placeUnits();
    };

    socket.emit('place units', units);

    socket.on('update positions', function (data) {
      socket.broadcast.to(socket.roomId).emit('update enemy positions',
 data);
    });
    playerId = playerId + 1;
    socket.on('disconnect', function () {
      socket.broadcast.to(socket.roomId).emit('user disconnected');
    });
  });
```

We start by determining the color and room id for the current socket. Next, we add these attributes to a player object, and then send that data in the `initialize player` message to the connected client socket. In the next line, we `join` the room with the current room id. This room feature of socket.io is one way of scoping messages to a subset of connected clients. Next, if the client connected has an even number, we initialize the placement of the units. We don't do this on odd numbers so that we can avoid re-creating the unit placement each time. If we redrew every time, the players would not see the same unit placement. Next, we create a handler for the `update positions` message. When we receive this message, we send the other player (via the broadcast mechanism) the `update enemy positions` message, and with it convey the new positions of the enemies.

Next we increment the `playerId` so that each connection gets a unique value and we are able to appropriately determine rooms and colors for players. If a player leaves the game, the last handler passes a message to the other player (again with the broadcast mechanism) indicating this.

Now for the game.js file. First, we have some changes to make to the `placeUnits` function. Let's address those with the bold lines in Listing 10.15.

**Listing 10.15** Updates to the placeUnits Function

```
var placeUnits = function(units){
  player.units = [];
  player.enemyUnits = [];
  for(var i = 0; i < units.length; i++){
    var unitInfo = units[i];
```

```
    var controllable = unitInfo.color === player.color;
    if(controllable){
      unitSprite = unitInfo.color + " _ " + unitInfo.type;
    }else{
      unitSprite = "selected _ box";
    }
    var componentList = "2D, DOM, Mouse, Tween, " + unitSprite;
    var unit = Crafty.e(componentList)
          .attr('z',100)
          .areaMap([7,0],[8,0],[14,3],[14,8],[8,12],[7,12],[2,8],[2,3]);
    unit.controllable = controllable;
    unit.trueSprite = unitSprite;
    unit.xPosition = function(){
      return this.x;
    };
    unit.yPosition = function(){
      return this.y;
    };
    unit.bind("Click", function() {
      if(unitClicked){
        if(unitClicked !== this){
          moveUnit(this);
        };
      }else{
        if(this.controllable){
          this.removeComponent(this.trueSprite);
          this.addComponent('selected _ box');
          unitClicked = this;
        };
      };
    });
    iso.place(unitInfo.xPosition, unitInfo.yPosition, 0, unit);
    if(unit.controllable){
      player.units.push(unit);
    }else{
      player.enemyUnits.push(unit);
    }
  };
}
```

We start by creating some arrays of units and enemyUnits. The first will end up being sent to
the server to describe where this player has moved. The second array is used for processing the
other player's position when we get data back from the server. Next, we set a unitInfo as a
shortcut to referencing an element of an array multiple times. The controllable variable is set
based on whether the player's color matches the unit color. According to the next conditional, if
they match, then the player can see the unit's value. Otherwise, it will just look like a box.

We assign the controllable variable to be an attribute of the unit so that we can reference it outside of this scope. Similarly, we assign `xPosition` and `yPosition` functions as properties of the `unit` so that we can reference them later. Because these values will change, simple variables would not be good enough.

Inside of the click handler, we have a new condition for allowing a first click (the "grabbing" click rather than the second "placement" click). If the player cannot control this unit, it cannot be grabbed. This is the second half of controllable. The first was whether the player could see the unit's face value.

Next, when a player places the tile, we no longer reference an array index for the x and y positions but use the `unitInfo` variable instead. Finally, depending on whether the unit is controllable, we append it to the `units` or `enemyUnits` array.

Let's move onto the server communication code. New lines are bolded, but nearly everything is new. For safety's sake, you may want to replace everything beginning with the `place units` handler with the code in Listing 10.16.

**Listing 10.16**   Server Communication for Updated Positioning

```
var socket = io.connect('http://localhost:1234');
socket.on('place units', function(units){
  placeUnits(units);
  var updateInterval = 1000/Crafty.timer.getFPS();
  setInterval(function(){
    socket.emit('update positions', player.unitsWithLimitedData());
  }, updateInterval);
});
socket.on('update enemy positions', function(enemies){
  player.updateEnemyPositions(enemies);
});
socket.on('initialize player', function(playerData){
  player = playerData;
  player.unitsWithLimitedData = function(){
    unitsToReturn = [];
    for(var i = 0; i < this.units.length; i++){
      unitsToReturn.push({x: this.units[i].x, y: this.units[i].y});
    }
    return unitsToReturn;
  };
  player.updateEnemyPositions = function(enemies){
    for(var i = 0; i < this.enemyUnits.length; i++){
      this.enemyUnits[i].x = enemies[i].x;
      this.enemyUnits[i].y = enemies[i].y;
    }
```

```
    };
  });
  socket.on('user disconnected', function(){
    alert("Your buddy has left or refreshed.  Refresh to join a new
➥room.");
  });
};   //End of the file
```

We start with a `setInterval` call that is scheduled to run at 50 frames per second, as is the main frame rate. When this loop-like code is executed, it will describe the x and y positions of the player-controlled units to the server. Next, a handler is declared to update the enemy positions.

Following that, the `initialize player` handler is described. This sets up the variables used by the first two handlers. The `player` variable is set with data from the server. Next, the `unitsWithLimitedData` function is described, which sends the x and y positions of each unit under the player's control to the server. Following that, the `updateEnemyPositions` function is declared, which acts as the inverse operation of `unitsWithLimitedData`. This function sets the enemy positions according to what came back from the server.

In the last message handler, if the enemy player disconnects, the player is given a pop-up indicating that.

Now if you restart your server and load up two windows, you can play a game against yourself. Use different windows, not just different tabs. If you use tabs, the browsers won't take the updating seriously.

## tip

This goes for changing the code during development as well, but if you're at the stage where you have two clients and a server going, as we are now, this will keep you from getting lost. The alert statement should help you keep track of what browser window you need to refresh, but if you get confused, try taking the following steps:

1. Shut down the server.

2. Reload or change pages with the browser windows you are connected to the socket with. If you don't do this, the open clients will automatically reconnect with the server, and you may get unexpected data flowing in.

3. Restart the server.

4. Reload the pages to reconnect the clients to the server.

If you stack both players' windows on top of one another, you should now be able to see something like Figure 10.7 showing the game. Also, terminal output like Figure 10.8 indicates that your server is running.

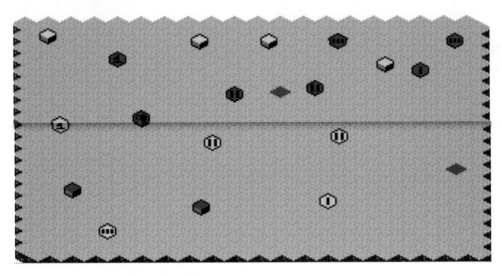

**Figure 10.7**  The game being played by two players

**Figure 10.8**  Terminal output from the socket.io server

# Recipe: Collisions for Destruction and Revelation

We have achieved nearly all of what we set out to do. We have just one task left: allowing units to attack each other. This won't require any changes in the server. We can rely on the message types that we are already passing back and forth.

Starting with the beginning of game.js, we have two new components to add. We can do this with the bolded code in Listing 10.17.

**Listing 10.17**   New components

```
window.onload = function() {
  Crafty.init();
  Crafty.c("blue");
  Crafty.c("red");
```

We introduce these components because crafty.js relies on components to detect collisions. We could bind the more specific components, but this ends up being longer (and slower) code.

With the bolded lines in Listing 10.18, we'll look at the changes we have to make to the placeUnits function.

**Listing 10.18**   Changes to the placeUnits Function in game.js

```
var placeUnits = function(units){
  player.units = [];
  player.enemyUnits = [];
  for(var i = 0; i < units.length; i++){
    var unitInfo = units[i];
    var controllable = unitInfo.color === player.color;
    unitInfo.trueSprite = unitInfo.color + " _ " + unitInfo.type;
    if(controllable){
      unitSprite = unitInfo.trueSprite;
    }else{
      unitSprite = unitInfo.color + " _ box";
    }
    var componentList = "2D, DOM, Mouse, Tween, Collision, " +
➥unitInfo.color + ",
" + unitSprite;
    var unit = Crafty.e(componentList)
            .attr('z',100)
            .areaMap([7,0],[8,0],[14,3],[14,8],[8,12],[7,12],[2,8],[2,3])
➥//(no ";" )
            .collision([7,0],[8,0],[14,3],[14,8],[8,12],[7,12],[2,8],[2,3]);
```

```javascript
      unit.controllable = controllable;
      unit.trueSprite = unitInfo.trueSprite;
      unit.xPosition = function(){
        return this.x;
      };
      unit.yPosition = function(){
        return this.y;
      };
      unit.hiding = true;
      unit.alive = true;
      unit.color = unitInfo.color;
      unit.type = unitInfo.type;
      unit.bind("Click", function() {
        if(unitClicked){
          if(unitClicked !== this){
            moveUnit(this);
          };
        }else{
          if(this.controllable){
            this.removeComponent(this.trueSprite);
            this.addComponent(this.color + '_box');
            unitClicked = this;
          };
        };
      });
      var collidesWithColor = (unit.color === "blue" ? "red" : "blue");
      unit.onHit(collidesWithColor, function(e){
        this.hiding = false;
        e[0].obj.hiding = false;
        if(this.type === "one"){
          if(e[0].obj.type === "one" || e[0].obj.type === "two" ||
➥e[0].obj.type === "three"){
            this.alive = false;
          };
        }else if(this.type === "two"){
          if(e[0].obj.type === "two" || e[0].obj.type === "three" ||
➥e[0].obj.type === "bomb"){
            this.alive = false;
          };
        }else if(this.type === "three"){
          if(e[0].obj.type === "three" || e[0].obj.type === "bomb"){
            this.alive = false;
          };
        }else if(this.type === "bomb"){
          if(e[0].obj.type === "one"){
            this.alive = false;
          };
```

```
        }else if(this.type === "flag"){
            if(e[0].obj.type === "one" || e[0].obj.type === "two" ||
➡e[0].obj.type === "three"){
                this.alive = false;
            };
        }
    })
    iso.place(unitInfo.xPosition,unitInfo.yPosition,0, unit);
    if(unit.controllable){
        player.units.push(unit);
    }else{
        player.enemyUnits.push(unit);
    }
  };
}
```

As an alternative to trusting that `unitSprite` and `trueSprite` are the same thing, we now differentiate between the two and keep a reference to `trueSprite` within the unit so that we can reveal enemies later on. Also, we now rely on the color of the sprite to determine the hidden box style (rather than using `selected _ box`). In our component list, we now add the color (for simple collision detection) and the `Collision` component. In the `collision` function, we pass a list of points that outline the hit box in the same way that we use `areamap` to specify the clickable area of the unit. The `hiding` and `alive` properties are added to the unit so that we can update a unit and pass information to the other player about its status. Using these, we can reveal any unit that collides with an enemy unit, and destroy those that lose to the enemy unit. The `color` and `type` properties serve as persistent references to these values. In the click handler, we now use this color property to determine what color the box should be when we click on the unit.

Next, we set up the collision handling, beginning by determining which color is the enemy. As the first parameter of the `onHit` function, we supply this color as the name of the component that we will handle a collision with. The second parameter is a function that reveals the value of both units and then handles the specifics for each type of enemy. In crafty's collision detection, `this` refers to the unit that the collision detection is bound to, and `e` is an array of collisions. We determine the unit type by getting the `obj` property of the first element of this array. If it is equal to any unit type that can beat this unit, then we set it for removal.

With our `placeUnits` function taken care of, let's address changes to the messages with the server that we pass and receive. In the `place units` handler, we need to make one minor adjustment with the addition of the bold line in Listing 10.19, which calls `updateCasualities`.

**Listing 10.19**   Update the place units Handler

```
socket.on('place units', function(units){
  placeUnits(units);
  var updateInterval = 1000/Crafty.timer.getFPS();
  setInterval(function(){
    socket.emit('update positions', player.unitsWithLimitedData());
    player.updateCasualities();
  }, updateInterval);
});
```

As our last set of changes to this file, we need to add the bold lines in Listing 10.20 to the
`initialize player` handler.

**Listing 10.20**   initialize player Handler Updates

```
socket.on('initialize player', function(playerData){
  player = playerData;
  player.unitsWithLimitedData = function(){
    unitsToReturn = [];
    for(var i = 0; i < this.units.length; i++){
      unitsToReturn.push({x: this.units[i].x, y: this.units[i].y, hiding:
➥this.units[i].hiding, alive: this.units[i].alive});
    }
    return unitsToReturn;
  };
  player.updateCasualities = function(enemies){
    for(var i = 0; i < this.units.length; i++){
      if(this.units[i].alive === false){
        this.units[i].destroy();
      }
    };
  }
  player.updateEnemyPositions = function(enemies){
    for(var i = 0; i < this.enemyUnits.length; i++){
      this.enemyUnits[i].x = enemies[i].x;
      this.enemyUnits[i].y = enemies[i].y;
      this.enemyUnits[i].hiding = enemies[i].hiding;
      this.enemyUnits[i].alive = enemies[i].alive;
      if(this.enemyUnits[i].hiding === false){
        this.enemyUnits[i].addComponent(this.enemyUnits[i].trueSprite);
        if(this.enemyUnits[i].alive === false){
          player.markToDestroy(this.enemyUnits[i]);
```

```
        }
        if(this.enemyUnits[i].reallySuperDead === true){
          this.enemyUnits[i].destroy();
        };
      };
    }
  };
  player.markToDestroy = function(enemy){
    setTimeout(function(){
      enemy.reallySuperDead = true;
    }, 1000);
  }
});
```

In the first bold line, we now indicate that we need to send the `hiding` and `alive` properties to the server along with each of the player's units. Next, we declare the `updateCasualities` function that we called in Listing 10.19. This function removes units of the player's that have been defeated by enemy units.

In the `updateEnemyPositions` function, we now use the `alive` and `hiding` properties that we passed. If the enemy unit is not hiding, we show its true sprite, and check to see if it's alive. If it is not alive, we mark it to be destroyed. The `markToDestroy` function waits for 1 second and sets a new attribute called `reallySuperDead`. If the enemy unit is marked with this `really-SuperDead` attribute, then we remove it. The reason for this indirection is that we want to show the defeated enemy unit so that a player can account for it in future attacks. It gives more information and makes for a more interesting game. The reason for introducing the new attribute is that if we just wait for a second and then mark for removal, other collisions will occur during that time and cause errors. `reallySuperDead` gives us a guard against that.

The game is complete! Now if you restart your server and load two separate browser windows, you will be able to play a two-player game where units can take each other out. After a few hits and revelations, the red player could see something like Figure 10.9.

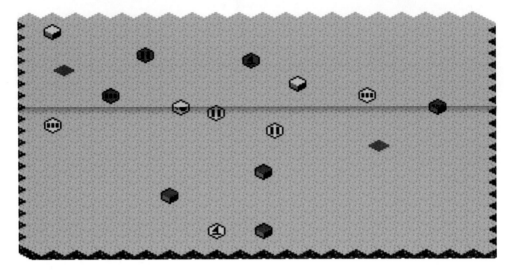

**Figure 10.9**  The game after a few hits. Notice the blue III has been revealed in the upper section.

## Summary

In this chapter, you created a networked, two-player RTS with crafty.js, node.js, and socket.io. You got our feet wet with crafty's Component/Entity system and had some exposure to working with the complexities and concerns using a server. In addition, you got to know npm, the node package manager.

If you want to get deeper into crafty, it has a number of features that were not addressed in this chapter. Between its storage and time capabilities, 2-D mathematics utilities, and additional features of the component/entity system and scene management, you could spend a good deal of time learning the full API. Moreover, craftycomponents.com features 16 (at this time) plug-ins that fill in some of the gaps that could improve the game. One of note that would be useful in an RTS is the AStar plug-in, which can help give your units more routing possibilities than traveling in a straight line. Using AStar, if you had holes or obstacles in the map, you could maintain your simple click-to-travel interface, but the units would take the fastest path around the places they shouldn't walk through.

There are plenty of other things that separate this from a fully featured RTS. Fortunately, many of them are not of a complexity to develop that we have not managed in other chapters. All of our units move, but RTS games often have "buildings" that stay put. Units and buildings typically have health, and attacking them reduces their health over time. In addition to health increasing the complexity of combat, units can often execute different types of attacks, including ranged and area-of-effect attacks. Units can, many times, be purchased and upgraded. There is often a currency (or multiple currencies) that can be gathered by certain types of units.

More features that incorporate the game's networking possibilities could also be explored. Instead of automatically connecting players, we could have a "game lobby" that allows players to manually decide who they want to play against. We could also open up a chat box so that players could type to each other while they play. Getting away from 2-player entirely, we could introduce a 1-player mode where one could play against an enemy AI.

# CHAPTER 11

# LEVELING UP

Congratulations on finishing the book. Thanks so much for reading it. For those of you who skipped ahead to see this, well, that's okay. I do that too. I'm going to talk to the first people now though, and I'll meet you back here when you finish.

There is no game in this chapter, which means it's fairly short. Hopefully, what it doesn't mean is that you are done making games. This chapter briefly recaps what you covered in the previous 10 chapters and wraps up with some thoughts on how you might take your game making to the next level.

# What Happened?

Let's recap what happened. You went through 10 chapters, which each covered a different genre of game along with a different JavaScript library to make it possible. You should now know how to break down a given type of game into smaller problems to solve. You should be comfortable with the terminology used in creating games such as sprite, collision, and parallax. You can claim a toolset, including a browser, text editor, terminal, JavaScript console, game genre, and game engine, as your favorites to work with. You might even have a favorite trig function. You don't need to have dogmatic preferences, but for many people, liking something demonstrates facility. If you like particular tools made for creating software, it's probably because you can create something with them that you value.

Beyond establishing a basic toolset and process that you are comfortable with, you also explored beginner-to-intermediate level HTML, CSS, and JavaScript. You also spent time with some of the things people like about HTML5 beyond canvas, such as CSS3 in the interactive fiction game and the local storage API. Also, you now should know that these things are not actually HTML, so they are part of "HTML5" (the marketing term) and not HTML5 (the technology).

# What's Next?

For starters, we covered 10 game genres, and there are more than that. You should be able to think of the games you made as "templates" and have some thoughts about how to break games into features such as sprites, tweening, frame rate, layers, events, scenes, inventories, collisions, maps, entities, and so on. If you can do that, a new game, even in a different genre, can be looked at as similar to something you have already built, but with different features. There are some genres that are fairly close to what you have. For example, if you turn the shooter 90 degrees, it's a top-down shooter. If you change the sprites around in the RTS and create a more complicated rule set, you could have a convincing NES-style football game. There are no "genres" that are far away, but certain features are. The blind spot in HTML5 right now is audio, and 3-D ratchets up complexity of a game immensely.

If you want to make a game in a new genre, you should go for it. And if you want to prove the author wrong about audio or 3-D being too unwieldy to do well and easily, that would be awesome. Besides bending the genres, you could add features to the games you already have. The summary of each chapter offers suggestions for interesting extra features. You could try those or create your own. You could put games inside of each other or link them together.

Beyond features and genres, these games lack certain qualities. You could say that they're not particularly artful. While they may be quirky or charming at times, they don't carry any particularly strong messages. Games can be artful, though, and they can challenge people to experience things that they otherwise couldn't.

Another thing is that these games lack is any sense of plot or character that isn't superficial or unnecessarily whimsical. An easy way to make them less abstract would be to draw from your own experiences. There aren't any games from your perspective unless you've made them already. Remember that games are not hard to make if you use a decent toolset (which could include these template games). If you've read and understood this whole book, you could easily spend more time on a well-crafted love letter, mix CD (or whatever the modern equivalent is), or even going to the store to buy a card than it would take to personalize one of these games for someone you care about.

Swinging in the complete opposite direction, there's probably some corporate fat cat out there smoking a cigar on the balcony of his penthouse who could use your skills, too. FatCatCo wants to keep people on its website to make people like them more. The only way to do that is to entertain them. "We'll give 'em games on the homepage! That'll increase profits by 14% in the next quarter alone by our projections! Brilliant!" is what they'd say. So that's another option.

Instead of focusing on the audience, there are plenty of ways for your desire to learn to be the motivating force behind making more games. If you want to produce games quickly, practice by creating the same small game over and over again and as quickly as possible. People are exceptional at things when they have a lot of experience doing it. Build it and throw it away a million times. Then pick a new type of game to do the same thing with. If the skills you exercise while you build are valuable, this will not be a waste.

Alternatively, some people take years of their lives trying to create just one perfect thing. This can work out well, but it can also be perilous. This requires believing in your vision, having others around who do, too, and not getting distracted, all while ensuring that at the end, whatever effect you are aiming for is still possible. And if not, you can live with that. Sometimes it works though, and that's how games like *Braid* happen.

From the technical side, in addition to creating the same game a million times, or creating a perfect game once, you can also focus on honing and deepening your knowledge in technical areas. There is always more you can learn about JavaScript, browsers, or other skills directly applicable to many types of games. However, you could also learn things that broaden your range of skills that are relevant to game creation by learning more about art, music, economics, writing, business, psychology, and so on.

In addition, game design itself is becoming a popular field of study. This area wraps these tangential disciplines up in one package, offering students a foundation to communicate their game ideas to many different people, while still (hopefully) giving them a chance to go deep in some technical area. A great book on game design is *The Art of Game Design*, by Jesse Schell. This book can teach you about things like playtesting your game, keeping it balanced, and making it fun. For some other resources you might benefit from investigating, look at Appendix C, "Resources."

Whatever path you take, even if it is a maximally introspective code-in-a-cave-for-5-years type of approach, you need other people. There are functional roles you need other people to perform if you aren't filling them yourself, which include designers, artists, programmers, writers, producers, composers, and playtesters. And even if you manage all that somehow, you still need people to keep you focused, people to distract you, people to believe in you, people to tell you it's good when it's not, people to tell you it's bad when it is, and people to push you when they think you can do better. And when they need you to do the same, you'll want to be that person for them. Overall, keep as many people in your life as you can fit. They're way more fun than games.

# JAVASCRIPT BASICS

If you don't have much JavaScript experience, this is the absolute minimum you should know for this book. If you can read JavaScript easily by virtue of knowing some other programming language, you may still find this useful as a reference for basic syntax. This doesn't reflect a full discussion of JavaScript concepts or even the subset found inside of this book, but if you understand the basic terms and structures covered here, you can progress through the chapters. Alternative syntax and adaptations for what is covered here are presented throughout the book. If you find yourself getting confused, come back here and see what basic structure you are building on top of.

# Main Types of APIs in JavaScript

API stands for Application Programming Interface and essentially what it refers to is what you have to work with in a given programming context. If you're wondering if you have access to a certain function or variable, this is a question of what is provided by the APIs you have available. For exploring and understanding an API, documentation is provided so that you know what you can do. Sometimes this documentation (the "docs") comes with the files you use; sometimes it's an online resource; and sometimes it's available through ancillary tools such as your text editor or terminal program. These methods are not mutually exclusive, and at times one access pattern of reading the docs is a just proxy (for example, to the online documentation).

In JavaScript, there are four main types of APIs to keep track of.

## The Native API

This is the basic agreement among people of what makes JavaScript JavaScript, and the building blocks for any program written in it—game or otherwise. This appendix covers the basics discussing things such as numbers, functions, arrays, and variables, but for a fuller reference, you should see the Mozilla Developer Network site at developer.mozilla.org.

## The Implementation API

Different browsers and nonbrowser implementations of JavaScript have different utilities available. If you run node from the command line, you should not expect the browser's objects such as `window` to somehow be available. When you use jQuery, a canvas element, local storage, or any browser-specific JavaScript feature, you rely on a browser's "implementation" of JavaScript. Similarly, when you call some specific feature of node on the command line, you rely on its implementation's API. As for demystifying the variations from browser to browser, and what can be relied upon, I would again recommend the Mozilla Developer Network.

## A Library API

Whether you call them libraries, packages, or "the source for X," external utility programs have some ways of interacting with them. The interaction that is possible is the "API" for that package. In JavaScript, this is often just one file but can be more complicated in order to include tests, build scripts, images, CSS, and so on. The newest open source tool sometimes has great functionality, and a well-designed API, but terrible documentation until a viable community rises up to support it. In reading the source code of a project, you can discover what is there and if you want or need it for your project. And if you decide to take on documentation efforts, it's usually appreciated, and a good first step to working on a project. By the way, all the game engines in this book are open source and on github. If you want to get to know their code better, you can help with documentation, submit bug reports, or work on new features, you should visit their github pages. For many of the code-based resources in section C, the github page (or Google Code in the case of Box2D) is linked to. Other times, it is the main website for the project, which usually contains a link to the source code.

## Your API

When you create a program, you are building up and using an interface to that program. Every time you write a function or declare a variable, this becomes part of your accessible list of tools, or in other words, your API. Any time you are calling these functions or referencing these variables, you are using your API. In truth, this is actually exactly the same as Library APIs, except you write the code.

As for how to construct your API, sometimes, the easiest way to write programs in JavaScript is to declare some semantic name for something (usually a function or a variable of some kind) that you imagine having a particular effect or containing some information, and then fill in the details later. On the other hand, breaking up problems into small pieces is another important, though contradictory, approach. Finding a balance and being able to bounce back and forth between those techniques is essential. Constructing an API and building a program are exactly the same thing, just from different perspectives. This goes for your programs as well as everyone else's.

# Statements

Also called a *line of code*, the *statement* is the most basic unit that you work with regularly in JavaScript. At the most basic level, statements appear on one line and end with a semicolon. If you want more than one statement on one line, you just put terminating semicolons on the same line like this:

```
x = "statement with one line";
y = "many"; z = "statements"; zz = "on"; zzz = "one"; zzzz = "line";
```

# Variables

Variables in JavaScript are a way of storing information for later use. Typically, they are preceded by the `var` keyword, which makes them *scoped* to the function they appear within. When they are not, your variable is *global*, meaning it can be accessed by anywhere in your program. Global variables can be trouble because you might accidentally use the same name twice. In larger systems, other people might also try to use this same name. This can overwrite your variables and result in a lot of confusion, so use the `var` keyword when declaring a variable.

A variable should be declared like this:

```
var myVariableName;
```

If upon declaration you want to assign your variable to 34212, the equals sign acts as an assignment operator:

```
var myVariableName = 34212;
```

Later in your program, when you want to change the value of your variable to something else, you should drop the `var` keyword. It is used for initialization.

There is a wide range of variable names throughout the book. Sticking to alphabetical characters (or numerical characters, but not at the beginning) is best for most standard variables. It is standard in JavaScript for variables to have *camelCase*, meaning they start with a lowercase letter, and any new words that follow are capitalizedLikeThis. Other languages (including CSS) sometimes use snake_case with underscores_like_this. This is a convention, rather than a requirement to have your programs work.

# Strings

When you put text in your program, you can't just write anything you want. The interpreter sees your text and tries to guess what it means in the context of the APIs it has available. To tell the interpreter that you want what you type to exist as text, to be passed, printed, and human readable, you surround it with quotes. Sometimes, strings use double quotes ("), and sometimes they use single quotes (apostrophes). If you want one of those symbols inside of the string, you must either use the other quote type, or "escape" the symbol by putting a backslash (/) in front of it.

# Numbers

There are two main types of numbers in programming: integers and floats. Integers don't have a decimal part, and floats do. If you want to treat your JavaScript interpreter as a calculator, you have access to the basic arithmetic functions (+, −, *, /), along with the rest of the Math library to perform different types of calculations on numbers. For instance, you could write a statement like the following and get 15:

```
5 * 2 + 8 - 3;
```

One special note here is to be careful with the + operator. If you put it between two numbers, it adds them. If you put it between two strings, it crams them together, so `"hello"` + `"world"` ends up being `"helloworld"`. If you add a number to a string (without careful thought), you might spend the next 20 minutes wondering why your program doesn't work.

# Arrays

Arrays are how you declare lists of things. Those lists can be numbers, strings, other arrays, objects, functions, and so on. If you want to declare a new array, you can use the literal syntax that has brackets with "elements" of the array separated by commas:

```
var myArray = ["this is my first value", 3, 1, 64, "this is my last
➥value"];
```

You can also set and retrieve specific positions in the array by specifying the index (which starts at 0). For example, if you want to know what the first value is, you can write the following:

```
myArray[0];
```

If you want to set the third element to something, you can write:

```
myArray[2] = "hello, set this here";
```

To figure out how long an array is, you can write:

```
myArray.length;
```

# Functions

JavaScript functions have a few different ways of being declared, but typically, you see something like this:

```
function(parameter1, parameter2){
  //what the function does goes here
};
```

This is a function declaration with two *parameters* (also called *arguments*) passed into it. Parameters have similar restrictions to variables as to what they can be called. The line with the two slashes is called a *comment*. The interpreter skips over comments. For a basic but real function, you can try something like this:

```
var addition = function(parameter1, parameter2){
  return parameter1 + parameter2;
};
```

By attaching the variable name `addition` to the function, you can call it. Without the `return` keyword, you would not see anything of consequence happen within this function. It would just return `undefined`. To understand better what that means, call a function with the following:

```
addition(5, 7);
```

This "returns" 12, and you can print the value, assign it to a variable, or use it in more functions.

# Objects

Objects are somewhat similar to arrays in that they store lists of things. What makes objects more flexible is that instead of numerical indexes, objects store mappings of keys and values that you define. Objects are surrounded by braces. There is a colon between each key and value, and a comma between each pair of keys and values. Here is an example:

```
var myObject = {value1: "hello", value2: 4343, anotherKey: 2, lastKey:
➥34};
```

To set and reference these values, you can use the bracket syntax, just like with arrays, but with the key names instead of numerical indexes:

```
myObject[value2]; //This will equal 4343
```

You can also use dot syntax:

```
myObject.value2; //This will equal 4343
```

One additional thing to note is that the values of objects can be functions. When you make a function a "property" of an object, you can also call this function a "method." It looks like this:

```
var myObject = {firstValue: function(){
              //whatever the function does
              },
              regularProperty: 4};
```

To call this method/function, you can write `myObject.firstValue()`.

# Conditionals

Sometimes, you need to know if values are the same or different, or if one is bigger than the other. To check this, you have comparison operators (`<`, `>`, `===`, `!==`) that you use in conditionals. The syntax of the most basic form looks like this:

```
if(x < y){
  //do something here if x is smaller than y
};
```

There are other forms of these as well. There is an if/else form:

```
if(x === y){
  //do something here if x is equal to y
}else{
  //do something here if x does not equal y
}
```

There is also an if/if else/if else.../else form where you specify additional conditions like this:

```
if(x === y){
  //do something here if x is equal to y
}else if(x > y){
  //do something here if x is larger than y
}else{
  //do something here if the above conditions aren't met
}
```

Comparison operators return booleans, which are either `true` or `false`. Everything in JavaScript has a boolean "truthiness" value inside of it. In general, you can assume that everything is truthy except for `false`, `null`, `undefined`, an empty string `" "`, `0`, and `NaN`. You can put anything into where you used a comparison before, and the `if` statement can happily discover the truthiness and evaluate. For instance, you could do something like the following:

```
if(5){
  //5 evaluates to true, so a statement here would execute
};
```

# Loops

In a program, you often want to do the same thing many times, either exactly or with slight variations. For that, you often use a loop. This is a basic `for` loop:

```
for(var i=0;i < 7; i++){
  //Whatever is here will happen 7 times
};
```

You declare "i" as a loop counter that start at 0. The second part inside of the parentheses is the termination condition, so here, as long as the loop counter is less than 7, you execute the code in the middle. The third part adds 1 to the loop counter on each iteration.

There are other kinds of loops, but this is the most common.

## Comments

Sometimes, you need to make a note to yourself or others about some code that has been written. Writing it on paper or emailing it are not as good as having it in front of you the next time you view the code. To accomplish this, you want a "comment." Comments are a way of annotating the code such that the interpreter ignores what has been written. Looking at some of the sample code in this appendix, you might be able to identify what these lines look like, but just to be clear, they look like this:

```
//I am a comment because I start with backslashes
➡3 + 5; // This part of this line is a comment too, but "3 + 5" still
➡runs
```

You can also have comments span multiple lines if you use this pattern:

```
/* Multiple lines with
backslashes and asterisks,
enable haikus */
```

# QUALITY CONTROL

If something isn't going right with your code, there can be any number of reasons. Sometimes, you spell something wrong or get two function names mixed up. Sometimes, you forget to load a library. Sometimes, one part of the code unexpectedly runs before another part. These are all called bugs, and you want to keep them out of your code.

# Browser Debugging Tools

In many programming languages, if you make a mistake, it is caught early by the compiler, or your run-time environment gives detailed feedback of why something didn't go right. What is awesome about JavaScript is that you don't need any special equipment to start. A text editor and browser are enough. What is not awesome is that by default, your development environment (a text editor and a browser) has no idea that you're a programmer trying to make something in JavaScript.

View Source is the simplest tool to use to see the HTML on the current page. It is not fancy. It doesn't let you edit anything, but it does come in handy at times.

There are many tools you can use to make your job easier, or at least possible. Some are hidden, and some you have to do a little work for. By default, the browsers assume you are just trying to look at pictures of cats, so it does not make the tools you can use completely obvious. In Firefox, you should get the Firebug add-on. You download this and learn to use it at getfirebug.com. In Chrome, the tools are in your browser already, but if you want to learn how to use and access them, you should visit developers.google.com/chrome-developer-tools.

These developer tools have similar features. There are tools to let you inspect the files (HTML, CSS, and JavaScript) used to make up the current web page. There is a DOM inspector that enables you to see how the elements on the page connect with one another. There is a network inspector that tells you all the URLs that were accessed to fully form the page you are on. Most important, there is a JavaScript console (interpreter) for you to use.

Using this console, you can create variables, call functions, and do all the things that you would expect to do in a programming environment. This is best for single statements. If you want to run a program, it's best just to bring the whole file in. When your script or statements on the console don't go right, the console gives you an error. When people "hate JavaScript," it may be that they don't use the console enough to their advantage and end up feeling like they are guessing.

Instead of using the console, some people try to debug by inserting "alerts" in their browser-based JavaScript. They look like this:

```
alert("print this in a popup box!");
```

You might do this sometimes when you want an instant indication that a particular part of the code is being accessed. The *feedback loop* on that is fairly tight: load the page, it ran/didn't run, back to code. However, using this to print the values of variables has an incredibly slow feedback loop and is not terribly specific. Consider this example:

```
alert(myObject);
```

The result of this alert statement code is shown in Figure B.1.

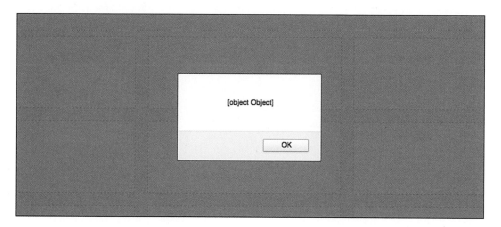

**Figure B.1**   An unhelpful alert box

That is incredibly unhelpful. You know that the object loads but cannot do anything with it. If the only inspection tool you knew about was the alert, you would keep guessing variable names, array indexes, and so on until you had an answer, requiring a code change every time you wanted to see a new aspect of your object.

A little better is using `console.log(myObject)` to print your object (and more of its details) in the console. This lets you click through its properties and subobjects easily. It is a little bit of a hack, but another option is to assign variables (or statements) that you want to see as global variables (just drop the `var` keyword). Then, you can inspect them as they were when they were assigned in your code. This isn't ideal because in addition to the problems around global variables discussed in Appendix A, "JavaScript Basics," you also must remember to remove these later. There is another option that the developer tools provide.

Stop everything. That's what *breakpoints* do. You know at what line of code things start to get murky ("I'm not sure what this variable does. Does this loop execute 10 times or 11?"). By setting a breakpoint at these confusing parts, you can execute any code inside the console that you would at that point in the JavaScript file that has the breakpoint in it. So to find out "what `thisThing` is," you just `console.log(thisThing);`, and to figure out what happens if you run the `doSomething` function, you can just type `doSomething();`.

Outside of the browser, for example, in the node run-time environment, you have a set of tools that are more standard for coding. When you run a file or line of code with the node program on the terminal, you can see errors show up there as they happen. Unlike the browser, it is not intended to be cat-viewing software first and development environment tool second.

# Testing

Appendix A discusses conditionals a little bit. Testing your code is a standard for asserting that some value has some relationship to some other value in a given context. These tests can be high-level code which asserts that "When someone clicks the button, there should be a dog on the page," or low-level code asserting something like "When this function is executed, x should equal 5."

The value of testing is that you are developing a contract with your code. Then, if you (or someone else) change(s) your code in a way that violates the contract, you have an early indication that something might be wrong.

QUnit is among the most popular frameworks for this type of "Does this do what it says?" testing. It can be found here: github.com/jquery/qunit.

Another category of testing is performance testing. When you build games in the browser, performance can mean many things. First, you have your general web type performance with questions such as "When does the user see the page start rendering," and "When is everything downloaded?" webpagetest.org can give you these types of metrics across many browsers.

In web games, performance matters the most for the number of frames per second you can draw. For a good look at this type of performance, the articles on html5rocks are excellent: html5rocks.com/en/features/performance.

Expanding testing to encompass quality control more generally, there a few other tools to be aware of. One is JSLint, developed by Douglass Crockford of "JavaScript: The Good Parts" fame. This tool checks to see if you're using any of the bad parts. It has been ported to various environments, but to get a basic idea of what it can do, you can just copy and paste your JavaScript into the window at jslint.com.

There are also automated ways to test your code for correctness (as you declare it in your tests) and code quality. These things build on each other, and you can make your environment complex. At a certain point, your "testing" becomes "tooling." Tooling in general is important. Knowing your tools, your editor, your terminal, your process, and ultimately your code can enable you to create and fix things quicker. Most developers go through periodic hot-rod building phases in which they tool out their environment with everything from terminal shortcuts to testing frameworks to in-editor games and animations.

On the downside, tooling (even when it masquerades as testing) can be a time sink and problematic if you rely on tools that you don't understand well or cannot function without. You probably like to make things through code. Tools can make you faster in the long run but slow you down in the short term. Consider tooling an exercise in reflection or self-improvement, but don't let it become your passion.

# Collaboration for Better Code

If you want to improve, pick a few heroes from the community. I wouldn't nominate myself for your list, but with this book, I'm offering you part of my list. It includes everyone who contributed to the game engines and other tools that made this book possible.

You are incredibly fortunate to have a hobby or profession in which the superstars are so accessible. You can go to conferences to hear these people speak and hang out with them at local events. You can contribute to their projects. Imagine this if it were true in the music industry. It would be like every aspiring singer having the chance to sing backup vocals on almost any CD they wanted to.

In no way am I suggesting that anyone has the right to demand anyone else's time, but rather that in many cases, there are incredibly talented people who are willing to lend a hand given the proper context. For some people, that means contributing to or seeking information on their open-source efforts. Github is a popular place for this sort of interaction. Often, projects have mailing lists that you can subscribe to if you want to stay up to date on the latest news.

You can also start your own project or community by building something other people want. Most great creators appreciate great tools, so if you make something great, people will probably want to use it. This goes for tools and games.

In spite of knowing how to stay up to date with your tools and APIs and crawling out of your coding cave every once in a while to get to know people (I don't mean that as an insult. I have a cave, too. It's okay.), sometimes you get stuck. You've read through everything you can find on the subject, and you're up to date on the latest news. It's time to ask someone who knows.

This can be intimidating depending on the forum. Mailing lists and Internet Relay Chat (IRC) can be unwelcoming. But in general, their helpfulness is directly proportional to the specificity of your question. "This tool won't work" in the best case will result in a polite request for more information but at times will be ignored or even derided (publically and permanently). Yikes. To avoid that, take some time to see if anyone has asked your question before, and give as many details as possible. I have had a few "oh no the Internet is going to think I'm stupid forever" moments because of asking a question too generally. If that happens, it's okay. If the feedback you get is "You need to be more specific in this way or that way," that may just be a sign that you don't yet know what aspects of your context are important. In the worst case, someone will be rude and say something like "lurk more" meaning read more of the posts before posting yourself, or RTFM, which means "read the frogging manual" (quite sure it's frogging).

At the risk of sounding self-helpy, for what it's worth, I have heard RTFM said (without irony) only one time in an offline context. That person wasn't terribly well respected or valued despite being competent. In any case, most people are nice, and most people are nicer in person.

In addition to project mailing lists and IRC, there are more general forums for help with coding. stackoverflow.com is great for general questions. jsfiddle.net offers a good way to show a live version of your code to other coders. If they are feeling benevolent, they might even edit it and send it back.

Between all the development and community tools available, if you are willing to study, and have a little courage, you can take on any problem you face while developing. It has never been easier to make games and get them into other people's hands.

# RESOURCES

There is no shortage of awesome places to find more information on everything you need to know to make games. Armed with the list of resources in this appendix, you should have no trouble hunting down ways to improve your approach beyond what is covered in this book.

# Game Engines

Some game engines are more standard than others. Some have a better community, or more features. They are all awesome though, and depending on what kind of game you build, any number of them could apply. At their core, they are just JavaScript, so if a good chunk of your game doesn't use an engine's features (as with the raycasting in FPS), you can use what you want of the engine and build the rest from scratch. Alternatively, as demonstrated in Chapter 1, "Quiz," you can easily load more than one engine and then pick what features you want from each of them.

- Akihabara at kesiev.com/akihabara

  This is possibly the first game engine that demonstrated the possibilities of HTML5 games. Some of the others in this book are easier to get up and running, but this engine inspired the arcade-style format in this book of creating different games in classical genres.

- Atom at github.com/nornagon/atom

  Not to be confused with other projects called "atom" on github, this tiny game engine demonstrates that a game engine doesn't need a lot of features to provide value to game creators. This is used for the party game.

- Crafty at craftyjs.com

  Great documentation, a solid feature set, a large plug-in archive, and an active community make this game engine stand out as one of the best. Plus the logo has a fox's tail that looks like a paintbrush, which is pretty great. The isometric map capability sold it as a solid choice to use for the RTS.

- Easel at easeljs.com

  Part of the create.js suite, easel provides a great API that sits on top of canvas. It doesn't call itself a game engine, but it worked out quite well for implementing the puzzle game.

- Enchant at enchantjs.com

  This game engine is big in Japan, with features that expand into Twitter integration and its own distribution platform. Did you know that you wanted an avatar animation server? Enchant thinks that you do. Of all the engines, this definitely has some of the more surprising features. It is used to build the RPG.

- Game.js at gamejs.org

  Based on the Python game library, Pygame, this engine is notable as being a port from another language. It also has a great demo page. This is used for the fighting game.

- GameQuery at gamequeryjs.com

  This game engine stands out among this list for two reasons. First, it is an engine that not only has a dependency, but also boasts about relying on jQuery in its name. Second, and partly as a consequence of this jQuery integration, it is based on the DOM, rather than the canvas. It is used for the shooter game.

- Jaws at jawsjs.com

  It's not as small as atom, but this engine's API doesn't try to match something as expansive as enchant or crafty either. It is a great middle-weight contender and keeps the FPS humming at a decent clip.

- Melon at melonjs.org

  This game engine has a ton of great features and useful documentation. It is used for the platformer game.

# Text Editors

Somehow, you have to write and edit code. Any of the following might end up as your favorite editor, or you might like something outside of this list. There are many choices. If you're just starting out, try a couple of these and stick with one for a while.

- Emacs at gnu.org/software/emacs/

  Due to its hackability for LISP programmers, this has a large following, especially among academics. It's available for Linux, Mac, and Windows operating systems.

- Geddit at projects.gnome.org/gedit

  This is the "official text editor of the GNOME desktop environment," meaning that it's fairly big in the Linux world. It's also available for Mac and Windows.

- Notepad++ at notepad-plus-plus.org

  This is a Windows-only editor. Windows users have fewer good options than available to Mac and Linux users. This is a simple, solid editor.

- Sublime Text at sublimetext.com

  This is a relative newcomer with great features and is meant to be "sophisticated." Put on your monocle, bust out the caviar, and give it a shot. A lot of people love this one.

- Vim at vim.org

  This is my favorite text editor. It's hard to use at first, and by at first, I mean for a couple of years. After that, it becomes a part of you.

# Browsers

In developing this book, the only browsers used extensively were Firefox and Chrome. They are both good in their own ways, reflect the modern state of the web, and are available on Windows, Mac, and Linux platforms. Beyond these two, Opera, Safari, and any number of mobile variants of these make up the rest of the list of reasonable browsers. Internet Explorer has a lot of quirks and doesn't always keep pace with the modern web. Depending on who will be playing your game and what features you need, you may choose to support as many browsers as possible or target only one in particular.

- Chrome at google.com/chrome

  This was the secondary engine used to develop these games. It is usually faster than Firefox.

- Firefox at mozilla.org/firefox

  This was the primary browser used to develop these games. It is not always as fast as chrome, but it experiments with different features and has a different ethos behind it.

# Assorted Tools

Here is a list of tools that are not game engines but proved to be useful while making the games in this book.

- CoffeeScript at coffeescript.org

  This is a language that compiles into JavaScript, which some people prefer to work with. You will likely encounter projects in CoffeeScript, so it doesn't hurt to be familiar with it. As far as this book's content is concerned, atom.js started as atom.coffee before we converted it in Chapter 3, "Party."

- Filtrr at github.com/alexmic/filtrr/tree/master/filtrr2

  This is used for the FPS to add the click-to-create-effect functionality.

- Firebug at getfirebug.com

  This provides the source inspection and JavaScript console for Firefox.

- Impress at github.com/bartaz/impress.js

  This is a great presentation tool. It's so good that it is treated as a game engine to tell interactive stories in Chapter 2, "Interaction Fiction."

- jQuery at jquery.com

  This is a JavaScript framework that used for its effects and DOM manipulation capabilities. It is used in a few chapters.

- Modernizr at modernizr.com

  This feature detection tool enables you to know what a browser can do so that you can fall back to various ways to do the same thing.

- Node at nodejs.org

  This is a server-side JavaScript framework that used in Chapter 10, "RTS."

- NPM at npmjs.org

  This is the node package manager used in Chapter 10 to download socket.io.

- Raptorize at zurb.com/playground/jquery-raptorize

  This jQuery plug-in accounts for the big finale in Chapter 2.

- Socket.io at socket.io

  This NPM package provides an interface for setting up communication in real-time in the RTS.

- Tiled at mapeditor.org

  This is used in Chapter 5, "Platformer," to create the sprite layer, create the collision layer, and place the entities.

- Yabble at github.com/jbrantly/yabble

  This is a dependency of the game.js game engine, used in Chapter 6, "Fighting."

# Art Creation/Finding

You might have a great concept for a game and create what would be an excellent challenge and experience overall, but if the art doesn't support the game, you will have a hard time bringing people into the world you made. With the resources in this section, you should find some way that works for you to build or buy assets for your game.

- Etsy at etsy.com/search?q=pixel

  The amount of tangible pixel art found here is absurd and awesome.

- Gimp at gimp.org

  This is not a great pixel art creation tool, but it is the most Photoshop-like free and open source tool around. (After all, not all game images have to be circa 1994 like the author prefers.)

- Inkscape at inkscape.org

  This is a good cross-platform tool for creating SVG images.

- Open Game Art at opengameart.org

  Most of the art here is available to remix and use but not necessarily to sell along with your game.

- Pickle at pickleeditor.com

  This is the best sprite editor the author could find and was used to make all the sprites in the book. It is free but asks you for a suggested donation of $9 every once in a while. Definitely worth having and paying for.

- Pixel Joint at pixeljoint.com

  A good number of pixel artists hang out here. You probably know this already, but it's worth saying if someone hasn't seen this situation play out anywhere. If you ask artists to create assets for your game without offering them money, they might take offense, and that is their right.

- Sprite Database at spritedatabase.net

  If you're looking for inspiration, this is a great place to see some of the best artwork in retro gaming. Keep in mind that most of these sprites will have copyright restrictions, so don't expect to get rich from selling MegaMan 47: I Built This On My Couch Edition.

## Demos and Tutorials

The author chose engines that were accessible so that you can have an easy time installing the engine, looking up the documentation, and working with decent sample code. In all cases, the artwork, code, and concepts for the games in this book are all original. In some instances, code samples were so helpful that they deserve attribution every bit as much as the game engines themselves.

- Platformer at melonjs.org/tutorial/index.html
- Shooter at gamequeryjs.com/documentation/first-tutorial/
- FPS (DOM-Based Raycaster) at dev.opera.com/articles/view/creating-pseudo-3d-games-with-html-5-can-1/
- FPS (Canvas-Based Raycaster) at developer.mozilla.org/en-US/docs/HTML/Canvas/A_Basic_RayCaster
- RPG at https://github.com/wise9/enchant.js/tree/master/examples/expert/rpg

## Books

These are books that I had in mind when writing, but the material they cover was sufficiently out of scope. I learned radically different things from all of them.

- *The Art of Game Design* by Jesse Schell

  This book covers everything you need to know about game design in an insanely thorough way. It is incredibly rare to walk away from a book feeling like all your questions were answered, but *The Art of Game Design* can do this.

- *JavaScript: The Good Parts* by Douglas Crockford

  This book is deceptively short, but it has a ton of depth. It convinced people that JavaScript was a reasonable language in spite of the bad parts. This was a watershed book, and the web would not be the same without its influence.

- *Learning JavaScript* by Tim Wright

  This book is awesome for covering basic through intermediate JavaScript. It covers modern web techniques and gracefully addresses both the bad parts and the good parts that you encounter when you program JavaScript in the browser.

- *Rise of the Videogame Zinesters* by Anna Anthropy

  If you want to learn about the value of designing in a personal way, and seeing a raw, uncommon point of view from the deep underbelly of the indie games scene, this is the book for you. It makes an awesome case for why anyone should imagine game-making as a powerful way to convey a message, whether the message is simple, complex, uncommon, or incredibly personal. If you don't run away from this book, it will compel you to discover your own stories to tell through games and challenge your ideas about what games can and should be.

# Websites

This book presents music and 3D as too hard to worry about. That's not entirely true: They are complex and are changing rapidly, like many things with HTML5 games. This list contains websites covering topics that were either too complex or shifty to try and pin down in paper form.

- Box 2D Web at code.google.com/p/box2dweb/

  box2d is a popular choice for implementing realistic 2-D physics in games.

- Can I use at caniuse.com

  This has tables for every browser of note shown in the context of what browser features (such as the Web Audio API) are supported in each version.

- Daily JS at dailyjs.com

  If you want to learn about everything cool that happened in JavaScript today (and yesterday, and the day before, and the day before...), this is the best site around. The frequency and quality of the posts are unmatched.

- HTML5 Audio at html5audio.org

  This is a blog covering the latest and greatest in browser audio tech. In addition to high-lighting cool audio stuff from around the web, when a big event happens, such as when Firefox finally gets around to implementing the Web Audio API, it'll be the first ones to report on it.

- HTML 5 Game Development at html5gamedevelopment.org

  This site is great for staying up to date on all things HTML5 games. If you want to understand all the issues and tools surrounding the community, this site is fantastic.

- HTML5 Rocks at html5rocks.com

  If you want well-researched articles detailing things such as caching and other millisecond level information about how browsers work with HTML5 technologies, this is the site for you.

- three.js at mrdoob.github.com/three.js

  If you want to start with 3-D, this is a good place to start. three.js sits on top of WebGL to provide a simplified API. As you can see in the demos on that site, you can do amazing things with it. Also, the three.js author has more incredible experiments at mrdoob.com.

- TIGSource at tigsource.com

  If you want to stay up to date on indie game development news, or get inspiration for your next game, this is a great place to check out.

# INDEX

rendering
    with easel.js file, *87-91*
    multiple objects, *91-94*
  time limits, 102-106
pygame, 142
Pythagorean theorem, 220

# Q-R

quality control. *See* debugging
question-making in quiz game, 6-12
questions
  determining correct answers, 21-24
  getting back, 14-16
  hiding, 15
  showing, 16
quiz game, 5-25
  determining correct answers, 21-24
  getting questions back, 14-16
  hiding and showing quiz, 12-14
  making the questions, 6-12
  shopping list, 16-21
QUnit, 328

random color, adding on page load, 90
random pairs, creating, 95-97
raptorized index.html, 56
raptorize jQuery plug-in, 56, 335
raycaster object, 204
raycasting, 194, 203-208
  creating 2-D maps, 196-199
  fake 3D with, 208-212
raytracing, 194
reading from Local Storage API, 276
real-time strategy game. *See* RTS game
recipes. *See names of specific game types*
  (e.g. fighting game, FPS game, etc.)
refactoring, 68, 146
referencing array literals, 78
refreshing browser windows, 303
registering
  hits, 165-166
  input, 156, 201
relational data storage options, 277
reloading server file, 291
removing
  caching, 108
  highlight variable, 101
  pairs, 97-100
  text, 247

rendering. *See also* drawing
  sprites, 146
  squares, 93-94
  types of, compared, 172-173
replacing previous and next with change, 155
replay function, 114
replaying games, 105
requiring JavaScript files in index.html, 18-19
resetting
  coins, 138
  CSS, 31
resources for information
  art creation, 335-336
  books, 336-337
  browsers, 334
  demos and tutorials, 336
  game engines, 332-333
  text editors, 333
  tools, 334-335
  websites, 337-338
resources.js file, 121
return values in JavaScript, 42
RGB color values, 22
*Rise of the Videogame Zinesters* (Anthropy), 337
role-playing games. *See* RPG game
RPG game, 231-277, 336
  adding players, 237-243
  battle interface, creating, 263-274
  collision detection, 243-244
  enchant.js, 232-233
  inventory, creating, 251-254
  map, creating, 233-237
  saving game, 274-277
  shops, creating, 254-263
  status screens, 244-248
  talking to NPCs (nonplayable characters),
    248-251
RTS game, 279-311
  collision detection, 305-310
  creating isometric maps, 288-291
  drawing units, 291-295
  moving units, 295-298
  node.js, 282-285
  player-specific control and visibility, 299-304
  servers, terminology, 280-282
  socket.io, 285-288

USING JAVASCRIPT AND HTML5 TO DEVELOP GAMES

*THE WEB GAME DEVELOPER'S COOKBOOK*

Evan **BURCHARD**

## FREE Online Edition

Your purchase of *The Web Game Developer's Cookbook* includes access to a free online edition for 45 days through the **Safari Books Online** subscription service. Nearly every Addison-Wesley Professional book is available online through **Safari Books Online**, along with over thousands of books and videos from publishers such as Cisco Press, Exam Cram, IBM Press, O'Reilly Media, Prentice Hall, Que, Sams, and VMware Press.

**Safari Books Online** is a digital library providing searchable, on-demand access to thousands of technology, digital media, and professional development books and videos from leading publishers. With one monthly or yearly subscription price, you get unlimited access to learning tools and information on topics including mobile app and software development, tips and tricks on using your favorite gadgets, networking, project management, graphic design, and much more.

## Activate your FREE Online Edition at
## informit.com/safarifree

**STEP 1:** Enter the coupon code: PJKSUWA.

**STEP 2:** New Safari users, complete the brief registration form.
Safari subscribers, just log in.

If you have difficulty registering on Safari or accessing the online edition,
please e-mail customer-service@safaribooksonline.com